AF248633

Kimio Kase and Tanguy Jacopin
CEOs AS LEADERS AND STRATEGY DESIGNERS
Explaining the Success of Spanish Banks

M. Mansoor Khan and M. Ishaq Bhatti
DEVELOPMENTS IN ISLAMIC BANKING
The Case of Pakistan

Mario La Torre and Gianfranco A. Vento
MICROFINANCE

Philip Molyneux and Munawar Iqbal
BANKING AND FINANCIAL SYSTEMS IN THE ARAB WORLD

Philip Molyneux and Eleuterio Vallelado (*editors*)
FRONTIERS OF BANKS IN A GLOBAL WORLD

Anastasia Nesvetailova
FRAGILE FINANCE
Debt, Speculation and Crisis in the Age of Global Credit

Dominique Rambure and Alec Nacamuli
PAYMENT SYSTEMS
From the Salt Mines to the Board Room

Catherine Schenk (*editor*)
HONG KONG SAR's MONETARY AND EXCHANGE RATE CHALLENGES
Historical Perspectives

Andrea Schertler
THE VENTURE CAPITAL INDUSTRY IN EUROPE

Alfred Slager
THE INTERNATIONALIZATION OF BANKS

Noel K. Tshiani
BUILDING CREDIBLE CENTRAL BANKS
Policy Lessons for Emerging Economies

Also by C. R. Schenk
BRITAIN AND THE STERLING AREA:
From Devaluation to Convertibility
HONG KONG AS AN INTERNATIONAL FINANCIAL CENTRE:
Emergence and Development 1945–65

Palgrave Macmillan Studies in Banking and Financial Institutions
Series Standing Order ISBN 978–1–4039–4872–4

You can receive future titles in this series as they are published by placing a standing order. Please contact your bookseller or, in case of difficulty, write to us at the address below with your name and address, the title of the series and the ISBN quoted above.

Customer Services Department, Macmillan Distribution Ltd, Houndmills, Basingstoke, Hampshire RG21 6XS, England

---

Hong Kong SAR's Monetary and Exchange Rate Challenges

Historical Perspectives

Edited by

Catherine R. Schenk

palgrave
macmillan

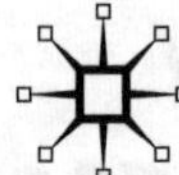

First published 2009 by
PALGRAVE MACMILLAN

Palgrave Macmillan in the UK is an imprint of Macmillan Publishers Limited,
registered in England, company number 785998, of Houndmills, Basingstoke,
Hampshire RG21 6XS.

Palgrave Macmillan in the US is a division of St Martin's Press LLC,
175 Fifth Avenue, New York, NY 10010.

Palgrave Macmillan is the global academic imprint of the above companies
and has companies and representatives throughout the world.

Palgrave® and Macmillan® are registered trademarks in the United States, the
United Kingdom, Europe and other countries.

ISBN-13: 978-0-230-20946-6   hardback
ISBN-10: 10: 0-230-20946-7   hardback

This book is printed on paper suitable for recycling and made from fully
managed and sustained forest sources. Logging, pulping and manufacturing
processes are expected to conform to the environmental regulations of the
country of origin.

A catalogue record for this book is available from the British Library.

Library of Congress Cataloging-in-Publication Data

Hong Kong SAR's monetary and exchange rate challenges : historical
perspectives / edited by Catherine R. Schenk.
        p. cm. – (Palgrave Macmillan studies in banking and financial
institutions)
    Includes bibliographical references.
    ISBN 978-0-230-20946-6
    1. Foreign exchange–China–Hong Kong. 2. Finance–China–Hong Kong.
    3. Monetary policy–China–Hong Kong. I. Schenk, Catherine R.
    (Catherine Ruth), 1964–
    HG3981.H66 2009
    332.4'56095125–dc22   2008030097

10   9   8   7   6   5   4   3   2   1
18 17 16 15 14 13 12 11 10 09

Printed and bound in Great Britain by
CPI Antony Rowe, Chippenham and Eastbourne

Contents

List of Illustrations

List of Tables

List of Figures

Notes on Contributors

Catherine R. Schenk FRHS, AcSS is Professor of International Economic History at the University of Glasgow. She has published widely on Hong Kong's banking and monetary history in international academic journals and is the author of *Hong Kong as an International Financial Centre; Emergence and Development*. In 2005 she was Visiting Professor at the History Department, University of Hong Kong. She was Research Fellow at the Hong Kong Institute for Monetary Research in 2005 and 2008.

Ming K. Chan is Research Fellow, Hoover Institution, Stanford University. He taught in the History Department, University of Hong Kong during 1980–1997, and was Visiting Professor at UCLA, Duke, Swarthmore, Mount Holyoke and Grinnell. He is General Editor of the multi-volume Hong Kong Becoming China series published by M.E. Sharpe. His recent books on Hong Kong including *China's Hong Kong Transformed: Retrospect and Prospects Beyond the 1st Decade* (2008), *Crisis and Transformation in China's Hong Kong* (2002), *The Challenge of Hong Kong's Reintegration with China* (1997), and *Precarious Balance: Hong Kong between China and Britain: 1842–1992* (1994).

Leo F. Goodstadt is an adjunct professor in the School of Business Studies, Trinity College, University of Dublin. He has been appointed to three research fellowships at the Hong Kong Institute of Monetary Research and is an honorary research fellow at Hong Kong University's Centre of Asian Studies. He was chief policy adviser to the Hong Kong Government 1989–97 and headed its Central Policy Unit. As a private-sector economist, he has been retained by leading banks in the Asian region. His career has also included the posts of deputy editor at the *Far Eastern Economic Review* (1969–74), editorial director of *Asiabanking* and Hong Kong correspondent for *Euromoney*. He is the author of *Uneasy Partners: The Conflict between Public Interest and Private Profit in Hong Kong* (2005) and *Profits, Politics and Panics: Hong Kong's Banks and the Making of a Miracle Economy, 1935–1985* (2007).

Tony Latter is an economist and central banker. He spent much of his career at the Bank of England, including spells at the Bank for International Settlements and the OECD. In the early 1990s, following the breakup of the Soviet Union, he was involved in providing technical advice on monetary reform to a number of its former component republics and satellite states; for a time he served as the International Monetary Fund's resident adviser to the governor of the National Bank of Ukraine. His association with Hong Kong dates back to 1982–85, when he was Deputy Secretary for Monetary Affairs. From 1999–2003 he was Deputy Chief Executive of the Hong Kong Monetary Authority. He then moved to the University of Hong Kong as a Visiting Professor and remains a senior research fellow of the Hong Kong Institute of Economics and Business Strategy.

John Greenwood OBE graduated from Edinburgh University and did his postgraduate economics studies at Tokyo University. In 1974 he joined G.T. Management in Hong Kong as chief economist. Between 1976 and 1996 he published *Asian Monetary Monitor*, a bimonthly journal specialising in monetary analysis of economics in the East Asia Pacific area. From 1986 until 1993 he was chairman of G.T. Management (Asia) Ltd. He was also a council member (director) of the Hong Kong Futures Exchange Clearing Corporation (1989–91) and the Stock Exchange of Hong Kong (1992–93), as well as an economic adviser to the Hong Kong Government (1992–93). He is now Chief Economist, INVESCO.

Joseph Yam joined the Hong Kong Civil Service as a statistician in 1971 after completing his university studies at the University of Hong Kong. In 1982 he was appointed Principal Assistant Secretary in the Monetary Affairs Branch and in 1985 became the Deputy Secretary for Monetary Affairs. In 1991 he was appointed Director of the Office of the Exchange Fund and in 1993 became the first Chief Executive of the Hong Kong Monetary Authority, which is his current post.

David Meyer has been Professor of Sociology and Urban Studies, Brown University, Providence, Rhode Island since 1997. In 2006–2007 he was Visiting Professor, Olin Business School, Washington University in St. Louis, Missouri. His books include: *Networked Machinists: High-Technology Industries in Antebellum America* (2006), *The Roots of American Industrialization* (2003) and *Hong Kong as a Global Metropolis* (2000).

Acknowledgements

The editor and publisher wish to thank the following for permission to reproduce copyright material: Colin Day at Hong Kong University Press has graciously provided permission to use material from T. Latter (2007) *Hong Kong's Money; The History, Logic and Operation of the Currency Peg* (Hong Kong: Hong Kong University Press) and from J. Greenwood (2008) *Hong Kong's Link to the US Dollar: Origins and Evolution* (Hong Kong: Hong Kong University Press). We are grateful also to *The South China Morning Post* for the use of images in Chapter 7. Every effort has been made to trace rights holders, but if any have been inadvertently overlooked the publishers would be pleased to make the necessary arrangements at the first opportunity.

The authors would like to thank the commentators and participants at the conference 'Banking and Monetary History of Hong Kong: Hong Kong's Current Challenges in Historical Perspective' in April 2007 and to thank the Hong Kong Institute for Monetary Research and the Centre for Asian Studies, University of Hong Kong for their contribution to the organization of this meeting and their gracious hospitality. The editor is grateful to Niall MacKenzie, Chris Munn, Leo Goodstadt and Matthew Yiu for their valuable assistance with this project.

Part I

Historical Perspectives

1
Hong Kong's Monetary Challenges in Historical Perspective

Catherine R. Schenk

Hong Kong SAR (Special Administrative Region) is almost unique in the world today with a highly sophisticated banking and financial system and a very open economy but still operating within a currency board framework. Moreover, the system pegs the HKD to the USD despite the dollar's dramatic and sustained decline since 2002. In its purist form, a currency board offers a cheap and automatic monetary mechanism whereby notes are passively issued and redeemed against foreign exchange at a fixed exchange rate. The narrow money supply is thus determined by the inflow and outflow of foreign exchange in response to the balance of payments and the government is unable to exercise monetary discretion. During the 1990s there was considerable enthusiasm for currency boards, particularly for small open economies, until the collapse of the Argentine system in 2001–2 and the subsequent decline of the USD.[1] Since then, currency boards have been used mainly by colonies, by countries seeking to dispel the shadow of chaotic monetary episodes, and by aspirants to membership of the European Economic and Monetary Union. Table 1.1 shows that Hong Kong SAR is now by far the largest economy to operate a currency board, although it no longer conforms either to the colonial rationale, or to the regime change rationale for a currency board.[2] Instead, the reasons for the persistence of the system reflect the historical development of the monetary system and the unusual process of decolonization as well as Hong Kong's geopolitical situation.

The modern currency board had its origins in the British colonial system. In 1913 the West African Currency Board began operations and formed the model for subsequent colonial monetary systems in the Caribbean, East Africa and Southeast Asia. The rationale was to provide a system to issue local currency that was protected from

Table 1.1 Economies Operating Currency Board or Quasi-Currency Board Systems December 2007

Country	GDP ($ Billion)	Currency Peg
Djibouti	0.834	USD
Gibraltar [UK]	1.1	£
Faroe Islands [Denmark]	1.7	DKr
Cayman Islands [UK]	1.9	USD
Bermuda [UK]	4.5	USD
Brunei	12.5	Sing$
Bosnia	14.2	Euro
Estonia	21.2	Euro
Latvia	27	Euro
Lithuania	28.6	Euro
Bulgaria	39.1	Euro
Hong Kong [China]	203	USD
Falkland Islands [UK]	n/a	£
Saint Helena	n/a	£
Eastern Caribbean	n/a	USD

Source: Countries identified by Kurt Schuler, http://users.erols.com/kurrency/intro.htm He excludes Latvia. GDP from CIA Yearbook and relates to 2007 except Gibraltar, Faroe Islands 2005 and Cayman Islands, Bermuda 2004 PPP.

inflation and from speculation by being pegged resolutely to the pound sterling, which at that time was the major international currency. The Board issued local currency against sterling on demand at a fixed rate and kept at least 100% sterling reserves, held by the Crown Agents for the Colonies in London. Hong Kong was a rather late adherent, beginning its currency board based on sterling only in 1935. The colony's economic integration with Mainland China, which operated a silver standard, delayed the adoption of a sterling standard in Hong Kong. However, as Chan describes in his chapter in this volume, by the early 1930s monetary instability on the Mainland prompted reforms there which offered an opportunity for Hong Kong to adapt its monetary system to the British colonial model. After the end of the Second World War, British colonies became part of the Sterling Area system of countries that pegged their exchange rates to sterling and retained sterling as their main reserve asset.[3] Currency boards continued to operate in colonies as part of this system.

In the period of decolonization during the 1950s, most British territories sought to establish central banks as an emblem of constitutional independence. Their rationale was often rhetorical – to eliminate the Queen's image from notes and to have a fresh national currency for the new state – but more fundamentally these institutions were also considered vital for the operation of expansionist economic policies aimed at development. Still, the economic realities of operating small open economies during the Bretton Woods system of pegged exchange rates meant that in practice these central banks had limited powers and tended informally to retain many of the rules of the currency board; keeping 100% sterling reserves and issuing currency only against foreign exchange at a fixed exchange rate.[4] Nevertheless, the institutional structure for monetary independence was put in place as part of the process of political independence for most territories, a major exception being Singapore where uncertainty over the future political relationship with Malaya prolonged the currency board. For Hong Kong, constitutional independence was never a viable option because of the lease arrangement with Mainland China, but the continuation of colonial status alone does not explain why a central bank was not introduced.

At several points during the 1950s and 1960s the Bank of England and the British Treasury were very keen for a central bank to be established in Hong Kong to exert monetary and exchange control and also to regulate the banking system, but this was vigorously resisted in Hong Kong itself.[5] The government had little interest in creating an official institution (with its attendant administrative costs) that would take over the note-issue from designated commercial banks. Successive Financial Secretaries also resisted repeated suggestions that they issue Treasury Bills to allow open market operations as a monetary tool since the government ran persistent surpluses and had no interest in issuing debt or influencing liquidity.[6] Interest rates were governed by a banking cartel and notes were issued along the lines of a currency board system leading to a perception that the monetary system was automatic and self-regulating, as Goodstadt argues in this volume. The note-issuing banks (HSBC, Chartered Bank and Mercantile Bank) credited the Hong Kong Exchange Fund's account in London with sterling and received in return HKD-denominated Certificates of Indebtedness (CoI) to the value of these sterling deposits at the pegged exchange rate. They were then entitled to issue this value of HKD notes. When the banks wanted to withdraw notes from circulation CoIs could be redeemed through the Exchange Fund at the cost of a slight exchange margin. This was not a perfect example of a colonial currency board, since commercial banks issued the notes rather than the Exchange Fund directly, but it still operated similarly to other colonial monetary systems where local currency was issued on demand against sterling lodged with the Crown Agents for the Colonies in London at a pegged exchange rate. There is every indication that these arrangements suited the non-interventionist philosophy of the government very well and they were not sympathetic to suggestions to change them.

As several papers in this volume note, as the Bretton Woods pegged exchange rate system crumbled in the late 1960s and early 1970s, various amendments were made to the operation of the Exchange Fund that fundamentally altered its operations. In response to the global lack of confidence in the sterling exchange rate, in 1968 the Exchange Fund borrowing limit was increased to allow it to provide forward cover for commercial banks' holding of sterling.[7] This involved swaps of the banks' sterling assets for HKD denominated assets issued by the Exchange Fund. The sterling was then re-deposited with the banks on account of the Exchange Fund. Soon after, when sterling was floated against the USD and other currencies in June 1972, Hong Kong was faced with the choice of whether to maintain the peg to sterling and float against most currencies, to float independently, or to peg to another currency. The decision was made to peg to the USD and at the same time to alter the operation of the Exchange Fund so that it accepted HKD balances rather than sterling as backing for the note issue. Note-issuing banks credited special deposit accounts ear-marked for the Exchange Fund and received the equivalent value of Certificates of Indebtedness against which they issued notes. This marked the end of the formal currency board rules that required foreign currency backing for the note issue.[8] By transferring the assets of the Exchange Fund from London to the Hong Kong banking system, this innovation fundamentally changed the nature of the monetary system. When the HKD floated free of its pegged rate in November 1974, the government was left with no mechanism to control monetary expansion. The instability of the international economy in the late 1970s and renewed inflationary pressure brought the system to a crisis just when the return of Hong Kong to Mainland China was being discussed in 1982. This exchange rate and monetary crisis was resolved by a return to a currency board system that pegged the HKD to the USD in October 1983 at HKD7.80 = USD1.00. Which has been sustained to the present day.

Figure 1.1 shows how the HKD performed on a monthly basis against the RMB and the USD from 1973–1983. Since a large proportion of Hong Kong's food was imported from the Mainland, the cost of living and inflation rate was sensitive to the RMB/HKD exchange rate as well as the USD/HKD rate. Hong Kong was thus adversely affected by the over-valued rates set by the People's Bank against the USD during

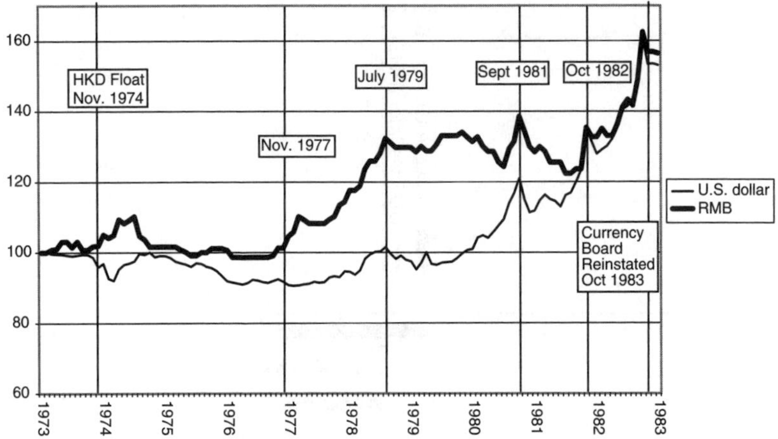

Figure 1.1   Nominal HK$ Exchange Rates (Dec 1973=100) End Month

the initial years of the open-door policy. The first year of floating was one of volatility against both the RMB and the USD as they moved in opposite directions and the HKD strengthened against the USD. For two years after September 1975, the RMB/HKD rate was very stable at the pre-float rate, while there was a slight appreciation against the USD. In the fourth quarter of 1977, the money supply ballooned, inflation began to accelerate in Hong Kong, and there was a rapid depreciation against the RMB over the following 18 months. A period of relative stability ensued until the depreciation against the USD began to accelerate in 1981. This depreciation was spread to the RMB/HKD rate during the crisis of October 1982 until the currency board was reinstated a year later.

In the 25 years since the currency board was introduced the Hong Kong economy has been transformed but, remarkably, the exchange rate of HKD7.80 = USD1.00 has been maintained. As Meyer's chapter in this volume shows, during the late 1980s and early 1990s there was a dramatic decline of manufacturing as factories were moved across to the Pearl River Delta, offset by the rise of commercial and other services in the economy. Nominal growth rates averaged 12% from 1983–1997 and inflation declined under the new currency board. However, after 1997 the Hong Kong economy suffered a downturn from which it recovered only in 2004–5 as is evident in Figure 1.2. The last decade of turbulence has not, however, resulted in a currency crisis or a failure of confidence in the HKD exchange rate.

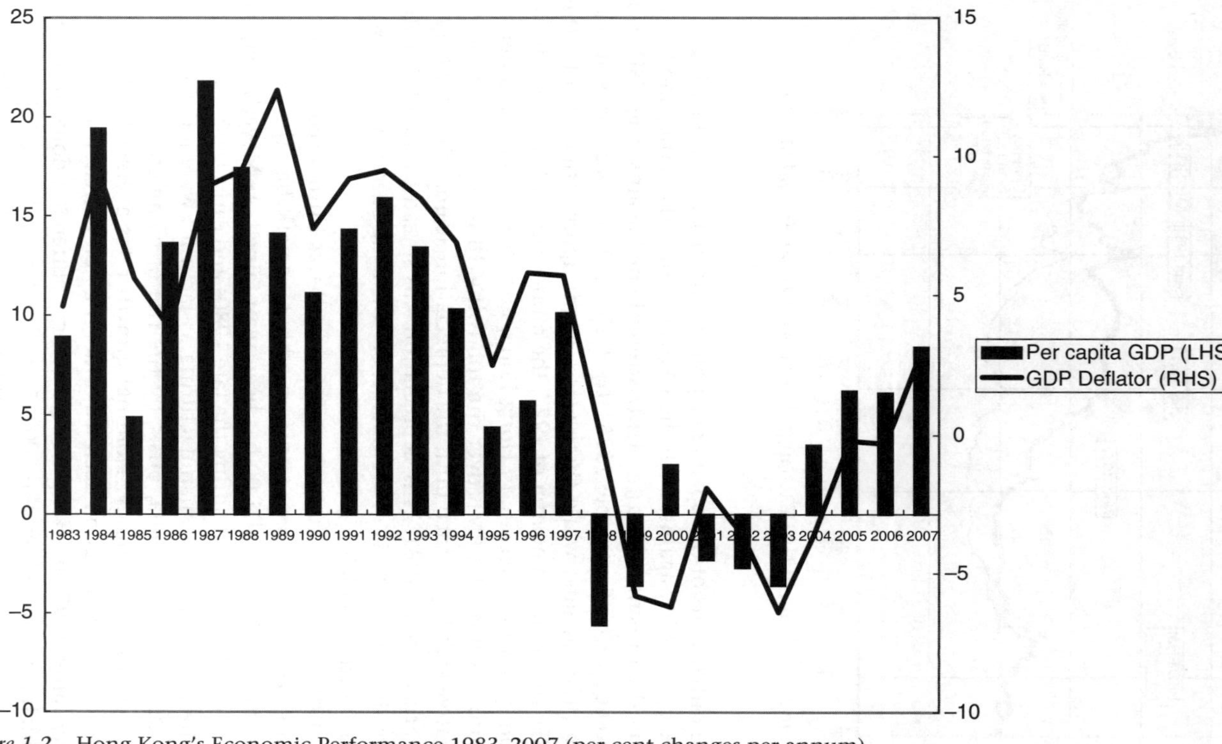

Figure 1.2 Hong Kong's Economic Performance 1983–2007 (per cent changes per annum)

Hong Kong SAR is a monetary anomaly in another way since it forms part of the People's Republic of China (PRC) but the operation of a separate currency is enshrined in the Basic Law setting out the terms of Hong Kong's return to China. The terms of the Basic Law were negotiated between 1984 and 1990 when the economic fortunes of Hong Kong seemed brighter than the Mainland and the continuation of economic and political institutions from the colonial period was considered vital to the prospects for Hong Kong as an international financial centre. However, we have seen that the current Exchange Fund is not merely a continuation of the colonial monetary system that operated in Hong Kong from 1935, since it was suspended from 1972 until the banking and exchange rate crisis of 1983. That the currency board was reintroduced in October 1983 during a crisis caused partly by political uncertainty arising from the negotiations over the return to China exemplifies the political importance at this time of Hong Kong's monetary independence from the Mainland. More recently, the monetary relations between Hong Kong SAR and the Mainland have become increasingly controversial because of the intensified economic integration with the Mainland, the decline of the USD on world markets, and the appreciation of the RMB against the HKD since it moved to a flexible basket peg in July 2005.[9] Figure 1.3 shows the depreciation of the RMB against the HKD during the currency board years, including

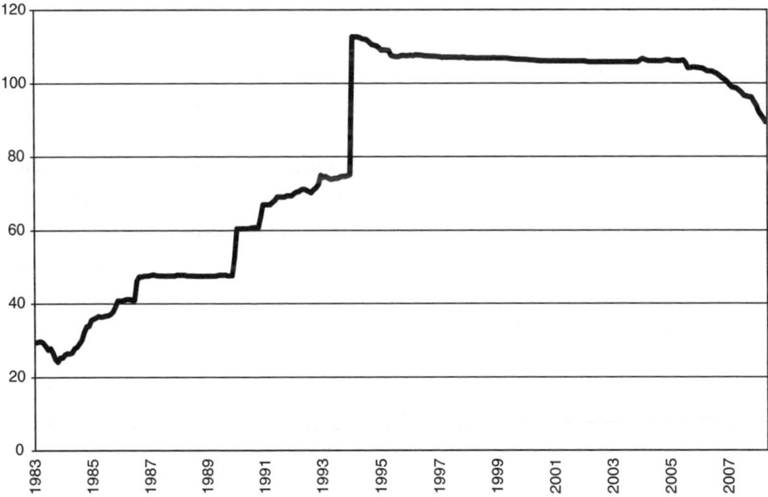

Figure 1.3 Monthly Hong Kong Exchange Rate 1983–May 2007 (RMB per HKD100)

the major RMB realignment in 1994 that informally pegged the RMB to the USD, stabilizing the RMB-HKD rate. Since July 2005, however, the RMB has appreciated so that since January 2007 HKD100 has been worth less than RMB100.

Since 1997 the economic performance of Hong Kong and the Mainland have diverged. Mainland China felt little impact from the Asian Financial Crisis given its strong underlying economic conditions and the tight exchange controls on the RMB that protected it from speculative pressure. Hong Kong's open system felt the crisis more deeply, partly through expectations that the HKD would follow other currencies in the region and devalue. The Hong Kong Monetary Authority (HKMA) did not bow to the pressure and took the extreme position of intervening in the stock market to crush speculation through this avenue so that the HKD retained its peg of HKD7.80 to the USD.[10] This was not the end of the difficulties for Hong Kong as the downturn in the regional economy, the collapse of property and stock markets and the SARS outbreak led to a prolonged downturn with slower growth, deflation and unemployment. During these years of recession, Mainland China boomed with the accession to the WTO, a surge of FDI and a dramatic increase in the current account surplus. The changing fortunes of the Mainland *vis-à-vis* Hong Kong SAR made it clear that Hong Kong's economic prosperity depended on the vibrant Mainland economy and the pace of integration was hastened by the signing of the Closer Economic Partnership Agreement in June 2003.

The economy of Hong Kong has clearly been shaped by the process of its transformation from British colony to Special Administrative Region of the PRC. To fully understand the nature of Hong Kong's monetary challenges, however, it is necessary to look further back into the historical record to acknowledge the long-term nature of the monetary integration between Hong Kong and the Mainland. It is the purpose of this book to examine the historical evolution of Hong Kong's monetary system in the context of its relations with the Mainland, before 1997 and after, to allow us to better appreciate the foundations of the system that operates today and the ways that it might respond to future challenges.

One major theme of the current volume is that the economic, financial and monetary integration of Hong Kong with Mainland China, and the influence of Mainland Chinese policy on Hong Kong, extend back to the founding of the colony in the 19th century. Ming Chan's chapter elucidates the close and sometimes troubled monetary relations in the early 20th century and the political and social upheaval that arose from disturbances in that relationship, which need to be borne in mind when devising responses to future challenges. He highlights the blurred identity of the population as Hong Kong residents and as Chinese and how this was reflected in the use of Chinese coinage. Schenk pursues this theme into the later 20th century to bring to light the sensitivity of Hong Kong to the Mainland's exchange rate policy during the first era when the RMB appreciated against the HKD, as well as the persistence of cross border banking links even during the height of the Cultural Revolution. Together these chapters emphasise that monetary relations between Hong Kong and the Mainland have had important social and political effects. Also, these underlying monetary relations were sustained despite political upheavals that disrupted other relations between the two economies.

A second major insight is that the present currency board system is not merely a carryover from the colonial monetary system. Hong Kong abandoned the currency board for over ten years during the 1970s and this era can be compared with those before and after. Goodstadt explores the operation of the monetary system during the early currency board period, emphasizing the lack of economic expertise and the costs that this posed on Hong Kong's economic stability. Latter looks forward to the evolution and adaptation of the currency board system from 1983 until April 2007 to show how it adapted to the challenges of globalization, the Asian financial crisis and the return to China. Greenwood returns to the origins of the currency board in 1983 to show how it arose from the failure of Hong Kong's monetary institutions to allow an effective monetary policy once the exchange rate was floated free from the USD in 1974. Yam reflects also on these years from a different perspective, emphasizing the importance of the political and economic context in which adaptations to the currency board were made in the 1980s and 1990s.

The chapters in Part II give the point of view of some of the key protagonists and on-lookers in the reform of the monetary system in the 1980s. Leo Goodstadt was a journalist for the *Far Eastern Economic Review* in Hong Kong during the 1970s and then joined the government to become head of the Central Policy Unit from 1989–1997. Tony Latter was Undersecretary for Monetary Affairs from 1982–1985 and so took part in the restoration of the currency board in 1983. He returned to Hong Kong in 1999 to take up the post of Deputy Chief Executive of the HKMA until 2003. John Greenwood arrived in Hong Kong in the 1970s to work in the financial sector and began to publish a regular newsletter on Hong Kong's monetary system that successfully made the case for re-introducing the currency board in 1983. Finally, Joseph Yam was Principal Assistant Secretary for Monetary Affairs from 1982–1985 and then Deputy Secretary for Monetary Affairs before becoming Director of the Office of the Exchange Fund in 1991. In 1993 he was appointed as the first Chief Executive of the HKMA, a post he continues to hold. Together these chapters provide a mix of academic, journalistic and personal recollections of the policy making challenges for Hong Kong during the critical post-war decades and the continued evolution of the monetary system after 1983.

The final chapter looks to the future to examine one of the most pressing questions, which is whether Hong Kong will sustain its leadership as a regional financial centre, and how this might be achieved. The changing nature of international financial services and the rising competitiveness of Mainland centres pose serious challenges for Hong Kong's pre-eminence in the region, although Meyer is optimistic about the future.

The future of Hong Kong's monetary system is certainly one of challenge. The USD peg has proved controversial as the USD's value in international markets fell, bringing the HKD with it. The exchange rate regime became even more widely discussed after the RMB was let loose from its USD peg in July 2005 and adopted an adjustable system based on a basket of currencies. As in the 1960s, the resulting appreciation of the RMB against the HKD raised the spectre of potential costs from exchange rate instability. In this context, Hong Kong's monetary options are limited. The difficult experience of the floating regime in the 1970s has convinced many observers that a stable exchange rate is fundamental to Hong Kong's viability as an international financial centre.[11] There is no obvious alternative international currency anchor other than the USD; Hong Kong's pattern of trade and payments would not suit the Euro peg adopted by other economies. The inconvertibility of the RMB and the shallow and illiquid nature of RMB financial instruments renders it ineligible for the time being. Nevertheless, the research presented in this volume should convince readers of the long-standing and deep integration of Hong Kong with Mainland China that predates the constitutional changes of 1997. Hong Kong will remain sensitive to monetary policy on the Mainland and will need to be adaptable and innovative in its responses to future challenges. Finally, the evidence presented here suggests that, overall, the currency board system has served Hong Kong well throughout the past quarter of a century and that there are perils to changing the monetary system fundamentally in response to what may prove to be short-term shocks.

Notes

1 Kurt Schuler and Steve Hanke were the most vociferous advocates. K. Schuler, *Should Developing Countries Have Central Banks? Currency Quality and Monetary Systems in 155 Countries*, London Institute of Economic Affairs, 1996. S Hanke, 'Reflections on Exchange Rate Regimes', *Cato Journal*, 1999.
2 Hanke finds that after 1992 Hong Kong did not operate a strict currency board because the HKMA supervises banks and is committed to only 100% reserve backing for the local currency. The financial secretary is also able to use the Exchange Fund to maintain financial and monetary stability, but only 'with a view to maintaining Hong Kong as an international financial centre'. S. Hanke, 'On dollarization and currency boards: error and deception', *Policy Reform*, 2002, 5(4), pp. 203–22. However, since the Exchange Fund does publish a target of 110% cover and does not regulate banks, we might consider it a currency board, although the HKMA takes on other roles more similar to a central bank.
3 The Sterling Area included members of the Commonwealth, British colonies and protectorates as well as Ireland, Iceland, Iraq, Persian Gulf. It was only disbanded in June 1972.
4 C.R. Schenk, 'Monetary Institutions in Newly Independent Countries: the experience of Malaya, Ghana and Nigeria in the 1950s', *Financial History Review*, (4) pp. 181–98, 1997. C.R. Schenk, 'The Origins of a Central Bank in Malaya and the Transition to Independence; 1954–60', *Journal of Imperial and Commonwealth History*, 21(2), pp. 409–31, May 1993.
5 See, for example, note by R.H. Hay, 14 November 1967. The National Archives, London, [hereafter TNA] T312/2636. Members of the Foreign and Commonwealth Office also hoped for a central monetary authority, Sir Arthur Galsworthy, Undersecretary of State, 30 July 1969. TNA FCO59/442. For a broader discussion see L. Goodstadt (2007) *Profits, Politics and Panics: Hong Kong's Banks and the Making of a Miracle Economy, 1935–1985* (Hong Kong: Hong Kong University Press).
6 G.R. Bell to Sir Philip Haddon-Cave, 24 November 1972. TNA T312/2963.
7 See correspondence TNA FCO59/441. The first swaps took place in November 1968 and the facility was generalised to all banks in March 1969. By July 1972 the Fund's borrowing limit was HKD7 billion compared to HKD30 million in 1967.
8 This was done without general discussion overnight on July 6 1972, contradicting the claims by Feuerstein and Grimm that it takes time to eliminate a currency board. S. Feuerstein and O. Grimm (2006) 'On the credibility of currency boards', *Review of International Economics*, 14(5) pp. 818–35.
9 Ma *et al.* recently found that Hong Kong's currency board peg to the USD resulted in poorer economic performance than Singapore's managed floating regime. Y. Ma, Y.Y. Kueh and R.C.W. Ng, 'A comparative study of exchange rate regimes and macro-economic stability in Singapore and Hong Kong', *Singapore Economic Review*, April 2007, Vol. 52 Issue 1, pp. 93–116. For another critique of Hong Kong's currency board see Y. Wu, 'A modified currency board system; theory and evidence', *Journal of International Financial Markets, Institutions & Money*, October 2005, Vol. 15 Issue 4, pp. 353–67.
10 C. Goodhart and L. Dai (2003) *Intervention to Save Hong Kong: The Authorities' Counter-speculation in Financial Markets* (Oxford: Oxford University Press).

11 Several authors who have noted the relatively poor performance of Hong Kong relative to Singapore have recommended a monitored band system similar to Singapore, but this was before the RMB regime was changed. Paul Yip (2005) 'On the maintenance costs and exit costs of the peg in Hong Kong', *Review of Pacific Basin Financial Markets & Policies*, 8(3), 377–403. R.S. Rajan and R. Siregar (2002) 'Choice of Exchange Rate Regime: Currency Board (Hong Kong) or Monitoring Band (Singapore)?', *Australian Economic Papers*, 41(4), 538–56.

2
Historical Dimensions of the Hong Kong-Guangdong Financial & Monetary Links: Three Cases in Politico-Economic Interactive Dynamics, 1912–1935

Ming K. Chan

Introduction

Much had been said on the extensive ties linking Hong Kong with Mainland China, especially neighbouring Guangdong. Interfaces with Guangdong have long constituted the most direct and discernible impact of the 'China Factor' on Hong Kong. Historically and geographically Hong Kong was an integral part of Guangdong until Sino-British treaties yielded British control of the island in 1841, the Kowloon peninsula in 1861, and the New Territories in 1898. Despite the jurisdictional demarcations that set the two apart, historical and geographical realities made colonial Hong Kong-Guangdong linkages more than neighbourly, but almost symbiotic functionally. The 'Hong Kong factor' has been significant to modern Guangdong while the 'Guangdong factor' has been a powerful element in Hong Kong's development since the mid-19th century.

Migration, trade, investment, services, employment, and environmental concerns often form the prime focus of Hong Kong-Guangdong narratives while the financial-monetary dimensions of their interactive dynamics have received less scholarly attention. This chapter aims to develop an informed appreciation of the historical roots of these monetary interfaces. Three historical case studies illuminate vital politico-economic dimensions of the Hong Kong-Guangdong interdependence through the intimate financial-monetary linkages during the early years of modern China's Republican era.

These three case studies are: the 1912–13 Tramway Boycott, the 1925–26 Canton-Hong Kong Strike-Boycott, and the 1935 Monetary Reform. Collectively, they highlight the historical patterns of collaboration and competition between Hong Kong and its Guangdong hinterland, emphasizing the financial-monetary interface that mirrored the fruitful, yet at times stressful, contemporary Hong Kong-Guangdong dynamics, punctuated by jurisdictional barriers and divergent visions. The 1997 retrocession that turned Hong Kong into China's Hong Kong SAR has yet to fully transform many of the features linking but also dividing Hong Kong and Guangdong.

Extra-territorial currency circulation between Guangdong and Hong Kong

As historical context for these case studies, it is useful to outline the extra-territorial currency circulation between Hong Kong and Mainland China. One consequence of the trading networks and human traffic linking Hong Kong and Guangdong was the free circulation of Chinese currency in Hong Kong and *vice versa*. Historically, as a major port for international maritime commerce, Guangdong's provincial capital Guangzhou (Canton) had witnessed a continuous influx of foreign silver coins, mainly from the Portuguese, Spanish, Dutch, British, French and American trading vessels in its harbour. For over three centuries (1550s to 1920s) the widespread use of foreign silver coins as a common monetary instrument for commercial transactions in Sino-foreign trade and domestic business among the Cantonese and through regional trade in the hinterland.[1]

When international maritime trade was confined to Guangzhou in early Qing, the Chinese gained a steady inflow of foreign silver due to favourable external trade balance until 1827, when massive opium imports triggered a net silver outflow to cover the trade deficits. Guangzhou enjoyed an annual average trade surplus of 6,063,064 tales of silver during 1817–33.[2] This trend was a key factor behind the Qing court's ban on foreign opium imports as contraband in 1839 that triggered the Opium War with Britain.

After the British took Hong Kong as a colony in 1841, the widespread use of foreign silver in Guangdong continued. Under the March 1842 currency ordinance, the colonial authorities permitted the circulation in Hong Kong of Spanish and Mexican 'Eagle' silver dollars, the British East Indian Company's Rupee notes, Chinese silver, copper and other metallic currency, and, the Pound. Two years later, to simplify and minimize the problems of a multi-currency situation, London ordered the adoption of Pound Sterling as Hong Kong's legal tender. Yet the popular use of other currencies and foreign silver bullion persisted in Hong Kong as it did in the Pearl River Delta (PRD), and the rest of Guangdong/South China coastal region. As trade with Mainland China and businesses run by local Chinese merchants increased in importance to the colony's economy, the British pound and Indian rupee gradually faded from daily use in Hong Kong. From mid-1862 onwards, the colonial regime began to use the silver dollar as the basic unit for all government accounts locally.[3] This shows that Hong Kong's economy had since its earliest colonial days been closely tied to China with a silver-based monetary system for centuries, and this meant that when Hong Kong began to develop its own currency, it had to be silver-based.

In 1863 Governor Hercules Robinson issued Hong Kong's first set of coins; 10 cents pieces in silver, 1 cent and 0.1 cent pieces in copper, all minted in London. The colonial regime in 1864 established a mint in Hong Kong to coin British silver dollars in an attempt to push out the 'miscellaneous currencies.' But this attempt did not fully achieve the desired effect and after releasing some HK$2 million worth of coins (in six denominations from 0.1 cent to 1 dollar) between 1866–68, the mint was closed in 1868 due to heavy losses. Afterward the Mexican Eagle dollars became Hong Kong's *de facto* principal currency in daily transactions. To solve the shortage of one dollar silver coins, in 1874 the regime imported US silver dollar coins for local circulation. A later effort at local coinage had some success in 1895, when the colonial regime entrusted a British India mint to produce a new Hong Kong silver dollar coin that became widely circulated in China and Singapore-Malaya. These popular Hong Kong one dollar coins were minted until 1935. After the 1935 off-silver standard reform, the 1937 monetary ordinance finally ended the local circulation of all silver currencies, British and foreign.[4]

By the end of the Qing, some HK$130 million worth of Hong Kong silver dollars were in circulation in Mainland China, of which about a third (HK$43 million) stayed in Guangdong. Hong Kong silver coins accounted for a sizable portion of the estimated CH$1,100 million total worth of foreign silver dollars that circulation in China with Guangdong absorbing CH$476 million.[5] After the 1856–60 Second Opium War, as China's previous surplus from its legitimate foreign trade evaporated with the large scale import of foreign goods through the new treaty ports under the treaty-stipulated low tariffs, the outflow of Chinese silver abroad became more serious after the 1860s.

Meanwhile, the Hong Kong bank notes issued by the British banks in the colony circulated widely in Guangdong. The earliest Hong Kong bank notes issued in 1845 by the Oriental Banking Corporation were recognized as legal tender in 1857. The notes (in seven denominations from $5 to $1,000) issued in 1865 by the Hong Kong branch (established in 1859) of the Chartered Bank of India, Australia and China (now Standard Chartered Bank) constituted the second type of Hong Kong paper currency. The third kind of Hong Kong notes appeared in 1860 from the Chartered Mercantile Bank of India, London and China (later Mercantile Bank) that started to operate in the colony in 1857. The last and best known Hong Kong notes were issued by the Hong Kong and Shanghai Banking Corporation (HSBC) starting in 1867, two years after its founding in the colony. The first local Chinese-owned bank, the Hong Kong National Bank of China (established in 1891) also issued its own paper notes until 1899 when the colonial regime restricted note issuing rights to only two banks, the HSBC and Standard Chartered.[6] Two of these four British banks had the word 'China' while another had 'Shanghai' in their official titles, which were also prominently displayed on their bank notes. From the start, as the British takeover of Hong Kong was aimed at the China market, these British banks' issue of Hong Kong currency notes had in mind their widespread circulation in China as part of British, and by extension colonial Hong Kong's, economic clout.

The unsettling socio-economic conditions in Mainland China due to foreign war defeats, a major civil war (the 1851–65 Taiping conflict) and other domestic upheavals in the final Qing decades had disruptive effects on trade and finances that undermined the exchange value of Chinese notes, which were supposedly silver-based. When the Cantonese regime started in 1905 to issue its own silver-based paper currency and authorized in 1909 the note issued by the new local branches of the Qing Imperial Bank and the Bank of Communications, Hong Kong bank notes had already established their dominance in the province. While the March 1911 uprising in Guangdong by Sun Yatsen's partisans did not immediately collapse the Qing regime, the ensuing panic led to a public rush to redeem the fast depreciating Cantonese notes into silver coinage or bullion.[7] In contrast, the Hong Kong notes became even more popular among Mainland Chinese as being extremely reliable with a stable exchange value.

The widespread use of Hong Kong notes further complicated an already chaotic Cantonese monetary scene during the first twenty five years of the republican era. There was a large assortment of foreign and domestic bank notes, silver coins, and copper coins circulating in Guangdong. Before the 1935 monetary reform, China was on the silver standard and basically utilized a silver and copper bimetallic system. Paper notes, however, were also legal tender. Until 1935 the Mainland notes technically could be redeemed in silver although often only at considerable discount. These coins and notes had various denominations, issuers, and silver content. After the Qing's demise, successive warlords in Guangdong issued a large amount of paper notes without sufficient silver or hard currency cover. The value of these provincial notes continued to fluctuate, sometimes sliding down to non-acceptance as 'worthless' due to regime changes, recession, and over-issue against inadequate silver reserve. Many Cantonese silver coins were minted below the standard silver content, so they were accepted only at a discount. The domestic copper coins shared the same devaluation over time. Worse still, almost every Cantonese political crisis led to a serious currency crisis, often coupled with a bank run in Guangzhou, especially during the warlord era in the first republican decade.[8] The mid-1920s saw improved provincial finances under Guomintang (KMT) rule.

Under militarist Chen Jitang's 1929–36 reign, Guangdong became semi-autonomous beyond the control of Chiang Kai-shek's KMT central government in Nanjing. The Chen regime did attempt a banking and currency reorganization, beginning with a renamed Guangdong Provincial Bank (founded in 1924 by Sun Yatsen as the 'Central Bank' but renamed 'Guangdong Central Bank' in 1929) as the provincial central bank in January 1932. Yet, the notes issued both by the Central Bank of China and the Guangdong Provincial Bank depreciated sharply. The Cantonese rushed to exchange their paper notes for silver. As Guangdong was plagued by successive currency crises, the Guangdong Provincial Bank had to direct most of its resources to the note issue, value maintenance and currency stabilization efforts instead of promoting the Chen regime's planned economic development amid the Great Depression.[9] The popularity of Hong Kong notes in Guangdong and inland areas reflected the acute monetary instability and the serious problems stemming from rampant currency speculation on the Mainland.

A substantial demand for Hong Kong dollars was created as Cantonese merchants used them to purchase foreign goods. The value of the Hong Kong dollar against the Cantonese dollar varied due to demand and supply fluctuations. The situation was worsened by speculation of the exchange shops and money brokers who bought and sold Hong Kong notes betting for a quick profit. Hence, Hong Kong notes became a hot commodity that was traded everyday with wide ranges.

During the early 1930s, the currency used in Guangdong was different from that in the areas controlled by Nanjing. Guangdong had its own provincial notes while the Central Government used the national dollar (standard dollar). For much of this period, the Guangdong dollar on average was worth only 80% of the national dollar. After Chen yielded Guangdong to Nanjing in mid-1936, the national dollar gradually replaced the Guangdong dollar as the standard that would improve Guangdong's trade with other provinces. Seven months prior to Chen's fall from power, Nanjing had affected a full scale monetary reform to replace the silver standard with a managed currency 'Fabi' (legal notes).[10] As we shall see below, the HK$ soon also went off its silver base in late 1935.

It was estimated that of the HK$13,281,730 issued Hong Kong notes in 1890, HK$6,198,141 circulated in Guangdong, HK$1,770,898 higher than the total amount in circulation within the colony. The figures for 1911 were, of HK$31,577,478 in issued Hong Kong notes, HK$14,736,157 were in Guangdong that was HK$4,537,773 larger than Hong Kong's circulated pool and HK$2,717,977 larger than the combined total of Cantonese notes issued by the three Cantonese entities. In 1921, Guangdong absorbed HK$30.87 million of the total HK$66.15 million issued Hong Kong notes, HK$20.48 million larger than those circulated in the colony. By 1931, HK$71.69 million worth of Hong Kong notes circulated in the province, out of the colonial banks' total HK$153.61 million issued notes, a 130% increase within a decade.[11] Among the Hong Kong notes, those issued by HSBC dominated the field as it became the larger of the colony's remaining two local note-issuing banks by 1890. The HSBC notes were so popular on the Mainland that of the HK$43 million issued in 1926, some 70% circulated in China.[12]

In a sense, there was no better indicator of the close colony-province monetary links than the extra-territorial circulation of Hong Kong notes in Guangdong. The massive inflow of overseas Chinese remittance into Guangdong that was usually processed through Hong Kong banks and cashed out in HK$ helped to underwrite much of the infrastructure projects as well as new enterprises in the PRD. The HSBC's chosen Chinese name 'huifeng' literally means 'abundance of remittance' as since the late 19th century, Hong Kong capital, financial institutions, and bank notes had played a crucial role in Cantonese external economic interface.

On the other side of the coin, there was the reverse case of Mainland copper coins, especially those 'ten cash' (one cent) pieces minted in Guangdong since 1900, which circulated widely in Hong Kong where local residents used them in daily transactions.[13] But the proliferation of impure, poor quality copper coins minted by many other provinces during 1901–05 led to a deep devaluation (30% by 1905) of these copper coins that added to price inflation. Political instability right after the October 1911 Revolution that collapsed the Manchu dynasty, further depressed the copper cash's value in silver. Soon after the Chinese republic's birth, some 15.276 million pieces of new one cent copper coins were minted in Guangzhou, each with a new republican logo and 'First Year of the Republic' date to replace the Qing imperial design. China's epoch change from monarchial order into a new republic did not revive the value of its currency.[14] The colonial counter-measures against the Chinese copper coins' increasingly serious depreciation soon triggered an unexpected crisis in Hong Kong.

The 1912–13 Tramway Boycott

The depreciation of copper coins against the silver dollars since the turn of the 20th century became a burden draining Hong Kong's monetary resources. Starting from 1905 when some HK$44 million worth of Hong Kong's own copper coins were in circulation, which was far too much for local needs, the colonial regime had to recall through redemption in silver dollars a very large amount of them for demonetization in order to maintain these coins' value.[15] In April 1912, to strengthen the local monetary system against the flood of increasingly depreciated Chinese coins, the colonial regime passed a Foreign Copper Coin Ordinance banning the import and circulation of foreign copper coins in the colony. This was regarded by many local Chinese as an unfriendly act disrespectful of their new republic. The colonial regime's stern enforcement of this law provoked a fierce three-month-long Tramway Boycott during the winter of 1912–13.[16]

In November 1912, Governor Henry May persuaded the two tramways and the Star Ferry to refuse Mainland Chinese coins for fare payment. These public transport concerns had suffered from the depreciation of Mainland coins that were of the same denomination and size as the local coins. This new policy took effect on 18 November 1912 and created considerable problems as local coins were few and the colony was flooded with Chinese coins. Many European and Chinese passengers were unable to pay their fares in local coins. By the second week, a boycott of the tramway broke out, with trams frequently stoned. Local shopkeepers either refused service to those who got off tram cars or charged them exorbitant prices. After the police arrested some stone-throwers, the stoning ceased, but by then the tram cars had become almost empty, and even with a policeman or soldier riding on the car for protection, the only Chinese on board were the driver and the conductor. The proliferation along the tram route of Chinese characters posters threatening tramway riders with death indicated a deliberate boycott. Workers who used to ride the trams to and from work walked instead and the trams remained empty even in bad weather. The regime attributed this widespread boycott to the intimidation by the guilds and other local Chinese organs.[17]

After the local Chinese leaders tried ineffectually to break the boycott, Governor May had the Legislative Council pass in a single sitting on 19 December 1912, a Boycott Prevention Ordinance that defined a boycott as 'any act calculated to persuade or induce any persons not to make use or occupy any movable property in any lawful manner, or not to work for any persons in a lawful manner in the ordinary course of trade, business or employment.' Besides heavy penalties for threatening violence, picketing, and inciting to boycott, it authorized the governor to declare any area in the colony as a boycotting area, over which a special punitive rate could be levied and paid to persons or companies incurring loss due to the boycott. [18] On 4 January 1913, the regime publicized its intention to impose a special levy on all the areas along the tram route that were proclaimed 'boycott areas.' A twelve-day grace period was given to Chinese representatives and merchants from the affected areas to break the boycott. A solution was soon worked out: the Tramway Company issued tickets in bulk at a small discount to property owners and merchants for sale to their employees. Gradually more Chinese used the tram, and passenger traffic returned to normal by February. Hence, no penal rate was levied and the law was suspended a month later. The regime later paid HK$45,000 to the tramway to compensate its boycott losses.[19]

Other Hong Kong companies soon also openly refused Chinese coins. In mid-1913 the colonial regime enacted two related bills, the Foreign Notes (Prohibition of Circulation) Ordinance and the Foreign Silver and Nickel Coins Ordinance.[20] Cantonese coins and notes from Macao gradually vanished from the colony.

The local Chinese community was divided in this episode due to divergent economic interests. Some elites collaborated with the regime to end the boycott by riding the trams to set an example. Some wealthy businessmen, being tram company share holders, also tried to defuse the crisis lest their share value and profits be affected. Among the tram boycotters, many of whom grassroots elements, were also businessmen with vested interests in continuing the circulation of foreign coins

– owners of small native banks, exchange shops, currency brokers, and money/bullion speculators who thrived on the overseas Cantonese remittance that cleared through Hong Kong. Also supporting the boycott were merchants in Southeast Asian and North American trade and suppliers from overseas Chinatowns who also engaged in money exchanges. Those who profited from Hong Kong currency-Chinese coins exchange normally netted over HK$2 million in processing overseas remittance then worth US$56 million per year. Conflicting local Chinese interests were at play in this boycott that was propelled by the forces of pocket book concerns and nationalistic sentiments.[21]

By solving his predecessors' perennial problem of Chinese coins inundating the colony, the breaking of the tramway boycott enhanced Governor May's authority. Stemming from his 'old police instincts' (as head of police, 1893–1902) May struck back firmly at challenges to British rule and assumed wide emergency powers.[22] The weakening of the Chinese state since the 1911 Revolution afforded him greater latitude to respond with force to threats originating from China. In flinging down the gauntlet with the Boycott Prevention Ordinance, May set a draconian precedent for the colony's statute book.[23] This unfair requirement of collective responsibility for all the inhabitants in the chosen area, implicit in section 9, was contrary to the presumption of innocence in the common law, the foundation of the colony's British-style legal system. It was closer to the traditional Chinese *baojia* system of neighborhood collective security and mutual guarantee in both rural and urban areas. As an observer commented, 'It was the kind of measure an occupying army might use to enforce its will.'[24] A disturbing rationale behind this ordinance was the colonial regime's overemphasis on the intimidation efforts of the guilds, secret societies, and fraternal associations.

In adopting this strong boycott-breaking measure, the colonial authorities ignored the genuine nationalistic pride among the local populace, who saw in the outlaw of Chinese coins a real insult to *their* new republic. In paying HK$45,000 from public funds to cover the tramway's loss and thereby intervening directly in private enterprise, the state might have violated its own sacred *laissez-faire* precepts. The ordinance only increased local Chinese anti-colonial hostilities but did not end the use of boycott as a highly effective economic weapon against British rule in Hong Kong.

The 1925–26 general strike-boycott

Based in Canton under Sun Yatsen's control, the Guomintang-Chinese Communist Party (KMT-CCP) United Front formed in January 1924 was committed to an anti-imperialist national revolution. Hong Kong as the citadel of British imperialism in China was a natural target of Chinese patriotic assault. Against such strained Hong Kong-Guangdong relations, a storm broke out in 1925 engulfing Hong Kong in its worst socio-economic crisis. The 1925 May 30th incident in Shanghai triggered a nationwide anti-British protest movement encompassing some 130 reported strikes throughout China.[25] The most significant, longest-lasting event and the climax of this movement was the Canton-Hong Kong General Strike-Boycott from June 1925 to October 1926 that came close to destroying Hong Kong and liquidating British interests in South China. As a gigantic political protest sponsored by the United Front using economic warfare against British imperialism, this strike-boycott drove 250,000 Hong Kong strikers and their families (1/3 of local populace) back to Guangdong and paralysed the colony.[26] While the full magnitude and severity of the strike-boycott's impact on Hong Kong were absolutely devastating, the focus here is on the contrasting economic realities between the colony and Guangdong during 1925–26.

Economic crisis in Hong Kong

In a nutshell, the British colony had to endure for 16 months an unprecedented economic nightmare of total economic warfare waged by its neighbour.[27] A most apparent result was the drastic decline in shipping through the colony that had thrived as South China's leading international port. As the Harbour Master reported, 764,492 vessels (56.7 million tons) cleared Hong Kong in 1924 but decreased to 379,177 vessels (41.4 million tons) in 1925 and 310,361 vessels (36.8 millon tons) in 1926. All shipping concerns in Hong Kong suffered great losses and failed to pay any dividends during these years.[28]

While shipping tonnage declined some 40%, Hong Kong's total trade fell nearly 50% during the strike-boycott. A precise measure of its full impact is impossible due to the lack of official trade data after September 1925. Some suspected a key factor behind Governor Reginald Stubbs' decision to abolish the Statistics Office and stop the compilations for budget saving was to conceal the strike-boycott's true effectiveness.[29] From other data on Hong Kong's trade with China (which normally claimed a 41% share of the colony's import-export business), the damages inflicted by the boycott were clear. In 1922-24, China received about 25% of its imports from Hong Kong, but this dropped to 18.6% in 1925 and 11.1% the next year. In 1924, 22.4% of China's total exports went through the colony, falling to 14.8% in 1925 and 10.9% in 1926.[30] According to Chinese Maritime Customs records, the total value of China-Hong

Kong trade declined from 1924's 411.5 million Haikwan Taels (1 Hk Tael = Ch$1.5) to HKT287 million in 1925 and HKT214 million in 1926.[31] Hong Kong's trade with other major partners also declined by 36% from the 1921–24 average while its trade with the UK was particularly hard hit with a 48% decline due to the boycott against British goods. Hong Kong's total loss in trade with all markets during the strike-boycott was estimated to be at least US$300 million.[32]

The months from mid-1925 to late 1926 was widely acknowledged as an exceptionally bad period for Hong Kong's business community. Besides the strike-boycott, the economy fell victim to the colonial regime's counter-productive embargo against Guangdong that became a self-inflicted wound. The ban on exporting foodstuffs and fuel from Hong Kong, aimed at hurting Guangzhou, instead further disrupted the colony's dwindling trade. Hong Kong soon lost its role as the rice distribution hub for South China.[33] As Guangdong had been Hong Kong's main meat and vegetables supplier, the vigorous Cantonese embargo on food exports hit the colony hard with a food shortage that drove prices up by half. The price of fuel increased more than 50%.[34] The colony's lucrative silk trade was 'literally dead.' as silk traffic from Guangdong through Hong Kong to overseas markets stopped.[35]

When the strike-boycott broke in late June 1925, the stock market collapsed and the regime was forced to close the Stock Exchange. After it was reopened in late October, stock prices continued to plummet. Particularly hard hit were the shipping companies' shares. Even the share price of the giant HSBC, a pillar of colonial finance and a major instrument of British economic activities in China, dropped 11.5%. There was an overall depreciation of 40% in the value of shares, a loss of £100 million for the speculators, a vast majority of whom were local Chinese businessmen.[36]

Another symptom of the colony's financial fabric unraveling under great strain was the 1925 banking crisis induced by the strike-boycott. Immediately after the strike broke out on June 19, there was a serious run on the local banks coupled with a general loss of confidence in the value of their notes. During 19–22 June, a total of HK$16 million was withdrawn in panic from these banks, converted into silver coins and exported from the colony before the imposition of an official embargo on gold and silver bullion and currency notes above five dollars in face value. Soon, of the total HK$65 million issued bank notes, at least HK$40 million went out of circulation, much of which was hoarded. What was left could not suffice for local needs. Ultimately, the colonial regime had to restrict withdrawals from bank accounts (not to exceed

10% of any depositor's total account) and grant a banking moratorium. Payments suspension or contract postponements were legalized. Even the credit of the powerful British banks was affected, while cash was required in most transactions.[37] As Bank of East Asia director Fung Ping-shan said, 'The strike erupted suddenly, shocking the whole of Hong Kong and commerce became stagnant. Those firms with insufficient cash flow were forced to close down. Banks, the pivot of financial operations, were most immediately affected. I, being the chairman of the Yik On native bank owned by the Yu Hing Company, had to be doubly careful in all the transactions. Luckily I had been very cautious in business and frugal in my personal life so that I was able to sail through the storm.'[38]

The impact of the banking crisis deepened the colony's trade depression. Unable to cope with the extremely adverse economic conditions, many business concerns declared insolvency. On September 1925, the bankruptcy court dealt with a daily average of 20 cases and by the year's end, bankruptcies numbered more than 5,000, including some of the colony's largest firms.[39] The strike-boycott's stranglehold on the mobility of goods continued to affect the liquidity of the local banks. In September 1925, another run on the banks occurred and seven banks were suspended.[40] Even the HSBC became very reluctant to advance any money to the colonial regime.[41] The situation became so critical that Governor Stubbs had to request a £3 million loan from London in October 1925 to relieve economic distress. The news of London's loan approval helped to soothe somewhat the colony's tight financial situation, but the economy as a whole began to recover only after the strike-boycott was terminated by the Cantonese in October 1926.[42]

The colonial government itself was forced to operate with huge budget deficits. Instead of the surplus of HK$2 to $3.1 million in 1921–23, the colony incurred a budget deficit above HK$5 million in 1925 and almost HK$2.4 million in 1926. The deficits were due to the decline in official revenue as well as various emergency expenses. Whereas total revenue reached HK$24.2 million in 1924, it fell to HK$23.2 million in 1925 and declined to HK$21.1 million in 1926 as revenue dropped half a million dollars per month since the strike-boycott. Drastic measures were adopted to trim spending; public works in progress were suspended and many public school teachers were dismissed.[43] During 1921–24, the regime gained an annual average of HK$2.5 million from public land sales but fetched only HK$510,243 in 1925 and HK$286,342 in 1926.[44] They vividly portrayed the ruinous 40% to 60% drop in local property value and the drastic 60% decline in rents.[45] An authoritative source estimates that the depreciation in property value and industrial shares was US$500 million.[46]

While all these statistics may indicate the magnitude of Hong Kong's financial and trade losses, they do not fully reflect the actual suffering due to bank and business failures, lost wages and lost working days. The estimates that place the colony's total economic losses at between HK$2 million per day or over HK$5 million per week seem quite conservative.[47] Figures alone cannot convey the physical destitution, material discomfort and socio-political consequences of Hong Kong's economic calamity amid the strike-boycott.

Guangdong's unexpected prosperity

In sharp contrast to Hong Kong's devastation, the strike-boycott brought unexpected prosperity to Guangdong. Despite the ban on British shipping, there was an unprecedented shipping boom as vessels that had previously docked at Hong Kong came instead to Canton, where an average 40 vessels called daily as 45 ocean-going steamers regularly running direct service. Canton harbour became so crowded that some ships had to anchor outside awaiting an available berth.[48]

The strike-boycott also led to much greater economic independence for Guangdong. The colonial embargo intended to starve the Cantonese and disrupt their economy was a failure as the British could not prevent supplies from reaching Canton directly, short of an unfeasible naval blockade.[49] After having endured some initial hardship at the start of the strike-boycott the Cantonese soon overcame the stoppage of food and fuel consignments that used to come through Hong Kong. By July 1925 the Cantonese succeeded in shipping rice directly from Thailand and Indochina while flour was shipped directly from Shanghai. Due to an effective counter-embargo on food exports, a surplus of fruits and vegetables led to lower local prices. Coal continued to be obtained from Indochina and with large supplies of Russian petroleum and kerosene, Canton was well-fuelled.[50] The initial trade dislocation due to bypassing Hong Kong was soon overcome and the local economy prospered as shown in Canton Maritime Customs statistics.[51]

The inauguration of direct shipping links between Canton and other ports and the suspension of the Guangdong-Hong Kong traffic contributed to a Cantonese wholesale boom. Because Hong Kong was boycotted, many of its former trading partners turned to Canton for direct trade.[52] This situation helped to create a larger Pearl River Delta market for native producers and retail business. For Chinese firms long accustomed to a marginal share of the Cantonese market because they could not compete with foreign concerns with better communication and financial support, the strike-boycott yielded an excellent opportunity to redress the balance as the Cantonese founded new firms to engage in coastal trade.[53]

The unification of Guangdong under the KMT enabled the extension of the boycott to the whole province and created a larger internal market to enhance Cantonese economic independence.[54] The KMT regime's finances improved considerably because of its expanded jurisdiction. Guangdong provincial revenue averaged CH\$833,000 per month in 1922 and was CH\$665,000 in 1924 but increased to CH\$1.47 million in August 1925, and reached CH\$3.82 million the next month, with total 1925 provincial revenue at CH\$19 million, more than double 1924's CH\$7.98 million.[55]

The KMT regime's position was further buttressed by a Cantonese financial boom since the boycott. Local banking business, no longer dominated by the Hong Kong banks, became much more active in a trade boom, especially in drafts and transfers. The Central Bank notes issued in Canton were in full circulation at face value. Previously, Cantonese notes had been accepted at a 40% discount of their face value as local business preferred Hong Kong notes. After the colonial embargo on the export of Hong Kong notes and silver and gold bullion, the Cantonese fell back on domestic notes. This situation, coupled with KMT finance minister T.V. Soong's management that reformed the provincial fiscal structure and backed the issue of notes with silver, enabled the Cantonese to have greater confidence in local notes.[56] Such developments were key factors in the KMT regime's willingness and ability to support the strikers financially. Guangdong had attained a high degree of economic independence.

Communist labour organizer Deng Zhongxia's claim that the strike-boycott freed Guangdong from the economic domination of Hong Kong was not unjustified.[57] Indeed, Guangdong's unexpected prosperity demonstrated the extent of British and Hong Kong domination over the Cantonese economy prior to the strike-boycott. Articles in the Anglo-American press, after questioning the basis of the Hong Kong-Guangdong economic relationship, concluded that the colony's past prosperity was won at Guangdong's expense.[58] As British Consul-General Jamieson pointed out, Guangzhou could carry on without Hong Kong indefinitely.[59] But the reverse is questionable.

The 1935 monetary reform: abandoning the silver standard[60]

Caught between the crosscurrents of the China market and world economic forces, Hong Kong, then and now, must strike a fine balance to safeguard the stability of its monetary system and maintain its international trade and financial hub functions. Amid the World Depression, the 1929–31 and 1934–35 silver crises that severely affected the value of the Chinese and Hong Kong currencies (both silver-based) eventually resulted in sweeping reforms in their monetary systems by late 1935 with lasting effect.

Hong Kong was fortunate enough to have survived the drastic decline in the value of silver against the gold during 1929-31 with only relatively minor administrative measures to cope with the crisis situation. Then, two years after the World Depression's adverse impact had finally hit China and Hong Kong in 1932, the US silver purchase policy triggered a second silver currency crisis that yielded a wholesale monetary reform in late 1935 by the Chinese government which pushed the Chinese currency off the silver standard and replaced it with a new managed currency system. This directly affected the local monetary systems in Guangdong and Hong Kong, and each in its own way responded with extensive reforms measures that paralleled China's new national currency system. Measures such as the establishment of the Exchange Fund to manage the local currency by issuing Certificates of Indebtedness (CoIs) to the note issuing banks according to the amount of silver or foreign currency that they deposited with the Fund as the base for their notes, laid the foundation of modern Hong Kong's monetary system.

Hong Kong and the 1929–31 silver crisis

Since the late 19th century the value of silver against gold (which was the currency standard of Hong Kong's European and North American trade partners) had been falling internationally due to a continuous oversupply. By the 1900s, as silver-gold bimetallism was given up in the West and other Asian countries turned to a gold standard, China remained one of the few major economies where silver was still the common means of payment in both domestic transactions and foreign trade. This long-term downward trend in silver's value not only impacted the Chinese economy but very directly affected the Hong Kong dollar exchange rate against the pound sterling, for instance, it declined two thirds from HK$1 = 4s/4d in 1872 to HK$1 = 1s/7d in 1902. Then a sudden rise in silver's value during the First World War reversed the trend to reach HK$1 = 4s/10d in 1919 before it declined again.[61] Against this silver devaluation, many countries either demonetized silver or decreased the fineness of silver in their coins during the 1920s. The average annual price of fine silver dropped drastically from US$6.3 per ounce in 1921 to US$0.29 in 1931.[62]

The silver price's drastic fall in 1929–31 had a direct impact on the Chinese and the Hong Kong economy. The premium of their bank notes over silver rose to an abnormally high level. The Hong Kong note's premium over silver reached 20% by end-September 1929 with disastrous consequences for government revenue and for many traders, especially exporters to China who had to compete with Shanghai and other Treaty Ports.[63] The depreciation of the Hong Kong dollar by nearly one half led to a brief trade boom in the early 1930s. These fluctuations in the value of silver and the disturbance to the local economy led to a heated debate over the local currency standard. Some major British merchant houses called for the adoption of a gold standard even if China remained on a silver standard, while many Chinese merchants reaffirmed the importance of keeping the same standard as China.[64]

By late 1929, the colony was flooded with Mexican dollars, mostly imported from Shanghai for speculative purposes. Silver was also accepted in payments due to the colonial government. The HSBC reported that its stock of such silver coins had risen to about 21.5 million from under 15 million on 1 January 1930. Accepting the HSBC's recommendation, the colonial regime soon banned the import without official permission of Mexican silver dollars in excess of $50 by anyone at a time. This curbed the inflow of silver coins into Hong Kong.[65] The fall in silver price also directly increased the colonial regime's expenditures as a substantial annual contribution to cover the British military's local presence and the salaries of British colonial officials were both paid in gold-based pound sterling. The Executive Council in March 1930 appointed a Committee of Inquiry and it submitted a report in July 1931 reaffirming the belief that Hong Kong's currency standard should follow that of China to facilitate trade. Governor William Peel concurred with the report that the low dollar was due to the fall in silver value and 'it was beyond the power of Hong Kong to remedy this.'[66]

The Report argued against the suggestion that the government should take over the note issue as additional official expenditure would be incurred and also the regime and indirectly the taxpayers would be exposed to great risks of heavy losses due to fluctuations in the value of silver and securities. Such risks would be more competently dealt with by the bankers. Yet, three committee members shared the view of many local Chinese businessmen and bankers that the regime should take more direct control over note issue as the existing system was defective and the fate of the people should not be vested in the hands of a few bankers.[67] Note issue remained the task of the three British commercial banks, in particular the HSBC, which had assumed some of the vital functions of a central bank that colonial Hong Kong never had.

A commission sent from London in April 1931 to study Hong Kong's currency situation upheld the committee's views that: Hong Kong should remain on the silver standard so long as China did, all bank notes be convertible to silver bullion and made unlimited tender and the supervision of the issue of notes and the reserve of silver bullion be undertaken by a Hong Kong Currency Board.[68] However, none of these proposals were immediately adopted except that Hong Kong remained on the silver standard. The report did not reach the Executive Council for consideration until April 1932. By then, world silver prices had steadily risen after the abandonment of the gold standard by Britain, Japan and the US while the Hong Kong dollar exchange rate had fallen to within the silver points and the premium minimized. The silver crisis appeared to be over and the colonial regime took no further action.[69]

Cantonese response to the mid-1930s silver crisis and currency reform

During 1931-33, when most of China and Hong Kong's major trading partners like Britain, Japan and the US went off the gold standard with a consequent pound, yen and US dollar depreciation, there was an upward appreciation of the Chinese and Hong Kong dollars' exchange value. As silver prices began to rise internationally in 1933, China suffered a deflationary crisis (Shanghai price index fell from 120 in 1930/132 in 1931 to 100 in 1935).[70] In 1935, the value of Hong Kong's total trade value retreated to the 1931 level.[71]

Besides domestic monetary problems that troubled China in the early republican years, the rapid rise in the international silver price since 1934 triggered a massive outflow of silver from China as a valued commodity that disrupted the silver-based Cantonese currency. In June 1934, US President Franklin Roosevelt enacted the Silver Purchase Act that stipulated the proportion of silver to gold in the US official monetary reserve was to be increased until 25% of the total reserve was in silver.[72] This immediately led to a rapid rise in world silver prices and the subsequent overvaluation of the silver dollar.

As the silver value of Chinese and Hong Kong dollar coins became far greater than the legal face value of the silver dollar, very soon a huge amount of silver was smuggled out of China and Hong Kong. The massive silver exodus led to a serious shortage of money supply in

China. After cash redemption of notes was suspended, the Chinese government in Nanjing imposed an export duty on silver to check the outflow in October 1934 and this immediately caused a 10% depreciation of the Shanghai dollar. The export of silver from Guangdong was huge. The provincial authorities had to issue a new series of treasury notes to stabilize the local currency, significantly increasing the money supply. Unable to arrest the continuous rise of silver prices and the silver exodus out of China through smuggling, the Chinese central authorities (on the advice of the UK Treasury's Sir Frederick Leith Ross) took a bold step on 5 October 1935 to depart from the silver standard and set up a managed, foreign exchange backed new legal currency (Fabi) at CH$1 = US$0.30 or 1s/2.5d sterling. This represented a 20% depreciation from the exchange rate kept by the Chinese government banks and HSBC since 1934, and was 40% below the silver par. It helped to re-inflate the Chinese economy as the Shanghai price index jumped to 112 in 1936 and 124 in 1937.[73]

Right after ordering nationalization of all silver within the country in early October, the Nanjing central government dispatched a special mission to Guangdong to take charge of the matter. However, the Guangdong government announced its own plans for monetary reform in early November. First, the paper notes issued by the two government banks (Guangdong Provincial Bank and Guangzhou Municipal Bank) would become legal tender. Second, an organizing committee would be established to administer the issue of bank notes and nationalization of silver. Third, the exchange ratio between the silver dollar and Guangdong note would be fixed at 1 to 1.2, and between the Fabi and Guangdong notes at 1 to 1.44. Fourth, all the silver coins and bullion would be nationalized according to their value. Fifth, all the contracts or debts negotiated in silver dollars would be converted into a new paper money basis. Sixth, foreign dollars could be traded freely in Guangdong but were not accepted as legal tender.[74] The effect was that the Cantonese currency was devalued by 20%. The subsequent inflationary effect was directly felt as the price of commodities like rice increased by 20% and flour by 15%.[75]

This provincial reform at first created a stir among the Cantonese populace who were sceptical of the real purpose of these measures. Many simply rushed to exchange their Guangdong notes into Hong Kong dollars and the premium on the Hong Kong dollars suddenly jumped from 40% to 80%. As silver ceased to be the currency, the public had to exchange their silver back into Cantonese notes but the notes of the two government banks were in short supply. The Hong Kong dollars were exchanged back to the Cantonese notes and the premium fell gradually from the peak at 80% to only 30%. The shortage of Cantonese notes was over by March 1936 when newly printed notes arrived. But during that summer, Hong Kong dollar notes again rose in value against the Cantonese notes because of the impending confrontation between Chen Jitang's forces and Chiang Kai-shek's central troops. The premium on the Hong Kong dollar reached as high as 60% in June–July 1936.[76] The Cantonese currency system gradually stabilized after the collapse of Chen's regime in mid-July and Nanjing's reassertion of control over the province. By autumn 1936 the Fabi became the dominant currency in Guangdong.

Hong Kong's November 1935 currency reform

Like Guangdong and the rest of China, Hong Kong also suffered from the rapid rise in the value of silver following the 1934 US silver purchase policy. The value of Hong Kong dollars rose against the pound sterling and the Shanghai dollar as shown below.

After an export duty was imposed on silver by the Chinese central authorities to check the outflow in October 1934, Hong Kong had to consider the option of imposing a similar export duty on silver in order to continue its general policy of keeping in line with China, thus preventing Shanghai from gaining any clear competitive advantage through currency depreciation. Opinions in the colony mostly opposed taking similar action as many doubted if China's policy could be effectively carried out by the Chinese government and whether the new exchange

Table 2.1   Average Monthly Rates for Sterling and Shanghai Dollar in 1935

	HK$ to Sterling (shilling and pence)	Shanghai$ to HK$ (SH$100 to HK$)
January	1/8	121
February	1/9	118
March	1/11	121
April	2/1	130
May	2/4	140
June	2/5	139
July	2/1	134
August	2/0	134
September	2/0	131
October	1/11	134
November	1/5	114
December	1/3	109

Source: Hong Kong Government, *Administrative Report, 1935*, Appendix, p. A19

rate could be maintained. The UK Colonial Office monetary experts agreed that it would be best to wait and see.[77]

The situation continued unchanged until April 1935 while the silver price kept on rising so that the Shanghai dollar depreciated 30% below its silver parity. By this time some circles in Hong Kong began to feel the need to depreciate the Hong Kong dollar and the UK Colonial Office recommended a limited depreciation of the Hong Kong dollar by imposing an export tax. The Hong Kong government accepted the suggestion from a London expert that they should take no immediate action until some emergency occurred.[78]

Unable to arrest the continuous rise of the silver price and the massive exodus of silver out of China through smuggling, the Chinese central authorities took a bold step to depart from the silver standard on 5 October 1935. The Hong Kong government followed suit by banning the export of silver on 9 November 1935. Then, on 5 December 1935, the colonial regime inaugurated a new linked currency system buttressed by a reserve and stabilization mechanism akin to a currency board operation. It recalled all the silver coins in circulation and purchased all silver bullion in private hands (at HK$1.28 per ounce). A Board of Exchange was established which was the only authority to have the power to buy and sell foreign exchange. The Board took over the silver bullion previously held as back-up by the note-issuing banks and issued CoIs according to the amount of silver or foreign currency that the banks had deposited with the Exchange Fund as the base for their issued notes.[79] These Hong Kong notes also became for the first time the colony's legal tender and were calibrated at a fixed exchange rate of HK$1 = 1s/3d or 1 Pound = HK$16, a rate (within a 1.25% margin) that was maintained through until November 1967 (and the sterling link lasted until mid-1972).[80] The colonial treasurer also began to issue new HK$1 dollar bills and new 5 and 10 cents nickel coins to replace silver dollars, which under law had to be exchanged for bank notes and nickel coins within a month.[81]

The colonial regime conceded that this reform had to be taken to follow China, but initially it was not fully confident that this new monetary system would be successful in the long term. As the colonial treasurer stated in his 1936 annual report, 'It is still too early to predict what effects Hong Kong's new monetary policy will have on the trade and prosperity of the Colony. It is felt that stability of exchange should result in improved trading conditions and in the last few months of the year signs of improvement were not lacking.'[82] As it turned out, the Exchange Fund did ensure every dollar of Hong Kong currency was adequately backed with a mechanism to maintain its stable external value.

To keep local price competitiveness, the HK$ experienced a new depreciation against the British pound (which had gone off the gold standard in 1931), from September 1935's 1 pound = HK$10 to December 1935's 1 pound = HK$16. This reform effectively stabilized Hong Kong's currency as the Hong Kong dollar exchange value that had soared to a peak of 2s/6d in April 1935 before the ban on silver export forced it down to 1s/4d. After the introduction of the new linked currency system, the Hong Kong dollar remained at a constant 1s/3d level. It enjoyed a fairly stable ratio against the new off-silver Chinese notes under a managed currency system until the Sino-Japanese War broke out in mid-1937.[83] The Japanese occupation of Guangzhou and costal Guangdong in October 1938 seriously disrupted the Hong Kong-Mainland trade, and then the outbreak of the Second World War in September 1939 (when the UK imposed foreign exchange controls) further impacted on the colony's financial scene.[84] The 1935 reform that occurred just ahead of the war years in effect detached Hong Kong's new non-silver currency (with a fixed pound sterling peg) from the Mainland's new Fabi as their previous common monetary bond through a shared silver standard was broken.

The colony's monetary reform away from the silver standard, necessitated by both the Chinese national currency reform and the new Cantonese provincial monetary measures, came at a critical juncture to relieve the stress on Hong Kong's banking system. At this time the banks in Hong Kong, particularly the small savings banks, were not government-regulated. In an economic downturn, especially when coupled with a sharp property market slump, some of these banks went bankrupt. Since the onset of the Great Depression those banks that had extended loans too liberally on landed properties had been burdened with frozen and declining assets.[85] The bankruptcy of the Bank of Canton in September 1935 for instance, was precipitated by a property market downturn. Its deposit base depended heavily on overseas Chinese remittances that were abundant until 1931 but had declined since 1932 while local withdrawal of deposits increased especially after 1934. As its funds were lent out mostly as mortgages for properties, the local property market's one-third fall triggered a bank run.[86] Part of the bank's failure was attributed to the currency crisis that drained the bank's cash reserve. As the HK$ exchange rate rose sharply against other currencies, people rushed to the bank to cash in and exchange their foreign currency drafts for HK$.[87] Meanwhile, another run on the National

Commercial Savings Bank occurred as its liabilities totalled HK$4.7 million against HK$4.2 million in assets.[88] To a large extent it was victimized by the rumours and public panic incited by the Bank of Canton's closure.[89]

In fact, the question of regulating banking had been under consideration in Hong Kong earlier.[90] But even in 1930 the colonial administration still considered any such regulatory measures as impracticable, unenforceable or too difficult.[91] Only after the two bank runs occurred in 1935, the colonial regime revisited the banking regulation issue by appointing a Committee of Inquiry with only informal meetings in order not to arouse public unease.[92] The UK Colonial Office offered no opinions but sent over banking reform information on British Palestine. Sir Vandeleur Grayburn, HSBC Chief Manager and a committee member, argued against any Palestinian type banking reform as Palestine's banking was undeveloped while the Chinese had engaged in banking for centuries and knew their business without official interference. Behind this status quo conservatism was the fear of extra expenditure on the new regulatory machineries.[93] The colony's regulatory reform had to wait until after the War.

As a whole, these turbulent 1930s experiences clearly revealed the limited role played by a colonial regime that lacked both the will and the necessary tools decisively to affect the monetary and financial development with any long-term vision. It only acted according to the dictates of current circumstances as shaped by larger external forces from both Mainland China and the world beyond. In the 1930s the administration faced the task of stabilizing the exchange rate of the Hong Kong dollar. The Hong Kong public, the local and the UK governments did consider whether Hong Kong should discard the silver standard, but the colonial regime's delayed response in the 1929–31 silver crisis revealed its limited capacity and inadequate expertise on monetary matters. The appointment of a special committee indicated the lack of standing machinery and experienced officials to react promptly and effectively to the challenge. The 1935 currency reform showed that the colonial regime took action only when it was compelled to react to the change of circumstances. Had China not adopted the managed currency system, Hong Kong would most likely not have been prepared to reform its monetary system accordingly. Eventually the British did proceed to update and upgrade Hong Kong's capacity in this regard. In 1937, the colonial treasurer was elevated to a new post of financial secretary. Reflecting the growing importance of finance and money in local administration, these 1930s changes laid the foundation of Hong Kong's modern monetary system that still functions today.[94]

Concluding observations

These historical case studies have yielded keen insights into the unique Hong Kong-Mainland China financial and monetary interface. The first two cases were collective economic sanctions through boycott movements on the part of the local Chinese population (or in league with the Cantonese) against the colonial regime for politico-ideological reasons using financial and monetary weapons. The third case was an example of Hong Kong's monetary crisis management dictated by economic necessity and shaped by political considerations.

The 1912–13 tramway boycott revealed how the colonial regime's originally narrow and mainly administrative attempt to exclude the seriously debased and fast depreciating Cantonese copper coins from local circulation was transformed into a larger state-society conflict. Seldom mentioned publicly but definitely in the minds of many tramway boycotters, was the apparent unfairness in cross-border currency circulation. While Hong Kong notes enjoyed widespread popularity and common acceptance in Guangdong and other Mainland points, Cantonese coins were outlawed in the colony that was populated mainly by Cantonese immigrants/sojourners. Concern for the prestige of their new republic added fuel to the flame of monetary discrimination against the local Chinese users of 'their' homeland copper coins in the colony. The 1912–13 boycott, relatively small in scale and intensity, failed to achieve the boycotters' immediate objective to continue the use of Mainland coins in Hong Kong. However, the colonial regime's stern anti-boycott measures deepened the anti-colonial animosity among local Chinese and did not end the use of boycott as an effective Chinese weapon against British imperialism.

The effectiveness of Cantonese patriotic sanctions against British economic interests in the 1925–26 strike-boycott led to a reorientation of British policy towards China in late 1926. This paved the way for the UK to become the first major power to offer diplomatic recognition of the KMT regime under Chiang Kai-shek as China's legitimate national government in 1928. British diplomats and colonial officials were alarmed and impressed by Guangdong's remarkable performance during this protest movement. As part of the strike-boycott's October 1926 termination, the British accepted a 2.5%–5% surtax on the standard maritime customs duty imposed by the Guangdong authorities to support the remaining strikers. This British acquiescence was a significant breakthrough leading to China's tariff autonomy in 1929. To appease the local Chinese community, the first Chinese member (Chow Shou-san) was appointed to Hong Kong's Executive Council in 1926. The British humiliation in the hands of the aroused Chinese grassroots movement was not limited to the Pearl River Delta but extended further. Along with the victorious KMT forces in their Northern Expedition, the British concessions in Wuhan and Jiujiang were restored to China after being swarmed by local protestors.[95]

The 1925–26 strike-boycott's effectiveness highlighted the role of economics in China's international relations. As boycott tactics improved the Chinese became more interested in the use of boycott as an economic means for political ends, as seen in the many large-scale, nationwide patriotic boycotts against Japanese aggression during the 1930s.[96] Hong Kong's economic slump and Guangdong's unexpected boom, especially in finance and money, testified to the intimate functional interdependence between the two territories that was not of equal mutual benefit. It offered sterling proof that Mainland China could do without Hong Kong economically, but the reverse of this relationship was and is much harder to sustain.

In terms of monetary and banking policies in the 1930s, Hong Kong seemed more fortunate than Guangdong. The colony was not burdened by a sizable discount of its paper notes or occasional public refusal to hold local notes. Hong Kong notes were usually redeemed at a premium and enjoyed widespread popularity in Guangdong province. Relative political and social stability helped Hong Kong avoid the successive monetary crises experienced by the Cantonese due to the volatile political and military environment in the province. The Guangdong administration had to devote much greater effort to cope with the many difficult problems created in part by major international forces (like the World Depression and the US silver purchase) that also impacted Hong Kong. In addition, the Cantonese, already burdened with long standing problems of chaotic multi-currencies and banking systems, also had to confront the collapse of the silk export market and the sharp decline in overseas Cantonese remittances after 1932. Recurrent Cantonese monetary and banking crises were often triggered by domestic problems stemming from political disturbances exacerbated by Guangzhou-Nanjing hostilities.

The fall in the price of silver from 1929–31 affected Hong Kong more seriously than Guangdong because a large proportion of expenditure such as the military contribution to the UK and the salaries of British colonial officials was paid in gold-based pound sterling. The fall in the price of silver thus increased the colonial regime's expenditure. Abandoning the silver standard was regarded as unfeasible unless China also did so. Hence Hong Kong resorted to fiscal measures such as a tax rate hike and new taxes to solve its budget problem. Other than forming a committee to investigate, the colonial regime did almost nothing to cope effectively with the 1929–31 silver crisis.

As to the silver price rise in 1934–35 and the subsequent shift to a non-silver based currency, both Hong Kong and Guangdong governments merely reacted to the new directions initiated by China's central government in Nanjing. The colony and the province simply could not escape the powerful, direct impact of the Chinese national state. The late 1935 currency reform did achieve its immediate objectives and speedily stabilized the monetary system, instilling inflation to relieve the depressed Mainland and colonial economies. Both governments could claim only very meagre credit for their rather reactive monetary reforms.

Hong Kong was so intimately linked with the Mainland in economic and functional terms that it was not willing or prepared to change its monetary standard unless China took the first step.[97] Ironically, while China adopted a managed currency system after the October 1935 watershed, Hong Kong's post-silver monetary reform was a linked currency system pegged to pound sterling at a fixed exchange rate. This new system in effect directly integrated the colony into the British Empire sterling zone and further set Hong Kong apart from Mainland China.

While it might seem an inevitable and necessary decision for Hong Kong to follow China's footsteps in late 1935, the 'Hong Kong Factor' in the Cantonese economy as manifested in the popular acceptance and widespread circulation of Hong Kong bank notes, constituted the other side of the coin of their mutual influence and inter-dependence. After enduring three decades (1949–79) of ideo-politically dictated separation, the momentum for the re-integration of Hong Kong with the Mainland has been much advanced since the PRC's post-1978 market reform and Hong Kong's 1997 retrocession.[98] Hong Kong bank notes once again became popular on the Mainland, especially among the Cantonese, until the recent Renminbi appreciation over Hong Kong dollar. In turn, Beijing's permission for Hong Kong SAR banks to conduct Renminbi business and to open branches in the Mainland became further helped promote the HKSAR economy's integrative links with the Mainland.[99]

Indeed since July 1997, without the dark shadow of Cold War East-West antagonism and the British colonial-imperialist overtones, Hong

Kong and Guangdong should enjoy the opportunities to develop even more intimately together as the core of a South China economic powerhouse. The old Cantonese saying of 'the province and Hong Kong are one family' (sheng gang yija) may soon find new patterns for fruitful actualization during the early decades of the 21st century. Amid a long history of economic and functional interdependence, today's intra-Pearl River Delta cross-border monetary links can trace some of their historical roots to the pre-Second World War repertoire of extensive Guangdong-Hong Kong interfaces that were punctuated by much larger economic, political and social forces beyond the South China region.[100] This dynamic interactive relationship will definitely expand into new dimensions in the decades ahead.

Notes

1   *Guangdong wenshi tziliao* V. 69 (1992) (Guangzhou: Guangdong renmin chubanshe), p. 17.
2   *Guangdong wenshi tziliao*, V. 69, p. 18.
3   Yao Chishun (Kay F. Yiu) (1930) *Xianggang Jinyong* [Hong Kong Money Market] (Hong Kong) 13; Zhou Liangquan (1997) 'Xianggang jinrong tixi' in Wang Gungwu, (ed.), *Xianggang shi xinlun*, V. 1 (Hong Kong: Joint Publishing), p. 326.
4   Zheng Bohong (1996), *Tuplan Xianggang huobi* (Hong Kong: Joint Publishing), pp. 52–7; Zhou 'Xianggang', pp. 326–8.
5   *Guangdong wenshi tziliao*, V. 69.
6   *Ibid.*, pp. 68–95.
7   *Ibid.*, p. 29.
8   Aaron Kwong Tak Chan (1995) 'A Warlord Regime and a Colony: A Comparative Study of the Economic Policies of the Canton and Hong Kong Governments, 1929–1936' (M. Phil. thesis, history, University of Hong Kong), pp. 2–4.
9   Aaron Chan, 'A Warlord Regime', pp. 15–17.
10   Aaron Chan 'A Warlord Regime', pp. 4–5; also see Guangdong sheng donganguan, comp., *Chen Jitang yanjiu shiliao 1928–1936* (Guangzhao: Guangdong sheng donganguan, 1985), p. 161.
11   Deng Kaizong and Lu Xiaomin (eds) (1997) *YueGang quanxi shi, 1840–1984* (Hong Kong: Qilin Books), pp. 161–2.
12   Zhou Liangquan, *Xianggang*, p. 330.
13   *Guangdong wenshi tziliao*, V. 69, pp. 3–10.
14   *Ibid.*, pp. 7–10.
15   Zhou, 'Xianggang', p. 328.
16   Norman Miners (1987) *Hong Kong under Imperial Rule, 1912–1941* (Hong Kong: Oxford University Press), p. 5.
17   R.L.P. Atkinson and A.K. Williams (1970) *Hong Kong Tramways* (London: Light Rail Transport League), p. 28.
18   Atkinson and Williams *Hong Kong*, pp. 28–9.

19 Atkinson and Williams *Hong Kong*, pp. 29–30; Martin Barnett (1984) *Tramlines: the Story of the Hong Kong Tramway System* (Hong Kong: South China Morning Post), pp. 39–40; Geoffrey R. Sayer (1968) *Hong Kong 1862–1919* (Hong Kong: Hong Kong University Press), p. 114.

20 Robert Peng-fai Lam (1983) *Currency of Hong Kong* (Hong Kong: Urban Council), pp. 14, 24.

21 Jung-fang Tsai (1993) *Hong Kong in Chinese History: Community and Social Unrest in the British Colony, 1842–1913* (New York: Columbia University Press) pp. 277–8.

22 Sayer, *Hong Kong*, pp. 111–13.

23 Sayer, *Hong Kong*, p. 114

24 Alan Birch (1991) *Hong Kong: The Colony that Never Was* (Hong Kong: Guidebook), p. 38.

25 On the May 30th Movement, see Richard Rigby (1980) *The May 30th Movement* (Canberra: Australian National University Press) and Jean Chesneaux (1968) *The Chinese Labor Movement, 1919–1927* (Stanford: Stanford University Press), chapter 1.

26 On the general strike-boycott, see Ming Chan (1975) 'Labor and Empire: The Chinese Labor Movement in the Canton Delta, 1895–1927', (PhD dissertation, history, Stanford University), chapter 11.

27 Ming Chan, 'Labor', pp. 325–31.

28 This report is included in Hong Kong General Chamber of Commerce's *Annual Report* and Hong Kong Government, *Hong Kong Administrative Report*. The figures are from the 1924–26 editions.

29 Dorothy Orchard (1930) 'China's use of the boycott as a political weapon', *Annals of the American Academy of Political and Social Sciences*, p. 259; *Hong Kong General Chamber of Commerce Annual Report, 1925*, p. 113.

30 C.F. Remer (1933) *A Study of Chinese Boycott* (Baltimore: Johns Hopkins University Press), pp. 123 4.

31 *China; The Maritime Customs Statistical Series*, no. 3–5, *The Foreign Trade of China: 1926*, Part I, p. 25.

32 Orchard, 'China's use', p. 259.

33 *Hong Kong General Chamber of Commerce Annual Report*, 1925, p. 123. Stubbs to Amory, 8 August 1925. The National Archives, London [hereafter TNA] Colonial Office [hereafter CO]129/489.

34 *South China Morning Post*, 14–21 August 1925; *China Mail*, 12 June and 23 September 1925; Deng Zhongxia (1953) *Zhongguo zhigong yundong jianshi (1919–1926)* (Beijing: Renmin chubanshe), p. 230 on the lack of food supplies and high prices in the colony.

35 *Hong Kong General Chamber of Commerce Annual Report, 1925*, pp. 18–19; 1926, pp. 142–3; *Hong Kong Daily Press*, July 24, 1926.

36 The share prices of the HSBC and other firms before and since the strike appeared in *China Mail*, 17 July and 26 October 1925. For the strike-boycott's impact on the stock market, see Rosemary L. Chung (1969) 'A Study of the 1925–26 Canton-Hong Kong Strike-Boycott' (MA thesis, history, University of Hong Kong) pp. 104–8, 138–40.

37 Stubbs to Amory, 8 August 1925, TNA CO 129/489; *SCMP*, 26 June 1925; Chung 'A Study', pp. 103–8; and Elizabeth Sinn (1994) *Growing with Hong*

     Kong: The Bank of East Asia, 1919–1994 (Hong Kong: The Bank of East Asia),
     p. 33.
38   Sinn, *Growing*, p. 33.
39   *Hong Kong Telegraph*, September 12, 1925; Deng Zhongxia, p. 195.
40   Stubbs to Amory, Hong Kong, September 18, 1925, confidential dispatch.
     TNA CO 129/489.
41   Stubbs to Amory, Hong Kong, October 2, 1925. TNA CO 129/489-C49489.
42   Sinn, *Growing*, p. 35; Ming Chan, 'Labor', p. 330. The loan was approved
     after long negotiations and at high interest, and it came too late to be of
     much direct assistance to uplift the depressed Hong Kong economy.
43   Stubbs to Amory, 4 September 1925. TNA CO129/489. Hong Kong Govern-
     ment (1932) *Historical and Statistical Abstract of the Colony of Hong Kong
     1841–1930* (Hong Kong) Appendix, 9. Budget figures are in H.G. Woodhead,
     (ed.), *China Year Book* (Tianjin: annual editions, 1901–1928).
44   *Hong Kong General Chamber of Commerce Annual Report, 1927*, p. 124.
45   Chung, 'A Study' p. 157; Motz (1972), p. 80; and Deng, *Zhongguo*, p. 232.
46   Orchard, 'China's use', p. 260. This estimate was made by the head of a
     large British firm.
47   The $2 million per day figure is from Ta Chen (1927) 'Analysis of Strikes
     in China from 1918–1926', *Chinese Economic Journal*, 10–11, p. 216; the
     £2.5 million per week figure is the Hong Kong Stock Exchange chairman's
     estimate, see Chan, 'Labor', 331.
48   For Canton's shipping boom see *China Year Book* 1926, pp. 827–8; *China
     Year Book 1928*, pp. 663–5.
49   See Motz, pp. 83–8, on British contemplation of military action against
     Guangzhou.
50   'Trade Conditions in Canton,' *Chinese Economic Bulletin*, v. 8, no. 254
     (January 1926); pp. 3–5; *China Year Book 1926*, p. 828; Jamieson to Palairet,
     14 July 1925. TNA Foreign Office [hereafter FO] 405/248.
51   *China Year Book 1928*; p. 1338; Jamieson to FO, 22 February 1926. TNA
     FO 405/250.
52   Remer, *A Study*, p. 113.
53   *North China Herald*, May 1, 1926; Motz, p. 82.
54   Deng, *Zhongguo*, pp. 233–5, 241.
55   Deng, *Zhongguo*, pp. 240–1; *North China Herald*, May 1, 1926.
56   Deng, *Zhongguo*, p. 241; *China Year Book 1928*, p. 1340.
57   Deng, *Zhongguo*, p. 241.
58   *The New Leader*, 28 August 1925; *The New Republic*, 9 September 1925;
     see also Motz, p. 107.
59   Jamieson to FO, Canton, January 18, 1926, TNA FO 405/250-8.
60   In this section, the author is indebted to the M. Phil. thesis of his former
     student Aaron Kwong-tak Chan (1995), 'A Warlord', chapter 4.
61   Zhou, *Xianggang*, pp. 331, 334.
62   Aaron Chan, 'A Warlord', pp. 38–9; Michael Blaine Russell (1972) 'American
     Silver Policy and China, 1933–1936' (Ph.D. thesis, University of Illinois),
     pp. 6–7.
63   Hong Kong Government (1930), *Report of the Currency Committee* (Hong
     Kong), p. 103.
64   *Report of the Currency Committee*, pp. 103–4.

65 Dispatch from Peel to Passfield, 23 July 1930. TNA CO129/523/12.
66 Aaron Chan, 'A Warlord', pp. 40–4; Peel to Passfield, 23 July 1930. TNA CO129/523/12.
67 *Report of the Currency Committee*, pp. 105, 109.
68 Aaron Chan, 'A Warlord', p. 42; Wilfrid Victor Pennell (1961) *History of the Hong Kong General Chamber of Commerce, 1861–1961* (Hong Kong: Cathay Press), p. 49.
69 Aaron Chan, 'A Warlord', pp. 42–3.
70 Frank King (1968) *A Concise Economic History of Modern China* (New York: Praeger), pp. 137–8.
71 Steve Tsang (2004) *A Modern History of Hong Kong* (London: I.B. Tauris), pp. 108–9.
72 Aaron Chan 'A Warlord', pp. 21–2; Russell, pp. 30–7, 52–3.
73 King, *Concise Economic History*, p. 138.
74 Aaron Chan, 'A Warlord', pp. 22–3. Shao Zhongchi (1987) 'Shougou baiyin qianhou yishu', in *Guangzhou wenshi tziliao*, v. 37 (Guangzhou: Guangdong renmin chubanshe), pp. 214–15.
75 Aaron Chan, 'A Warlord', pp. 22–3.
76 Aaron Chan, 'A Warlord', p. 24.
77 Colonial Office 'Memorandum on Hong Kong currency policy in the last two years.' TNA CO129/558/11.
78 *Ibid.*
79 Aaron Chan, 'A Warlord'. p. 46; Hong Kong Government, *Administrative Report, 1935*, Appendix, p. A20.
80 Zhou, *Xianggang*, pp. 334, 337.
81 Zhou, *Xianggang*, p. 334.
82 Hong Kong Government, *Administrative Report 1936*, Appendix, p. A42.
83 Hong Kong Government, *Administrative Report 1936*, Appendix, p. A26.
84 Zhou, *Xianggang*, p. 334.
85 Hong Kong Government, *Report of the Economic Commission, 1935*, pp. 93, 104.
86 *Xianggang gongshang ribao*, 5 Sept 1935.
87 Hong Kong Government, *Administrative Report, 1935*, Appendix A, p. A24.
88 *Xianggang gongshang ribao*, 7 Sept 1935, 17 Sept 1935.
89 Hong Kong Government, *Administrative Report, 1935*, p. A24.
90 Gillian Chambers (1991) *Hang Seng: The Emerging Bank* (Hong Kong: Hang Seng Bank), p. 14.
91 'Report by J.H. Kemp, Attorney General, to the Colonial Treasurer dated 15 February 1930', enclosure in Young to Vernon despatch, 24 September 1935. TNA CO129/555/6.
92 *Ibid.*
93 Frank H.H. King (1988) *The Hong Kong Bank Between the Wars and the Bank Interned, 1919–1945: Return from Grandeur* (New York; Cambridge University Press) p. 238.
94 Leo F. Goodstadt (2007) *Profits, Politics and Panics: Hong Kong's Banks and the Making of a Miracle Economy, 1935–1985* (Hong Kong: Hong Kong University Press), offers a critical and sweeping account of the colony's post-1935 banking development.
95 Ming Chan, 'Labor', pp. 353–6.

96   See Remer, *A Study*, pp. 128–246 for the anti-Japanese boycotts.
97   Much of this summary section's coverage on the 1935 reform is based on Aaron Chan, 'A Warlord', chapter 4.
98   Ming K. Chan (1995) 'All in the Family: The Hong Kong-Guangdong Link in Historical Perspective', in Reginald Kwok and Alvin So, (eds) *The Hong Kong-Guangdong Link: Partnership in Flux* (Armonk: M.E. Sharpe).
99   Ming K. Chan and Sonny S.H. Lo (2006) *Historical Dictionary of the Hong Kong SAR and the Macao SAR* (Lanham: Scarecrow Press), pp. 60–8, 170–2 on the growing HKSAR-China Mainland economic ties.
100   Hong Kong Museum of History (2007) *The Development of Banks in Shanghai & Hong Kong* (Hong Kong: Hong Kong Museum of History) offers essays on and historical photographs of banking and currency in Hong Kong and Shanghai since the 1850s.

3
Banking and Exchange Rate Relations between Hong Kong and Mainland China in Historical Perspective: 1965–75[1]

Catherine R. Schenk

Introduction

The 'one country, two systems' structure established to govern the relationship between Hong Kong SAR and Mainland China was an innovative and comprehensive solution to particular economic and political challenges posed by the return of Hong Kong to the PRC in 1997. At the time of the drafting of the Basic Law, the integration of the colony into the regional economy of Southeast China through outward FDI had already begun, and from the mid-1980s this process facilitated the transformation of the Hong Kong economy from a manufacturing base to one dominated by financial and commercial services. It was recognized on both sides of the negotiations that the territory's viability and future prosperity relied on retaining independence over a range of key fundamentals, including a separate and independent currency and monetary system that was at the foundation of Hong Kong's attraction as an international financial centre for the PRC and also for the rest of the Asian region. An important credibility mechanism for the HK$ (as for the inconvertible RMB at this time) was the exchange rate link to the US$. Since this was also the anchor for the RMB after 1997, the linked rate system kept the relationship between the RMB and the HK$ stable.

While the rapid growth and development of the Mainland economy after 1999 outstripped many predictions, the relatively poor performance of Hong Kong from 1997 until 2003 has changed the context in which the one country two currencies system operates. The de-linking of the RMB from the US$ and subsequent appreciation from July 2005 has further complicated the monetary relations between Hong Kong SAR and the rest of China. Hong Kong's interest rates and monetary policy are now arguably more closely aligned with those of the USA than those of its main trade partner. The increased use of RMB in banking and other transactions in Hong Kong SAR is further evidence of the erosion of the barriers between the two currencies. In February 2008, RMB deposits in Hong Kong had reached RMB47.8 billion, an increase of 92% over a year, although this still represented only 0.8% of total deposits in Hong Kong. Cross-border financial flows within the banking system have also accelerated with the accumulation of net liabilities in Hong Kong to banks on the Mainland since 1999.[2] Once the RMB and the HK$ reached parity against the US$ in January 2007 there was a psychological shift in attitudes about the relative merits of each currency as well real concerns over the potential impact of the appreciation of the RMB on the cost of imports into Hong Kong from the Mainland.[3] The potential for further appreciation of the RMB against the HK$ poses challenges as well as opportunities for Hong Kong consumers and producers and heightens public attention on the implications of separate currencies within a single country.

The financial, monetary and banking relations between Hong Kong and Mainland China have a long and intimate history that should be borne in mind when assessing the challenges faced by the separate monetary systems operating today. As Chan's chapter in this volume shows, due to the commercial integration of the region, the HK$ circulated widely in Southeast China both as a store of value and as a medium of exchange. This monetary integration increased during the collapse of China's monetary system in the late 1940s.[4] With the establishment of the PRC, HK$ were collected by the new government of China and their use in private transactions was prohibited in order to promote the new national Chinese currency. Banking relations between the two territories were never severed but they were put under severe strain by the nationalisation of banking and commerce in the early 1950s. Nevertheless, this article will emphasize that there was considerable continuity in the banking relations between Hong Kong and Mainland China and will explore the operations and implications of exchange rate dynamics in the 1960s and 1970s when the global fixed exchange rate system collapsed, destabilising the exchange rate between the HK$ and RMB. An important contribution is to present new data on the activities of Mainland Chinese banks operating in Hong Kong during this period, collected from official archives. This data confirm the extent of cross-border activities throughout the 1960s and early 1970s.

International banking

Hong Kong has traditionally been an important international financial centre for the Mainland, surpassing Shanghai from the mid-1930s as military and political disturbances interrupted activity there. The monetary chaos of the 1930s also drew foreign banks into operating the exchange rate system. King recounts how during the crisis caused by the rise in the silver price in 1933–34 H.H. Kung and T.V. Soong of the Bank of China drew Henchman of the Hongkong Bank into a secret partnership to support the exchange rate of the Chinese dollar. His success earned him a gold wristwatch and the confidence of Soong and Kung that put the Hongkong Bank at the forefront of support schemes over the next few years.[5] Although the new Communist regime after 1949 severely restricted the activities of foreign banks and most extracted themselves from China during the early 1950s, the Hongkong and Shanghai Bank (HSBC) maintained its presence through these difficult years and was able to restore some of its business from the mid-1950s.

Relations between the Bank of China, the HSBC and the Hong Kong government were cordial and generally functioned well.[6] However, there were delicate political aspects of the Bank of China's role in Hong Kong. In 1961, the Bank of China requested subsidised land to build workers' accommodation but the project was delayed because the land needed to be cleared of 1500 squatters. The Political Advisor recommended to the Colonial Secretary that

> 'I feel that we should be no more or less helpful to the BoC than we would be to any other employer wishing to take similar action. What we want to avoid doing is creating the impression that for political reasons we are putting obstacles in the BoCs way.'[7]

Ten years later, however, when the question of land for workers' housing arose again, the Director of Special Branch advised that

> from an internal security viewpoint it is undesirable to allow the BoC or any other CPG [PRC] organization to build further large fortress-type buildings, especially on road junctions or other strategic locations. Hence Special Branch would wish to be consulted on any sites which may be offered to the bank.[8]

While the Bank of China was the most prominent Mainland-controlled bank in Hong Kong it was not the largest. Table 3.1 shows that by 1970 there were 13 PRC-controlled banks in Hong Kong with a total of 55 branches.[9] They included the Bank of China, other banks registered on the Mainland, and banks registered in Hong Kong but controlled by the PRC.

Table 3.1　Mainland Chinese Controlled Banks in Hong Kong 1970

	Number of Offices Jan 1970
Bank of China	2
Bank of Communications	6
China and South Sea Bank	5
China State Bank	5
Chiyu Banking Corporation	3
Hua Chiao Commercial Bank	4
Kincheng Banking Corp.	6
Kwangtung Provincial Bank	7
Nanyang Commercial Bank	7
National Commercial Bank	3
Po Sang Bank	1
Sin Hua Trust	7
Yien Yieh Commercial Bank	5

Classification based on Bank Returns to the Banking Commissioner for 1970. In 1967 Chiyu Banking Corporation was removed from the list of Mainland banks but reappeared in the list in 1969. Hua Chiao Commercial Bank was moved from local to Mainland in 1967. Branches from HKRS411/2/45.

The Bank of China was undoubtedly the most politically influential PRC bank in Hong Kong but Nanyang Commercial Bank (locally registered in Hong Kong) had the largest local deposits and advances. Figure 3.1 shows the growth in total assets and deposits of Nanyang Commercial Bank. The rate of growth was interrupted by the communist disturbances in Hong Kong in Spring 1967 that affected all PRC banks adversely, and it took several years to recover its position. In the boom of the early 1970s, however, the bank grew very quickly.

Based on archival data, Figure 3.2 shows the rise in deposits and advances for all PRC banks in Hong Kong from 1964–72. After growing quickly at the beginning of this period, deposits and advances declined in 1967 due to political disturbances in Hong Kong arising from the Cultural Revolution on the Mainland. It took two years for the Mainland banks to recover the 1966 level of deposits but the rate of increase then recovered quickly and by the end of 1972 Mainland banks in Hong Kong held over HK$2b (US$354m) of deposits. The fastest growing banks after 1967 in terms of deposits were Sin Hua Trust and Kwangtung Provincial bank, both of which (along with Nanyang Commercial) had significant branch networks in the colony. In 1964 and in 1972 these three banks accounted for over 40% of total Mainland banks' deposits in Hong Kong, although their share dipped below 40%

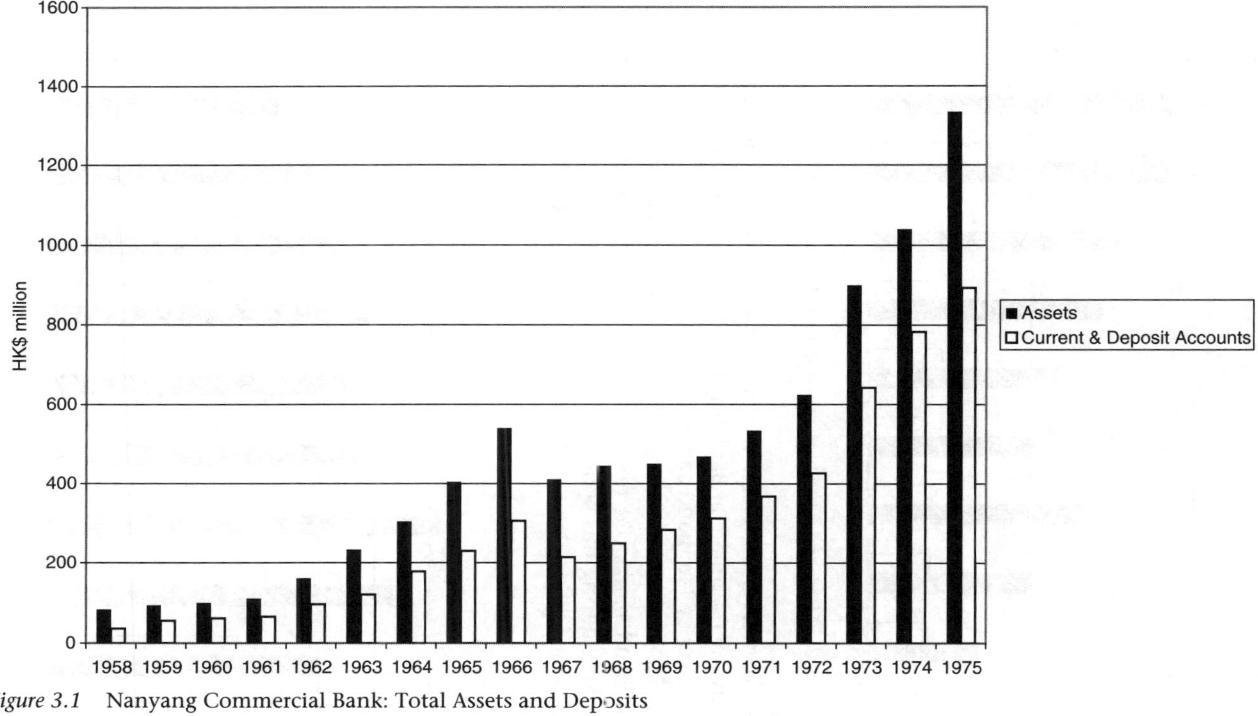

Figure 3.1 Nanyang Commercial Bank: Total Assets and Deposits

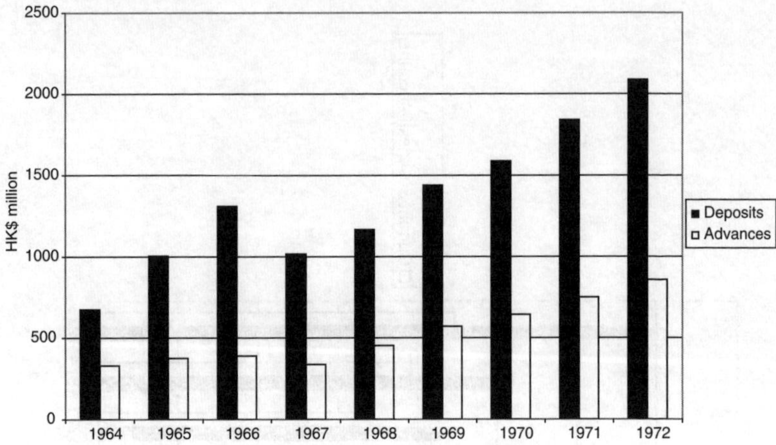

Figure 3.2   Mainland Chinese Controlled Banks in Hong Kong

in the intervening years. In terms of local advances, Sin Hua Trust and Nanyang Commercial Bank together accounted for about one third of advances by Mainland banks.

Despite an impressive overall performance, Figure 3.3 shows that the Mainland banks did not keep pace with the growth of Hong Kong banking during this boom period. After peaking in 1966 at 14% before the political troubles of 1967, their share of deposits declined steadily to

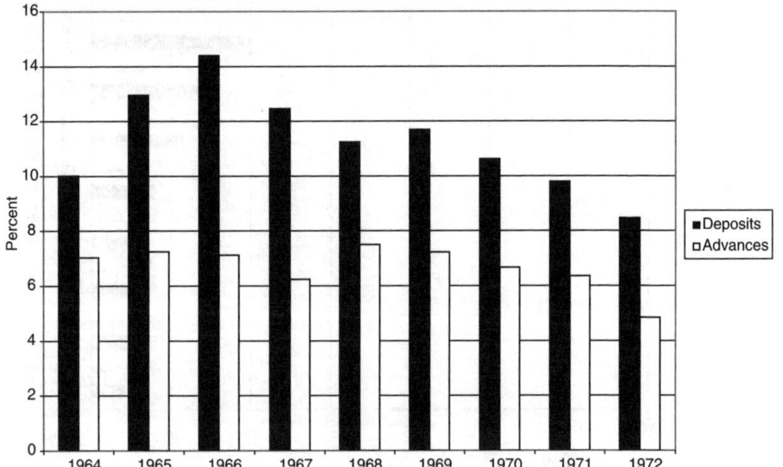

Figure 3.3   PRC Banks in Hong Kong: Market Share

below 9% by the end of 1972.[10] After making significant initial progress, confidence among depositors in the Mainland-associated banks never recovered from the disruptions of 1967 and the ensuing political strife on the Mainland. By 1981, after the Open Door policy was in operation, Mainland controlled banks restored their share of deposits to 14% and increased their share of advances to a historically high level of 15%.[11]

While the growth of deposits was sustained at the same rate as for the banking system as a whole through most of 1969, there was an absolute fall in the level of deposits from May to July 1970. The value of deposits then recovered, but no longer grew at the same pace as the banking system as a whole.

Another feature of the Mainland Chinese banks was the low ratio of local advances to deposits, which led to high liquidity ratios. Figure 3.4 shows that most PRC banks were not engaged in substantial lending to customers in Hong Kong but mainly collected deposits for other uses, particularly to be channelled overseas. Only three small PRC banks met the average ratio of loans to deposits of locally incorporated banks. When deposits were rising quickly in the years before 1967, advances lagged well behind.

Figure 3.5 shows the high levels of liquidity in Mainland Chinese banks compared with other foreign or locally registered banks. Information on the specific nature of the liquidity is available only for December 1966 when it was calculated that 80% of the overall liquidity of Chinese Mainland banks was held overseas. The other 20% was held in cash and net

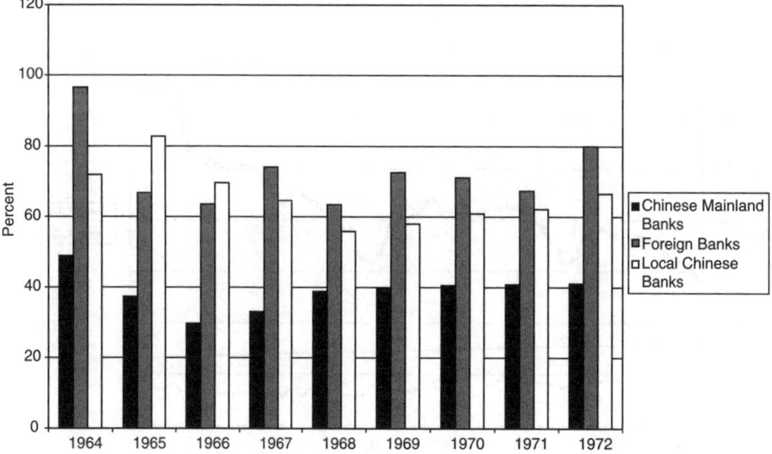

Figure 3.4   Ratio of Advances to Deposits

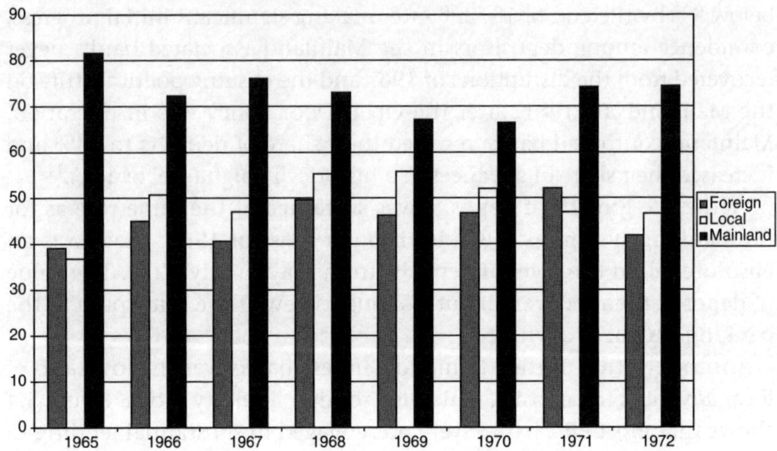

Figure 3.5   Hong Kong Banks' Liquid Assets as a Percent of Deposits

bank balances in Hong Kong. About 70% of these overseas liquid assets were held in China, and the rest in London.[12] As China's foreign trade bank, the Bank of China predictably held the largest balances on the Mainland, accounting for about 35% of the total and over half of Mainland banks' assets in the UK. While the Nanyang Commercial Bank was more heavily involved in local lending, it was also the next largest holder of overseas balances, accounting for 15% of the total held in China and 21% of the total balances in the UK. In all, 87% of Main-

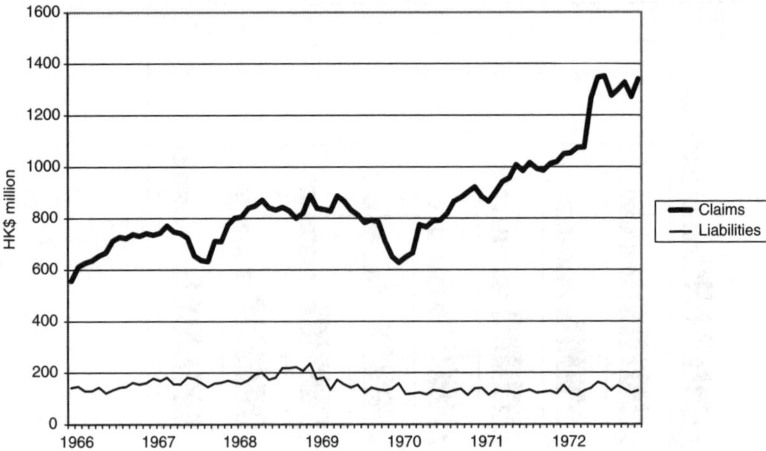

Figure 3.6   Hong Kong Banks' Balances with Banks in Mainland China

land banks' assets in China were bank deposits and money at call and only a small proportion were commercial bills.

Figure 3.6 shows that claims on banks in the Mainland represented a substantial proportion of the deposits collected in Hong Kong. PRC banks were the only group that held net claims on banks in China, while other banks held small net liabilities. Hong Kong banks' net claims in China declined temporarily during the political unrest in Hong Kong in the Summer of 1967, but then recovered until the last quarter of 1969. The decline in the claims on banks on the Mainland in the second half of 1969 was just as severe as during the May riots of 1967, but from the beginning of 1970 a steadily rising amount of funds was held in the Mainland, amounting to HK$1b (US$177m) by mid-1971 and HK$1.3b (US$230m) in 1972. Figure 3.7 shows the half-yearly data for PRC banks only.

In May 1967, the Economic Secretary noted that '[T]he money due from China amounts to an illegal (but countenanced) keeping of funds outside this Colony by the Mainland banks. Other banks which wish to keep their money outside the colony comply with the regulations by keeping it in London. The PG [PRC Government] is enabled by this to use the assets of Hong Kong banks for whatever purpose it likes in the medium of Hong Kong dollars or transferable sterling. A useful working capital.'[13] To put this into perspective, the value of HK$ held in China averaged 30% of exports to Hong Kong from 1965–72, and amounted to about one month of China's total import bill in 1968.

Figure 3.8 shows the relative magnitude of the net balances compared to the value of total deposits in PRC-controlled banks in Hong Kong. The rise in this ratio in the early years reflects the slower growth of deposits after the riots of 1967 up to 1970. From the start of 1970, an increasing proportion of PRC banks' liquidity was being channelled to the PRC, peaking at a net balance equivalent to 60% of total deposits by the end of 1972.

These cross-border balances can be compared with more recent experience. Since 1999 Hong Kong's current surplus with the Mainland has been offset by outward flows of capital that have led to accumulations of net liabilities by Hong Kong banks to the Mainland. In the 1960s, in contrast, investment from Hong Kong in the Mainland was prohibited so the trade surplus led to an accumulation of claims on banks in China. From 2000–07 net liabilities of Hong Kong banks to the Mainland amounted to an average of 3.7% of total HKD deposits. Figure 3.9 shows that net cross-border balances were much higher relatively in the 1950s. Even in the 1960s and 1970s, these balances amounted to at least 5% of

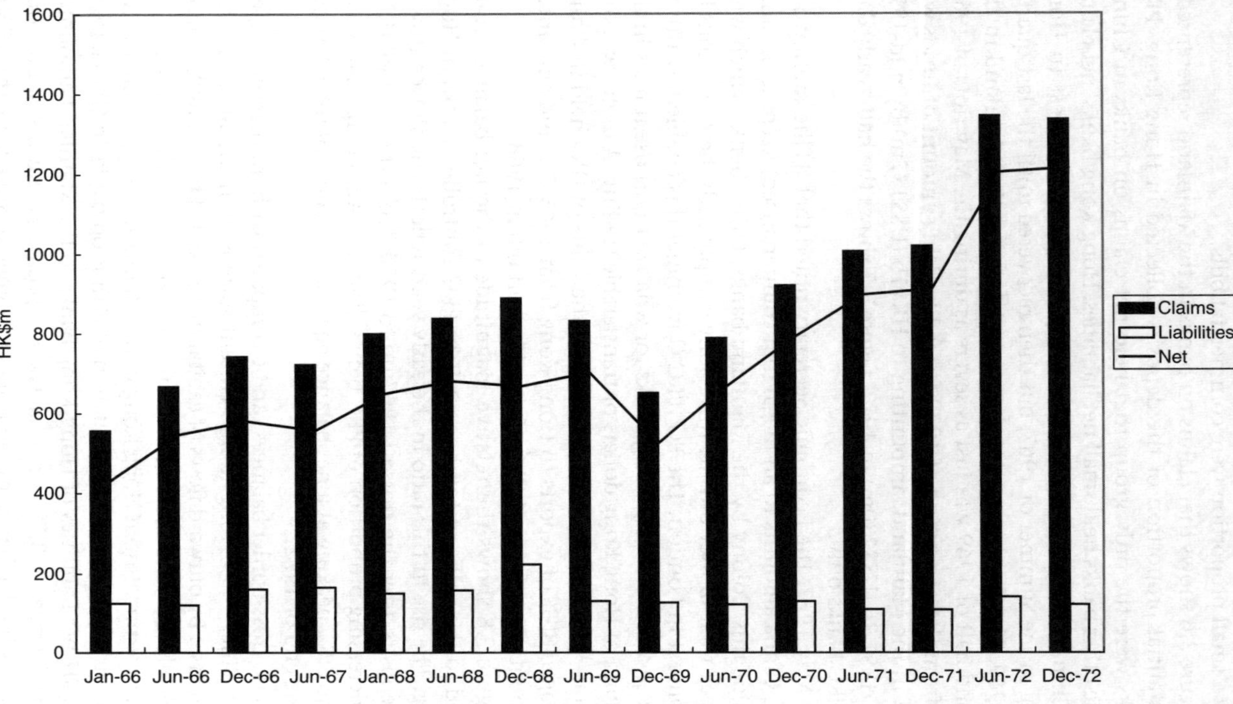

Figure 3.7   Mainland Banks in Hong Kong: Balances with Banks in Mainland China

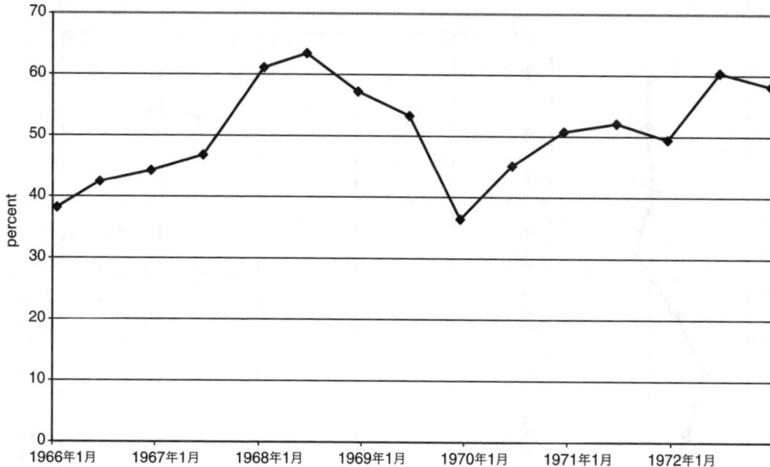

Figure 3.8 Mainland Banks net claims on Banks in China as Percent of Deposits in Hong Kong

HK$ deposits. Unlike the 2000s, however, changes in the net cross-border balances were not more volatile than overall deposits so they did not threaten monetary stability in the colony.[14]

The financial links between Hong Kong and the Mainland also operated through branches of Hong Kong banks there, but on a much smaller scale. From 1955 the Bank of China agreed to channel enough business through the Shanghai office of HSBC to allow it to cover its overheads in order to keep the office open. Chartered Bank also continued to operate in Shanghai on this basis (in premises below the HSBC). Both banks processed documents for exports to various countries, but not for imports. Business was very limited, both by the number of staff and by the amount of business directed to them by the Bank of China. Profits were only allowed to be remitted to head office from 1962 and revenues were taxed heavily.[15] Chartered Bank had a larger turnover than the HSBC office at this time and, indeed, the HSBC Board considered shutting the Shanghai Office in March 1962, but decided to remain open in expectation of long-term advantages.[16] Figure 3.10 shows the increase in business passing through the HSBC Shanghai branch on a half-yearly basis. From about 10,000 bills per year (worth £6m) in 1966, the number fell to a low of 5,500 in 1970, recovering to 7,700 (worth £7m) by the end of 1971. This pattern of business resulted in a rise in the pre-tax profit of the Shanghai branch from RMB108,000 in 1968 to RMB288,000 in 1971.

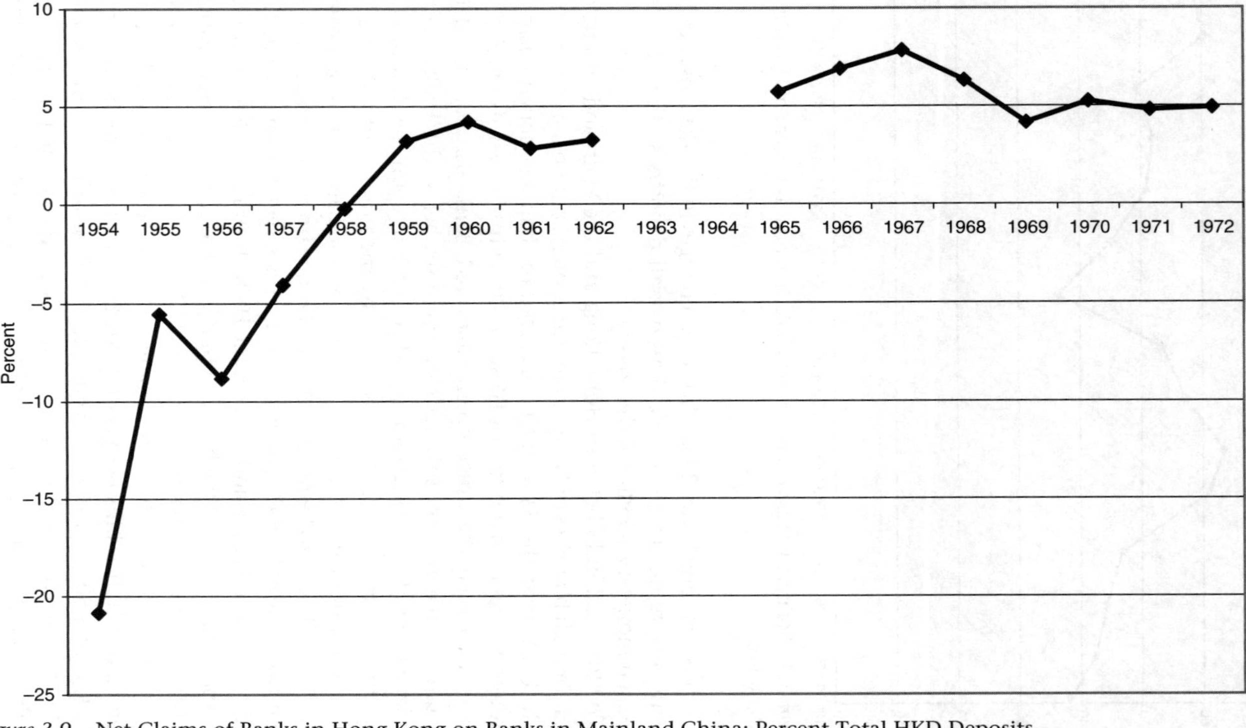

Figure 3.9   Net Claims of Banks in Hong Kong on Banks in Mainland China: Percent Total HKD Deposits

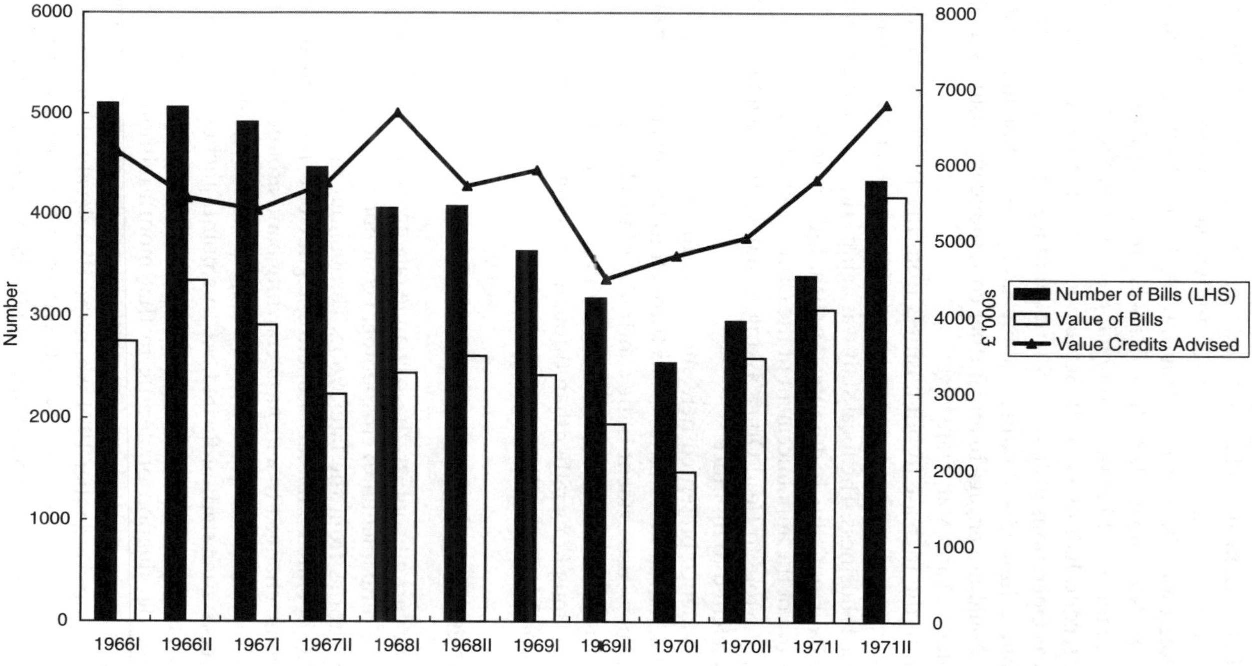

Figure 3.10   HSBC Shanghai Office Business 1966–71

Mostly, however, the Shanghai office was burdened with small and unprofitable Demand Debit (DD) and Mail Transfers. In 1974 the HSBC estimated that total remittances by individuals to the Mainland via Hong Kong was HK$1.9b (US$380m), rising to HK$2.13b (US$426m) in 1975.[17] By November 1978, the office was processing about 800 export bills per month, which was not much greater than the 700 per month in the second half of 1971. In September 1978 the General Manager Overseas Operations visited the Shanghai office and found it 'depressing', 'old fashioned and rather gloomy' and he recommended that the office should not engage in any further correspondent business (mainly low value DD and Mail Transfers).[18]

Despite the increase in bill business from the 1970s, the Shanghai office continued to be constrained by staff shortages and was unable to increase it business. The local staff was aging and new staff appointed by the Bank of China had limited English. Indeed, in November 1978 on the eve of the announcement of the Open Door policy the Shanghai Manager wrote to Head Office asking to reduce the volume of documents referred to his office.[19]

The evidence presented here shows the integration of Hong Kong with the Mainland from the 1950s through to the advent of the Open Door Policy. Also evident is the continuity of this link throughout the period, and that it operated mainly from the branches of Mainland banks in Hong Kong rather than through the residual offices of foreign banks on the Mainland.

Exchange rate policy

As in the current context, the exchange rate between the HK$ and the RMB was fundamental to cross-border economic relations between the two territories from the late 1960s. Throughout most of this period the PRC operated a managed floating regime but from January 1974 the regime changed to a *de facto* crawling band around the US$ with fluctuations of +/−2%.[20] The HK$ was pegged to sterling until July 1972, two weeks after sterling floated. At this point, anchor currency was changed to the US$. The HK$ was depreciated slightly in November 1967 after the devaluation of sterling in that month (although not by as much as sterling was devalued). Both currencies appreciated against the US$ from December 1971 when the USA devalued the US$. With the collapse of the Bretton Woods system in the Spring of 1973, the HK$ re-pegged to the US$ at just over HK$5 (an appreciation of 17%). The RMB was also stabilised against the US$ and the premium on the

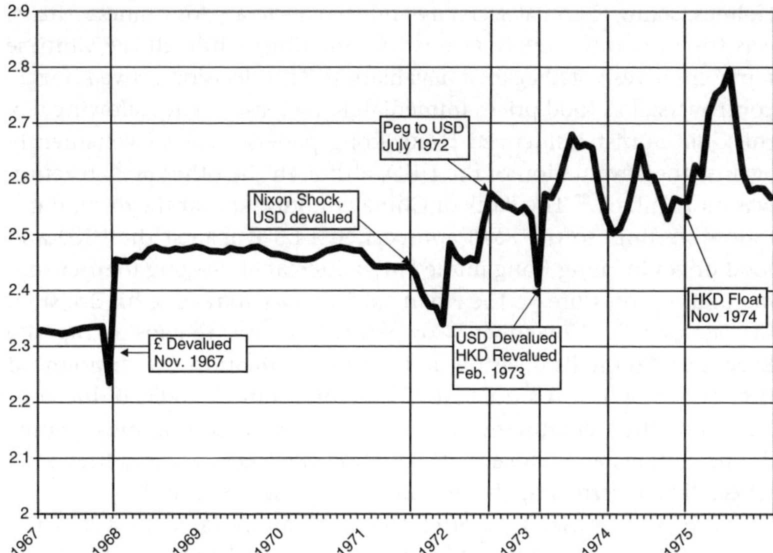

Figure 3.11   HK$ per RMB 1967–75

black market contracted. Figure 3.11 shows the monthly cross rate between the HK$ and the RMB.

Hong Kong's decision not to follow sterling in November 1967 owed much to the public sensitivity to the RMB/HK$ exchange rate at this time. London informed the Hong Kong government of its intention to devalue the pound at 1:30am on Sunday 19 November and an Executive Council meeting was convened that evening to determine Hong Kong's response. A Bank of England representative described the meeting as quite heated, with strong indignation expressed by the representative from HSBC in particular who objected to the lack of consultation and the loss in the foreign currency value of sterling assets. Malaysia and Singapore had already declared that they would not follow sterling, which surprised those in Hong Kong who now understood that there was a choice to make and they groped for an assessment of Hong Kong's own interests. The Executive Council debate was 'a struggle between the banking group and some official and the Chinese members who were particularly concerned with the prospects of rising costs' so the impact of increased prices from devaluing the HKD against its trading partners was clearly in the minds of legislators.[21] However, after only 45 minutes the Council agreed to follow sterling, in a decision pushed through by British official members of the Council (Ronald

Holmes, acting Colonial Secretary and later Secretary for Chinese Affairs, was the only one to vote against devaluation) while all the Chinese representatives voted against devaluation. This decision proved hugely controversial as food prices immediately increased. The following day the Communist influenced Hong Kong papers were all vehemently against the devaluation of the HKD, although the other press reaction was more mixed.[22] The Bank of China announced that they would not follow sterling, so the RMB appreciated 14.3% against the HKD and food prices in Hong Kong immediately increased, leading to intensifying political pressure on the Financial Secretary to reverse his decision. By Tuesday 22 November, Cowperthwaite was re-considering the Executive Council's decision and a 10% revaluation was announced the following day. A survey of 720 people from all walks of life conducted by the Department of Chinese Affairs noted that most people did not understand why any devaluation was necessary and they were especially concerned by the impact on the cost of living.[23]

Figure 3.11 shows that after the RMB appreciated in 1967, the exchange rate was stable until the suspension of US$ convertibility in the Nixon Shock of August 1971. Until the US$ was re-pegged at the end of 1971, the RMB was allowed to depreciate against the HK$. Once the US$ was stabilised the RMB began again to appreciate against the HK$. Of course the RMB was not convertible during this period so that the exchange rates were centrally determined rates rather than market rates. However it is clear that the rate between the HK$ and the RMB and the use of Hong Kong as China's international financial centre during the 1960s and 1970s had important implications for Hong Kong's own exchange policy.

By the end of the mid-1960s the USA was the largest market for Hong Kong's exports and Japan was the largest source of imports. These two trade relations suggested that a peg to the US$ would have made more sense for the Hong Kong dollar than a peg to sterling. Nevertheless, despite the falling proportion of sterling trade, Hong Kong's foreign exchange reserves remained 99% invested in sterling assets and sterling was the intervention currency. This was to some extent a legacy of historic trade patterns, but was also encouraged by contemporary circumstances including the market price of these British government securities, high interest rates on short-term sterling assets (by 1972 Hong Kong earned about £30m per year in interest on its sterling assets[24]), and the important role that Hong Kong played as a financial intermediary for China. Most importantly for this chapter, Hong Kong needed to be able to convert China's substantial HK$ earnings into sterling, which was China's preferred international currency. After sterling floated in 1972 and relations between China and the USA warmed, the supply of sterling through Hong Kong became less important to China and Hong Kong accelerated its diversification away from sterling.

Figure 13.12 shows Chinese banks' purchases of sterling through Hong Kong. Sales by HSBC alone accounted for slightly less than half on average. The total amount fell slightly in 1967 due to a shortage of sterling caused by local monetary conditions in Hong Kong after the riots of May-September of that year.[25] In 1968 and 1969 sales of sterling to the PRC recovered and then increased sharply in 1970 when China ran its first substantial trade deficit since 1960.[26] In the same year, purchases of sterling amounted to over a third of China's total import bill. By 1973 Hong Kong banks sold over £500m to the Bank of China, amounting to 25% of China's total import bill for that year.[27] Given this evidence of substantial purchases of sterling through Hong Kong, a stable exchange rate between the HK$ and sterling was particularly important for China.

Following losses sustained from the devaluation of sterling against the US$ in 1967, in 1968 China began to insist that its export contracts be denominated in (overvalued) RMB and conducted through foreign banks' RMB accounts with the Bank of China.[28] Moreover, between 1967 and 1968, Mainland banks reduced their net assets in London from HK$1.7b to HK$33m. By the end of 1973 the Bank of China claimed that over 60 countries used RMB in commercial transactions with the PRC.[29] Settlement took place through foreign currency accounts opened by the Bank of China with a wide range of correspondent banks, and RMB denominated accounts opened by correspondent banks at the Bank of China. Because of the dispute over frozen US$ assets from 1950, there were no direct correspondent relations with American banks, although the Bank of China had correspondent relationships with foreign banks located in the USA.

Exchanging RMB to hard currency was only possible for transactions related to an official export contract, which restricted the transferability and convertibility of RMB surpluses. Because the RMB was not convertible to US$, proceeds had to be converted first to sterling and then to the trader's domestic currency. Forward markets in some European currencies such as SwFr, DM and £ were created through Chinese banks in Hong Kong and through appointed correspondent banks. But China's largest trading partner, Japan, needed to exchange their RMB to sterling or change sterling for RMB to complete their trade contracts.

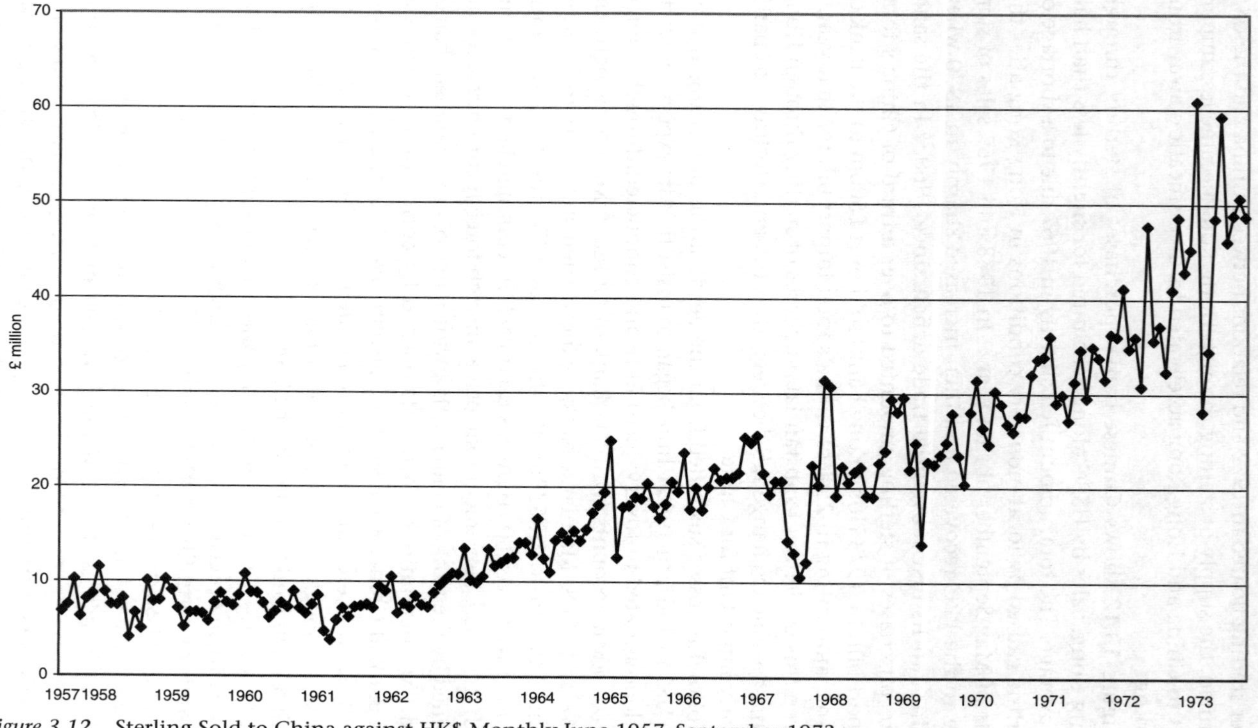

Figure 3.12   Sterling Sold to China against HK$ Monthly June 1957–September 1973

Until 1975 sterling was formally the final currency of settlement for trade contracts between Japan and China, a restriction that proved costly to Japanese exporters as Japan's trade surplus mounted and sterling weakened against the yen. Japan was China's largest non-socialist trading partner by 1969 and the largest supplier of iron and steel, exporting over 1 million tons per annum from 1968 which accounted for over 40% of Japan's exports to China in the early 1970s. In April 1973, China also signed a contract to supply Japan with crude oil from the Daqing oil field, just in time for the oil crisis that began in the autumn.

China earned a substantial surplus in foreign exchange from exports of price inelastic products such as food and water to Hong Kong.[30] The trade balance averaged HK$2.5b per year from 1966–69 but then increased sharply during the early 1970s to HK$5.4b in 1973. Moreover, the proportion of these exports that were consumed in Hong Kong rather than re-exported remained at about 75% until 1976. The exchange rate between the Hong Kong dollar and other currencies was therefore of vital interest to China since the surplus with Hong Kong was used to pay for imports from elsewhere. The proceeds of exports to Hong Kong were determined by the state-set RMB prices of exports to Hong Kong and by the exchange rate between the RMB and HK$. In common with other Comecon countries, to improve foreign exchange earnings China used a combination of exchange rate appreciation and price manipulation. Raising food prices generated friction between Hong Kong and China so the management of the balance between the two countries was a delicate matter.

Hong Kong's exchange rate policy and reserves policy was further complicated by relations with the UK. In July 1968 Hong Kong signed one of the first Sterling Agreements with the UK, by which they agreed to hold 99% their reserves in sterling (a proportion known as the Minimum Sterling Proportion [MSP]) in return for an exchange rate guarantee (for the value of £ against the US$) for 90% of those balances.[31] By the end of March 1970 Hong Kong held £422m in sterling and the colony was largest single holder of sterling reserves in the world.[32] In August 1971 after the re-negotiation of the three-year agreements, the British government (HMG) offered a reduction in Hong Kong's MSP by 10% to 89%, and this was accepted, but the high interest rates available in London encouraged the Hong Kong government to delay diversification.[33]

The re-emergence of China into the international economy co-incided with the collapse of the international monetary system. In August 1971 after a run on the US$, Nixon suspended convertibility to gold and threatened to impose a 10% surcharge on all imports into the USA unless other countries adjusted their exchange rates to ease the US balance of payments deficit. After frantic negotiations, the Smithsonian Agreement was signed in Washington that re-established the fixed exchange rate system at adjusted parities in December 1971. These new rates proved impossible for some countries to defend and from June 1972 sterling floated. Finally, in February 1973 the US$ was devalued again prompting most countries to break their pegs from March 1973 and the era of floating exchange rates began. The Chinese government viewed the collapse of the international monetary system as an example of the weakness of US hegemony, but it also created serious problems for China's trade links.[34]

This uncertainty and the changing paradigm of the international monetary system posed major challenges for Hong Kong as an important industrial exporter, a major regional financial centre, as a financial entrepot for Mainland China, and also as a colony linked to an imperial metropole. If the HK$ were pegged to a sinking currency (either sterling or US$), China would adjust their exchange rate or raise the price of exports to Hong Kong to protect the hard-currency value of its HK$ earnings. As Leo Goodstadt, then Deputy Editor of the Far Eastern Economic Review put it in 1972:

> Peking in the end decides which parity is correct for the colony. If the US dollar weakens, Peking will signal its desire for new arrangements for the colony's currency by devaluing the Hongkong dollar against the RMB. Unlike other economies, Hongkong cannot simply choose its own rate of exchange, or its links with other countries, on the basis of its export interests alone. Hongkong, to survive, must maintain its value to China.[35]

When the US$ was devalued against gold in December 1971, the HK$ continued at the same peg to sterling (a revaluation of 8.57% against the US$), citing the dangers to the cost of living posed by higher import prices if the HK$ were devalued against sterling, and therefore the RMB. The Financial Secretary revealed publicly that a lesser revaluation of perhaps 6% only had been considered by was rejected because of the projected rise in the import bill of 3.5%.[36] In January 1972 the RMB followed to keep in line with the HK$.

On 23 June 1972, sterling floated, launching a new round of problems and negotiations. When London told Hong Kong about the sterling float on 23 June (without any advance notice) they advised rather brusquely that 'HMG's action does not bind non-metropolitan territories. Your government should consider whether to follow the UK or to peg to the dollar. We shall need to inform the IMF [International Monetary Fund] of your decision'. Hong Kong's governor, Sir Murray MacLehose asked if the HK$ could be allowed to float freely, separate from sterling, but was told firmly that 'independent floating by HK dollar would not (repeat not) be appropriate, since present speculative pressure does not apply to Hong Kong'.[37] The IMF could be persuaded that sterling had to float in response to speculative pressure but a breach in the Bretton Woods rules for Hong Kong could not be justified. A week after sterling floated, the Governor of Hong Kong wrote to London 'we are veering to the view that our interests would best be served during the period of the sterling float (and only during that period) by pegging on the US$, at about the previous cross rate'. Hong Kong banks wanted to avoid the uncertainty of floating. Also, the Bank of China was unsettled by the floating pound and this undermined Hong Kong's traditional role as a supplier of foreign exchange for China. The HSBC reported difficulty selling sterling to the Bank of China because of conflicts over the rate quoted against the HK$. This enhanced the anxiety about the HK$ exchange rate and the continued usefulness of Hong Kong to China.[38]

The Governor insisted that 'I would of course deplore anything which appeared to reduce the link with the UK, but such a move could be presented as a purely temporary measure pending the return of sterling to a new fixed parity, and I feel sure it would be seen, just as the float is seen, as something ephemeral'.[39] The HSBC's view was that once the link to sterling had been broken, the government's stated intention to revert to sterling once that currency had stabilised was 'most illogical'.[40] The British Treasury and Foreign Office tried to persuade MacLehose to maintain the link to sterling but were not successful.[41] The Bank of England believed that the Hong Kong authorities would have preferred to keep the link with sterling, but were persuaded that if sterling floated down too low then this would cause inflation because of the rise in the cost of imports from China. Clearly the China factor was important.

China was the largest supplier of the imports that directly affected wage rates – food and water. From 1967–80 Hong Kong imported about 50% of its domestic food consumption from China alone.[42] China accounted for 80–85% of live animal imports at this time and Chau has argued that Mainland food products were particularly important for working class Chinese diets.[43] Figure 3.13 shows that the price of foodstuffs was rising in 1970–72 faster than the overall Consumer Price Index for

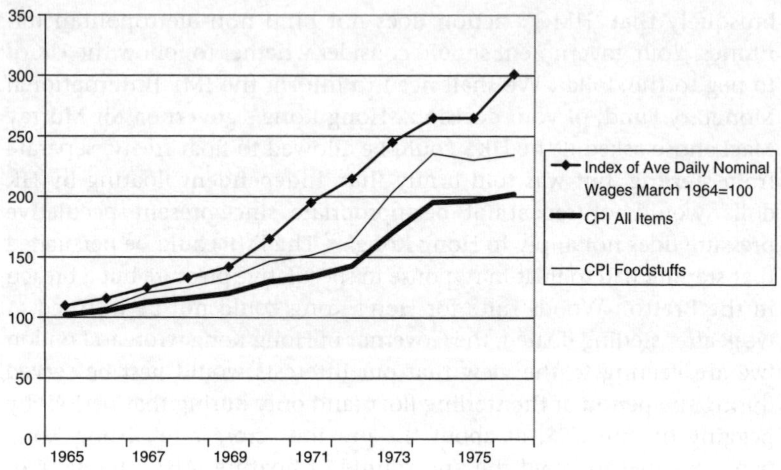

Figure 3.13   Hong Kong Indices: Wages and CPI for Low Income Households

low-income households, although the sharpest increase did not come until world prices rose in 1973.[44] Nominal wages, however, had reached an inflection point in 1970 to a higher rate of growth. These developments help to explain the enhanced sensitivity of the government and employers to the cost of living, although Chau did not detect a direct relationship between wages and prices.

The difficulties facing banks and objections from London were overridden by the importance of stable links with China and the threat to the cost of living in Hong Kong. Concern in the local press focused on rising prices of imported food and vegetables from China; on 29 June the wholesale price of imported vegetables from China increased from HK$53.79 per picul to $70 per picul.[45] On 6 July 1972 the Governor reported that after consultation with the Executive Council, the HK$ was to be pegged *temporarily* to the US$ at HK$5.65 = US$1 with a 2.25% margin either side of parity. This rate was 1.22% below Smithsonian rate of HK$5.5821 set in December 1971 and represented a revaluation against sterling of 5.2%.[46] A day later the Chinese revalued the RMB just over 1% against the HK$ to RMB39.73/HK$100 and 2.2% higher against the US$. As the Governor stated, 'in other words, their response to our announcement that we were temporarily pegging the HK$ to the US$ has been exactly as we predicted'.[47] He estimated that the revaluation of the RMB would raise import prices by 6% causing a 1.5% rise in the cost of living.[48] In 2007, Hong Kong imported about 70% of food from the Mainland, exaggerating the potential impact of RMB appreciation on the cost of living for lower income earners. It was estimated that a 5% appreciation of the RMB against the HK$ would generate a 1% increase in the Consumer Price Index (CPI).[49] There is, therefore, continuity in the sensitivity of Hong Kong's economy to exchange rate policy on the Mainland.

As July 1972 progressed the HK$ slumped to the bottom of its band against the US$ but Hong Kong did not have reserves of US$ to defend the rate. Instead, the Hong Kong government was forced to sell sterling for US$ to then buy HK$ to support the rate. At this point the Hong Kong government reported that they were running out of sterling cash and would soon need to liquidate sterling securities. Sandberg of HSBC believed that Haddon-Cave had picked the exchange rate of HK$5.65/ USD 'arbitrarily' and that the rate was too high from the outset. He advised Haddon-Cave that

> Cutting ourselves off from sterling, however, tempting it might seem to set the HK$ up as an independent currency instead of merely an adjunct of sterling which it has always been, was taking a risk when practically all of Hong Kong's reserves were in sterling. Secondly with the almost total lack of exchange control regulations here speculation against the HK$ (whether as an over or an under valued currency) could be a gnome of Zurich's dream and a Financial Secretary's nightmare.[50]

At the end of August 1972 the banks agreed that HSBC would have a monopoly on market intervention to support the exchange rate and discretion over when to intervene.[51] By mid-September Haddon-Cave was in London where he advised the Bank of England and UK Treasury that 'we are trying to explain to Hong Kong banks that the Hong Kong government runs the place, but it is rather difficult'.[52]

In February 1973 the US$ was further devalued by 10% but the HK$ was kept at its gold parity (revalued against the US$ to HK$5.085 = US$1) in order to maintain parity with the RMB. By July 1973 the HK$ was being dragged down against sterling partly by the continued devaluation of the US$ and partly due to the outflow of capital from the colony after the end of the stock exchange boom.[53] The Bank of England wanted to advise Hong Kong to float its currency or at least to revalue against the sinking US$ but the UK Treasury disagreed.[54] During the summer the RMB was appreciated against the HK$ and the US$ and at the same time RMB-denominated prices of Chinese exports rose dramatically, putting double pressure on Hong Kong's food costs.

At the beginning of August 1973, the Hong Kong government finally attempted to end the historic commitment to sterling reserves, announcing to the Bank of England that if a new sterling guarantee was not forthcoming within a week, it would diversify official sterling assets down to 50% of total reserves. At this point Hong Kong's sterling assets were £660m amounting to 88.6% of total reserves.[55] MacLehose remarked that 'we have held on out of loyalty and in the expectation of definite proposals from HMG, and required the banks to do so too. Because the guarantee itself is now of so little value we have long passed the point of commercial prudence.'[56] The reply from the British government was categorical that 'we cannot endorse any diversification of your own official reserves' because of the threat to the global sterling exchange rate arising from the sale of such large sterling balances. MacLehose and Haddon-Cave set out for London to take on their imperial leaders.[57] They left again empty-handed to the dismay of the legislative council, who wrote to the Acting Governor in strong terms that they were 'gravely dissatisfied with the attitude of the British government over a matter which is of vital importance to the economy of Hong Kong'.[58]

A week before all the sterling agreements were due to expire at the end of September 1973, sterling came under pressure in foreign exchange markets as traders worried about what would replace the Sterling Agreements. This prompted the British government to offer a unilateral agreement to guarantee sterling balances at a new slightly higher rate. Leo Goodstadt reported in the *Far Eastern Economic Review* that 'A sweaty hand pushed a tatty piece of paper at Hong Kong Financial Secretary Philip Haddon-Cave when he stopped at Bahrain recently on a flight back from London'.[59] This was the final offer of a sterling agreement to compensate Hong Kong if sterling should fall below US$2.4213 averaged out on the exchange rates that would prevail up to the end of March 1974. This was a slight improvement on the $2.40 threshold but nowhere near the $2.60 that Hong Kong had first claimed. In addition the guarantee was to be for official balances only with no consideration of commercial bank balances. At the end of December 1973, 76% of Hong Kong's official exchange reserves were still denominated in sterling.[60]

During 1974 there was further pressure on the HK$/US$ rate and the price of US$1 fell below HK$5.05 in July. From the 20–26 November 1974 the HK$ came under considerable pressure and was finally floated free from its link to the US$ on 27 November. The General Manager of HSBC was very aggrieved not to have been consulted formally in advance, although he had met with Haddon-Cave the night before the announcement.[61]

Conclusions

This paper has described in new detail the banking and monetary links between Hong Kong and Mainland China from the 1960s until the eve of the Open Door Policy. Hong Kong acted as a vital external partner throughout this period both in terms of sales of foreign exchange to the Bank of China, and also as a source of funds channelled through Mainland-controlled banks registered in the Colony. Indeed these cross-border balances were larger relative to total deposits than they are today. This paper has also shown how the disarray in foreign exchange markets complicated the delicate relationship between Hong Kong and Mainland China and affected Hong Kong's ability to adapt to the emergence of China into the international economy. Supplies of food from China were essential, particularly to the labour force in Hong Kong's rapidly growing industrial sector and this put Hong Kong at the mercy of China's exchange rate and pricing policy. Meanwhile, Hong Kong was caught by the legacy of colonial links to the UK and substantial sterling assets, without the independence to diversify its reserves once sterling was less important to China. The sterling link had been vital to Hong Kong's usefulness to Mainland China throughout the 1960s but with the collapse of the international monetary system, the complicated and prolonged extrication from sterling presented new problems for the colonial administration, both internally and externally as China diversified its own trade and payments.

Hong Kong's economic relations with the Mainland are now much more complex and comprise not only essential imports, but also processing trade, exports of services and flows of investment. The impact of the strengthening RMB on the Hong Kong economy, therefore, will be more widely distributed than in the 1960s and 1970s and the increased competitiveness of Hong Kong's exports of goods and services may well outweigh the increase in import prices. Nevertheless, this chapter has shown that the exchange rate between the HKD and the RMB first became an important policy issue forty years ago and promoted the further economic estrangement of the colony from the UK. Along with the rise in cross border bank balances, the disarray in exchange markets led to a closer realization of the continued importance of the Mainland to Hong Kong's longer-term economic viability even when China was relatively closed to the rest of the world. This reality is at the basis of the one-country, two currencies system that has sustained the relationship between Hong Kong SAR and the Mainland since 1997 and will continue to be fundamental to future changes in the currency arrangements between these territories.

Notes

1 Research for this paper was supported by the ESRC World Economy and Finance Programme, Grant RES-165-25-0004.
2 'Cross-border fund flows and Hong Kong banks' external transactions *vis-à-vis* Mainland China', HKMA Research Memorandum, June 2006.
3 J. Yam (2006) 'The RMB and the HK$', *Viewpoint*, November. (http://www.info.gov.hk/hkma/eng/viewpt/index.htm). Bank of China (Hong Kong) (2007) 'The RMB Appreciation and Its Impacts on Hong Kong', February. (http://www.tdctrade.com/econforum/boc/boc070201.htm)
4 C.R. Schenk (2000) 'Another Asian Financial Crisis: monetary links between Hong Kong and China 1945–50', *Modern Asian Studies*, 34(3), 739–64.
5 F.H.H. King (1988) *The Hongkong Bank between the Wars and the Bank Interned 1919–1950*, pp. 411–12 (Cambridge: Cambridge University Press).
6 For HSBC's relations with the Bank of China in the 1950s see, C.R. Schenk (2009) 'Sterling, Hong Kong and China in the 1930s and 1950s', in N. White and S. Akita (eds) *International Order of Asia in the 1930s and 1950s* (Aldershot: Ashgate Publishing).
7 Political Adviser to Colonial Secretary, 26 August 1961. Hong Kong Public Record Office [hereafter HKRS] 156-1-4850.
8 J.J.E. Morrin, Acting Director of Special Branch for Commissioner of Police, 10 September 1976. HKRS 156-1-4850. Agreed by the Colonial Secretary.
9 In 1970 there were a total of 73 banks registered in Hong Kong with a total of 326 branches.
10 For an account of the development of the Hong Kong banking system see, C.R. Schenk, 'Banking Crises and the Evolution of the Regulatory Framework in Hong Kong 1945–70' (2003) *Australian Economic History Review*, 43(2), 140–54. C.R. Schenk, 'Banks and the emergence of Hong Kong as an international financial centre', *Journal of International Financial Markets, Institutions and Money* 12(4–5), pp. 321–40. C.R. Schenk, 'Banking Groups in Hong Kong 1945–65' (2000) *Asia Pacific Business Review*, 7(2), 131–54.
11 L. Goodstadt (2005) *Uneasy Partners: The Conflict Between Public Interest and Private Profit in Hong Kong* (Hong Kong: Hong Kong University Press) p. 186.
12 HKRS 163-1-3274.
13 Memo, 3 May 1967, HKRS163-1-3275.
14 'Cross-border fund flows and Hong Kong banks' external transactions *vis-à-vis* Mainland China', HKMA Research Memorandum, June 2006.
15 In the first ten years of operations from 1955, the HSBC Shanghai Office's total bills purchased from Chinese export corporations was £19,175,600, HK$94,088,300, DM12,916,800, SwFr5,830,600, FFr6,554,200, CdnD27,500, CeyRps11,002,700, Iraq D474,700, Dirhams850,700, SwKr30,900. WA Stewart (Shanghai) to MW Turner (HK), 12 January 1965. HSBC Group Archive [hereafter HSBC] GHO158.
16 W.A. Stewart to F.J. Knightly 30 December 1964. HSBC GHO158. Paper for March 1962 Board Meeting recommended closing the branch. Letter from L. Kadoorie arguing to maintain the Shanghai office, March 1961. HSBC GHO157.
17 Correspondence between London Office and Head Office, HSBC GHO160.
18 Report of visit to Shanghai Office 9–13 September 1978 by I.H. MacDonald. HSBC GHO160.

19 Carey to I.H. MacDonald, General Manager, Overseas Operations, 2 November 1978. HSBC GHO 160. Carey was anticipating an increase in export business to offset the reduction in small remittance advices.
20 C. Reinhart and K. Rogoff (2002) 'A Modern History of Exchange Rate Regimes: a reinterpretation', NBER Working Paper, 8693.
21 Telegram from Haslem, Bank of England, 22 November 1967. BE OV44/258.
22 Review of Press. HKRS 160-3-27.
23 The survey was conducted the first week of December 1967 by regional Assistant Secretaries of Chinese Affairs and their liaison officers. The largest categories were hawkers, office clerks and housewives, amounting to 23%, 18% and 13% of the sample respectively. HKRS 160-3-27.
24 Haddon-Cave quoted in the *Far Eastern Economic Review [hereafter FEER]*, Vol. 78, No. 51, 16 Dec 1972, p. 40.
25 C.R. Schenk (2004) 'The Empire Strikes Back: Hong Kong and the Decline of Sterling in the 1960s', *Economic History Review*, LVII (3), 551–80.
26 In 1967 China ran a small deficit of US$5m and in 1970 a deficit of US$190m.
27 The sterling offtake from Hong Kong rose from 12% of China's import bill in 1959 to 42% in 1972, but then fell back to 25% in 1973. L. Goodstadt (2006) 'Painful transitions: the impact of economic growth and government policies on Hong Kong's Chinese banks, 1945–70', HKIMR Working Paper, 16, p. 22.
28 D.L. Denny (1975) 'International finance in the PRC', US Congress, Joint Economic Committee, *China: A Reassessment of the Economy*, 653–77, p. 663.
29 Cited in Denny, 'Recent Developments', p. 163.
30 Jao calculated that in 1977 about 30% of China's net foreign exchange earnings came from Hong Kong. Y.C. Jao, 'Hong Kong's Role', p. 58.
31 The British government agreed to compensate holders of sterling if the pound were devalued against the US$. These agreements were signed with all sterling area countries in the summer of 1968 as a counterpart to the Basle Agreement of that year.
32 Draft Sterling Area Working Party Report, 18 June 1970. Bank of England Archive [hereafter BE] OV44/120.
33 Telegram No 560 from Foreign and Commonwealth Office to Hong Kong, 2 August 1971. BE OV44/264. It was formally agreed on 20 August 1971.
34 The 'Trade and Tours' periodical of spring 1969 stated: 'At this time of complete chaos in the Western financial and monetary world, this is a good opportunity for our RMB to enter the world market and take the role of an international currency... After RMB's entry into the world market, the field of international settlements originally occupied or dominated by capitalist trading currencies must lose ground and contract gradually.' Quoted in I. Sharp (1970) 'Renminbi or Bust', *FEER*, Vol. 68, No. 19, 7.
35 L. Goodstadt (1972) 'The HK$ Compromise', *FEER*, Vol. 77, No. 29, 15 July, p. 38.
36 Leo Goodstadt (1971) 'Currency Realignments: Government Blow to Hongkong Exports', *FEER*, Vol. 74, No. 52, 25 December, p. 29.
37 Telegram correspondence between Sir A Douglas Home and Governor MacLehose, 23 July 1972. National Archives, London [hereafter TNA] T354/275.
38 Telegram from Hong Kong, 18 July 1972. BE OV44/266.
39 Telegram from Governor of Hong Kong to Foreign and Commonwealth Office, 3 July 1972. BE OV44/266.

40 Undated Report for the Board of HSBC, 'The currency situation' probably July 1972. HSBC Chairman's Files 1459 Box 2.14, Financial Secretary re: Devaluation and Compensation 1968–73.

41 Reply FCO to Governor of Hong Kong, 4 July 1972. BE OV44/266.

42 L.C. Chau (1983) 'Imports of Consumer Goods from China and the Economic Growth of Hong Kong', in A. Youngson (ed.) *China and Hong Kong: The Economic Nexus*, pp. 184–225 (Oxford: Oxford University Press).

43 *Ibid.*, p. 189. Rice imports were controlled by the government, which managed a geographically diversified sourcing policy. In 1972 1/3 of rice imports were from China. *Ibid.* p.188.

44 Data from Chau, 'Imports', pp. 202–3.

45 Answer reported to Sing Tao Man Po, 10 July 1973.

46 Telegram from Hong Kong to FCO, 6 July 1972. BE OV44/266.

47 Telegram from Hong Kong to FCO, 7 July 1972. BE OV44/266.

48 Haddon-Cave quoted in S. Dalby (1972) 'Riding the sterling crisis', *FEER*, Vol. 77, No. 28, 8 July, p. 21.

49 Bank of China (2007) 'The RMB Appreciation and Its Impacts on Hong Kong', February. (http://www.tdctrade.com/econforum/boc/boc070201.htm).

50 M.G.R. Sandberg to G.M. Sayer 27 July 1972, HSBC, Chairman's Files, 1459 Box 2.14.

51 D.A. Sharp to Fenton and Payton, 31 August 1972. BE OV44/266.

52 Haddon-Cave in London meeting with Bank of England and Treasury, 18 September 1972. BE OV44/266.

53 The *FEER* estimated the outflow due to the stock market at £400 m or US$1,040 m. Leo Goodstadt (1973) 'Soft spot for the HK dollar', *FEER*, Vol. 81, No. 26, 2 July, p. 31.

54 Note by Payton for the Governors of the Bank of England, 10 July 1973. BE OV44/267.

55 Telegram from Hong Kong, 26 July 1973. BE OV44/267. This compares to compensation paid to commercial banks after the 1967 devaluation of £10,587,268. Telegram from Governor Trench to Secretary of State for the Colonies, 17 January 1969. BE OV44/261.

56 Telegram from Governor of Hong Kong, 2 August 1973. BE OV44/268.

57 Reply to Hong Kong, 2 August 1973. BE OV44/268. The *FEER* reported that 'Sir Murray MacLehose, Hongkong's Governor, has been forced by London's failure to respond before now to interrupt a well-earned leave for a confrontation with the [British] Treasury', *FEER*, Vol. 81, No. 32, 13 August 1973, p. 37.

58 Letter from PC Woo to Sir Hugh Norman-Walker (acting Governor) transmitted in a telegram to FCO, 28 August 1973. BE OV44/268.

59 Leo Goodstadt (1973) 'Greasy Palms', *FEER*, Vol. 81, No. 37, 17 September, p. 55.

60 The proportion was 88.6% in July 1973, falling to 78.7% in September, Oct 79.2%, Nov 78% Dec 76%. Memorandum 12 September 1973. BE OV44/268.

61 J.L. Boyer, General Manager HSBC to Haddon-Cave, 29 November 1974. HSBC, Chairman's Files 1459 Box 2.14. GM Sayer's Financial Secretary File 1971–76.

Part II
The Currency Board

4

Laissez-faire's Limitations: The Evolution of Monetary Policy in Hong Kong, 1935–80[1]

Leo Goodstadt

Introduction

Hong Kong's path to prosperity has been very different from other Third World societies. Its economic performance in the second half of the last century was a record of sustained and largely self-financed success.[2] Its growth rates were, arguably, unparalleled in economic history, and real GDP increased each year without exception from 1961 until 1998.[3] Economic expansion was never hindered by a shortage of the capital needed to finance high-speed growth.[4] Also remarkable was how little change took place in the government's economic policies. *Laissez-faire* was discarded by the rest of the world but flourished in Hong Kong together with free trade, a belief in the efficacy of free market forces and minimal state interference with business. Hong Kong also stuck to the monetary arrangements of the past. It retained a 'currency board' system, and the government insisted that interventionist monetary policies were unnecessary because the Hong Kong economy was self-regulating.

Individual financial secretaries defined their responsibilities in narrow terms and were nervous about monetary economics, especially Keynesianism. In 1954, Arthur Clarke expressed his opposition to 'a policy of Government control of the money market and of the volume of money'.[5] In 1961, he defined 'a thoroughly sound monetary policy' as ensuring that 'the Hong Kong dollar is the most trusted currency in the East'.[6] Even this responsibility was more rhetorical than real, however, because in this period, British colonies had no opportunity for 'taking any ... measures that would affect the value of their own currencies'.[7] His successor, Sir John Cowperthwaite, insisted that the government could not espouse interventionist policies because 'the modern school' of economics did not apply to a small, open economy. Keynesianism, he claimed, would lead to financial irresponsibility and 'create an immediate balance of payments crisis'.[8] In the 1970s, Sir Philip Haddon-Cave declared that he avoided the term 'monetary policy' in public for fear of raising expectations of a Keynesian approach to public finance. He accepted that his fiscal measures might involve monetary policy but he disclaimed any capacity 'to manipulate – or rather try to manipulate – the rate and pattern of economic growth'.[9]

The management of Hong Kong's monetary affairs has to be seen in its colonial setting. In contrast to other colonies, policy-making in Hong Kong was, almost always, haphazard and piecemeal rather than a structured process that would offer a coherent guide for decision-making.[10] In addition, the fundamental data required as a basis for monetary and other policies started to become available only in the 1970s.[11] Hostility toward statistical information had been widespread within the colonial administration before World War II and remained pervasive during the 1950s.[12] In the 1960s, the Financial Secretary declared that, 'it is not necessary, nor even of any particular value, to have [GDP] figures available for the formulation of policy'.[13] His successor admitted in the following decade that he had tried to manage monetary affairs in a statistical void.[14] This state of affairs was facilitated by the colony's political arrangements.[15] Without either an elected legislature or political parties, the government was under little pressure to explain its policies or defend its performance. Public discussion of monetary policy was rare before the 1970s and not extensive after that date. The currency board system, for example, was at the heart of Hong Kong's monetary arrangements (except between 1974 and 1983). Yet, this term was mentioned in the legislature on only three occasions before the end of colonial rule in 1997.[16]

This chapter starts with a review of why colonial economies were regarded as self-regulating under the currency board system. It explains how this 'automatic' adjustment mechanism started to weaken once a colonial economy embarked on rapid growth. The discussion turns to whether Hong Kong's financial secretaries were correct in assuming that the currency board system made monetary policy unnecessary. It examines the historical background to the modern economy, the period between the world wars when the colony was integrated into the Mainland economy and the immediate post-1945 challenges of peacetime reconstruction and the Korean War embargoes. The chapter then offers an assessment of individual financial secretaries from 1950 to 1980.

The colonial background

Currency boards developed in an era in which most British colonies were pre-industrial, often semi-subsistence and usually dependent for growth on exports of a narrow range of agricultural commodities and mineral products. Cash dominated local business life, and banking services were limited. Banks maintained high levels of liquidity which restricted their creation of credit.[17] In many respects, the colonies could be regarded as an extension of the British economy, finding their major export markets and their principal sources of capital in the United Kingdom.[18] '[Colonial] banks were merely branches of London banks, maintaining their basic liquidity in London', so that integration into the British financial system was almost complete.[19] A currency board seemed to leave officials with little scope for discretionary policies or the market intervention typical of central banking.[20] Notes and coins were issued solely in exchange for sterling assets of equal value, so that the money supply was linked to the balance of payments. The assets backing the currency had to be held in sterling, which compelled the colony to accumulate surplus export earnings in London if it wished to increase the supply of currency. Under such conditions, currency boards managed the currency 'by a sort of mechanical process' but did not control the money supply.[21]

Hong Kong did not fit the colonial mould. Its economy was not pre-industrial, and it did not rely on British export markets and financial institutions. Hong Kong was integrated into the Mainland economy until 1949 and, thereafter, it sold the products of its rapidly expanding industrial sector not only to Britain but to North America and Western Europe. Hong Kong was dominated not by London banks but by HSBC, whose headquarters were in the colony and which had a long record of acting independently of the Bank of England and UK interests.[22] The colony had been a regional financial centre and home to major Mainland and foreign banks since early in the twentieth century.[23] The banking system's ability to create credit was not dependent on the volume of currency in circulation nor mechanically dictated by the balance of payments, as was the case for the rest of the colonial empire, a feature of Hong Kong's monetary arrangements that had been noted even of its pre-World War II economy.[24]

The case for self-regulation

Hong Kong officials' conviction that monetary policy was redundant and that the economy was self-regulating implied that a currency board created the conditions for automatic adjustment regardless of the level of economic development. This conclusion was misleading. Development economists noted relatively early that once a colony begins its economic take-off, monetary conditions alter substantially. As national income becomes less dependent on foreign trade, the money supply would cease to fluctuate automatically with the level of exchange earnings.[25] Liquidity could be created by the banks, and their loans and advances became significant components in the money supply.[26] At this stage, the self-regulating tendency of the currency board system would decline because 'a significant proportion of the money supply was not currency but bank credit over which the currency board had absolutely no control'.[27]

In general, however, little attention was paid to the importance of the commercial banks' freedom to create liquidity as colonial economies became more developed,[28] and Hong Kong officials and economists were no exception. They shared the view common throughout the colonial empire that, for the most part, monetary issues could be ignored. There was widespread confidence that problems would be temporary and self-solving because the currency board system would create the following conditions in Hong Kong:[29]

- overall liquidity would rise or fall in line with export performance.
- changes in the money supply would trigger any adjustments required within the economy to ensure a healthy state of the balance of payments.
- credit creation by the banking system was not a significant or separate source of liquidity.
- any inflation would be imported.

Although the colonial administration regarded the system as largely self-regulating, officials understood that they were not entirely powerless to intervene. The government's reserves could affect the money supply. Fiscal conservatism meant that the government accumulated considerable funds by underspending the annual budgets. While these surpluses remained in Hong Kong, they were deposited in the local financial system and could be used to support bank lending, which expanded the money supply. If they were transferred overseas, they left the local system, and the money supply contracted. The government could also place direct controls on bank lending. The imposition of statutory liquidity ratios would limit the banks' freedom to create credit. Hong Kong had no central bank or money market to provide a vehicle in which these liquid assets could be held locally. As a result, the bulk of them were transferred overseas which, under the currency board system, sterilised them very effectively and reduced the capacity of the banking system to create loans.[30] Financial secretaries made virtually no use of these two monetary levers, however, and they consistently argued that formal monetary policies had little or no part to play in Hong Kong.

China issues

In the years between the two world wars, Hong Kong was not committed to unconditional *laissez-faire* and favoured measures to encourage industrialisation and social development.[31] But there was no interest in activist monetary policies despite problems with the money supply. The banks amply met the demands of business, for industrial expansion in particular.[32] If anything, their credit policies were regarded as too liberal. The colony was not tied to sterling but followed the Mainland which was on a silver standard until 1935. During the 1920s, falling silver prices attracted an influx of Overseas Chinese money in search of foreign exchange gains, causing a surge in bank deposits that was difficult to manage, and banks were criticised for using these funds to finance alarming volumes of speculative activity.[33] When silver prices started to increase in the 1930s, a new banking boom started, with a rapid rise in the number of local Chinese-owned banks.[34] The complaint now was that these firms, tempted by high interest rates, made funds too easily available for dubious projects, particularly in the property sector.[35] The accepted wisdom during the period was that the remedy for the period's liquidity problems lay in prudent management by the banks themselves rather than direct action by the government.[36]

The monetary issue that the colonial administration could not ignore was the currency. Unlike other colonies, notes were issued not by a currency board but by HSBC and two other commercial banks. When they expanded or contracted the note issue, they made a commercial judgment about the benefits of tying up assets in silver to back their banknotes. In the 1920s, HSBC declined to increase the currency in circulation unless it made a profit from the new bank notes, a policy which aroused considerable public criticism.[37] As Ming Chan's chapter in this volume shows, an additional complication was that Hong Kong was economically and financially part of China so that demand for the colony's currency was generated not only within the colony but quite widely in southern China. The Chinese government abandoned the silver standard in 1935, and the colony followed suit. Hong Kong then had to decide between the gains from continuing to link the colony's currency to its Mainland markets and the advantages of improved financial stability which a relationship with sterling would bring. While the Chinese authorities hesitated about whether or not to establish their own link with sterling, Hong Kong made the switch, but the new connection with sterling was seen as a temporary break with the historical currency relationship with the Mainland. The understanding was that the colony would be free to follow whatever final decision China might make.[38]

The currency might well have become a critical monetary issue after World War II. The colony was a member of the Sterling Area which had introduced draconian exchange controls. However, when officials in London were planning for post-war economic reconstruction, Hong Kong was seen as a special case because of its dependence on China rather than on markets in the United Kingdom and the British Empire. It was taken for granted that its free-port status, free financial markets and commitment to *laissez-faire* should continue unchanged.[39] After the restoration of British rule, Hong Kong was able to maintain the colony's special exemption from the full rigours of Sterling Area regulations.[40]

After Japan surrendered in 1945, inflation became the immediate monetary challenge. Rising prices, rents and public utility charges provoked industrial disputes and social unrest which endangered the political legitimacy of British rule.[41] Shortages of machinery and raw materials were a threat to Hong Kong's manufacturing take-off and its growing domestic exports.[42] The government could not leave market forces to restore economic equilibrium because world trade was not operating normally; food and essential supplies were being allocated through international agreement; and foreign exchange and trade transactions were tightly controlled.[43] The colonial administration's solution was sweeping state controls. Although these were introduced as reluctantly and temporarily as possible, they did not completely disappear until 1954.[44]

The early post-war years were an important test of the government's understanding of the role of monetary policy. In May 1949, the exchange rate on the free market fell briefly to USD1 = HKD8 as the Chinese Communist Party's victory in the civil war became unmistakeable.[45] In the following year, Hong Kong's external trade started to collapse as the United States and the United Nations imposed an economic blockade against the

Mainland which was the colony's largest trading partner. Business confidence ebbed, and the banks started to reduce credit facilities.[46] As recession loomed, the government and the business community took very different views of the appropriate solution. Officials saw the danger as a general collapse of the economy and devised a series of largely impractical initiatives: make-work programmes and a campaign to persuade large employers not to lay off staff or close down.[47] Leading businessmen, by contrast, focused on the credit squeeze and pleaded in vain with the government for measures to maintain bank liquidity and halt deflation.[48] The government would not accept that the colony was suffering from an avoidable recession that was capable of a simple financial solution. Eventually, the banks recovered their nerve. Political and administrative solutions were found for the Korean War embargo. The manufacturing boom gathered momentum, and the economy did not collapse.

Financial secretary Arthur Clarke (1952–61)

In the 1950s, world and domestic markets returned to normal as the inflationary spiral subsided and rising prices ceased to be a major concern. Management of the government's reserves and their impact on the money supply became the chief monetary challenge. Under a currency board system, the almost annual budget surplus had no monetary implications in itself. As explained above, what mattered was where the surplus was held. If the government retained the funds in Hong Kong, they remained within the banking system and a part of the money supply so their impact on the money supply was neutral. If they were transferred overseas, the funds were removed from the banking system, and the budget surplus was deflationary. The colonial administration was free to choose whether or not to keep the funds in Hong Kong. This discretionary power to decide the size and location of the fiscal reserves gave the government direct monetary leverage.

The colonial empire's overseas reserves aroused considerable controversy, both in Hong Kong and overseas. These sterling holdings were attacked as forced loans to the United Kingdom which should return to the colonies to finance their economic development.[49] In most British territories, governments were expected to run down their overseas assets and to use budget deficits in order to finance the social and economic development programmes demanded by their electorates.[50] In Hong Kong, however, the unreformed political system allowed the government to control spending on economic development and social services, and the annual budget showed a surplus in most years. During the 1950s, the Financial Secretary rejected criticisms of holding the funds overseas and of his policy of building up the fiscal reserves until they equalled a full year's recurrent expenditure. The business community could not believe that budgetary prudence on this scale was justified especially when local industry was complaining of a shortage of finance.[51] Business leaders launched an unsuccessful campaign that was to continue into the 1960s for the government's sterling reserves to be brought back to the colony and invested locally.

These demands clashed with the government's desire to maximise its earnings from the reserves in the 1950s. Interest rates were higher in London than in Hong Kong, and Clarke thought it wrong not to take advantage of this profit opportunity.[52] His investment strategy, however, ignored the deflationary impact of transferring surpluses overseas, with painful consequences. In 1955, HSBC became nervous about soaring share and property prices which were probably fuelled by the bank's decision to redeem a significant quantity of banknotes in 1954, since under the currency board system the redemption of currency in circulation was inflationary.[53] With the Financial Secretary's approval, HSBC introduced a credit squeeze to stabilise the markets.[54] To the indignation of the business community, bank lending was cut back and liquidity started to shrink. Local Chinese-owned banks suffered a sharp decline in both deposits and profits as the stock market collapsed and turnover slumped on the gold and the foreign exchange markets. Liquidity tightened still further after six local Chinese banks failed in late 1955.[55] HSBC blamed the government for the mounting crisis on the grounds that the colonial administration had intensified the initial credit squeeze by transferring its fiscal surplus from local banks into sterling, thus reducing the money supply.[56] HSBC now urged the government to reflate the economy, and the Financial Secretary injected additional liquidity into the banking system by bringing funds back from London.[57] He explained publicly that the colonial administration accepted responsibility for ensuring adequate liquidity, and he seemed ready to acquire 'a much greater say in credit policy' for the government in future.[58] Henceforward, however, there were to be no more attempts of this kind to manage the money supply.

Financial secretary Sir John Cowperthwaite (1961–71)

There was another side to the liquidity issue. During the 1950s, the only constraint on a bank's lending was its own good sense. The government refused to believe that a bank's loans could exceed its deposits, and officials assumed that modern banks would automatically maintain a healthy level of liquidity to meet depositors' demands. In practice, foreign-owned banks persistently lent in excess of their deposits, and so did many local banks before the 1964 Banking Ordinance set minimum liquidity ratios.[59] During the 1950s, the absence of legal constraints on lending made it easier for the banks to play the major role in financing the sustained expansion of manufacturing.[60] In Hong Kong, industrial finance involved banking practices of the most conservative kind. In the early 1960s, however, the absence of constraints allowed banks to finance property and share activities on a reckless scale. The result was a major banking crisis in 1965 during which three banks failed, including the colony's second largest, the Hang Seng Bank.

These 'bubble' markets demonstrated the crucial weakness of the currency board system: its inability to control bank lending, which the 1964 Banking Ordinance came too late to remedy. Its minimum liquidity ratio of 25% was intended 'not only to ensure the ready availability of funds to repay deposits but also to prevent ... excessive bank lending'.[61] The 1965 bank runs convinced the Financial Secretary that the 25% ratio was not an adequate barrier to imprudent credit practices. He decided however not to raise the requirement because the banking industry as a whole was maintaining a much higher ratio on a voluntary basis.[62] This left a serious loophole in the statutory requirements. Banks with headquarters overseas were never subject to this legal constraint in practice, leaving a substantial segment of the industry free to create credit as liberally as it chose.[63]

The dangerous pressures created by the property 'bubble' had been obvious to officials well before 1965. Cowperthwaite admitted that, as early as 1963, there had been a strong case for direct measures to stabilise the property market.[64] He chose not to intervene, he said, because 'businessmen would have fiercely resisted' any government intervention.[65] Later in the decade, the stability of the financial system came under threat once more because of what Cowperthwaite described as 'a sudden, and inevitably ill-considered, expansion of [bank] advances'. He again preferred the banking system to find its own solution because 'we must be sure not to starve [the private sector] of funds if we are to maintain our rate of growth'.[66] Thus, Cowperthwaite's case for *laissez-faire* began with a belief that growth came first.[67] He also invoked a practical obstacle to intervention: the government was incapable of identifying 'what rate of expansion of the economy would be "right"

... [and how] to regulate it at that rate'. He saw no way of judging when an industry or market was suffering from 'over-expansion'. Thus, he preferred to stand aside even when, as he put it, the growth rate was threatening 'uncomfortable, even injurious, effects on some individuals or some sectors'.[68]

There was an important exception to Cowperthwaite's *laissez-faire* approach. He was adamant that the government had to let a recession run its course, unless deflation began in the financial sector. At the peak of the 1965 bank crisis, the government pumped funds equivalent to 9.7% of the total liquidity of the local Chinese-owned sector into the more vulnerable banks regardless of the quality of their management or their loan portfolios.[69] 'One of the few elements of modem monetary policy we can safely indulge in', he later argued, was to reverse a contraction in the banking system's liquidity by direct injection of government funds. For this reason, he adopted a strategy of maintaining what he described as 'abnormally high' levels of reserves by comparison with other governments, which should 'be held to a great extent abroad'.[70] This strategy meant that budgets had to be consistently deflationary to generate the surpluses for transfer overseas.

Cowperthwaite's commitment to growth as the first priority affected his attitude toward inflation. He knew that 'excessive bank lending' led to inflationary pressures.[71] Yet, he would do nothing to impede the fastest possible expansion of the overall economy even when liquidity was growing at an alarming rate.[72] When domestic rents rose sharply in 1961 causing widespread public discontent, the colonial administration at first tried to deny that the increasing cost of property was a matter for concern.[73] 'Rent increases are rather the result of pressures arising from our present prosperous economic condition', Cowperthwaite told legislators, 'they are one symptom of that prosperity rather than a cause of inflation'. The public was not convinced, and protests continued until legislation to restrict increases in domestic rents was enacted eight month later.[74] Rent controls were to remain on the statute book in some form or another for the rest of the century.[75]

Although retail prices proved relatively stable in the first half of the decade, the business community complained bitterly of inflationary pressures. The colonial administration was attacked for rising land and labour costs which were said to be undermining Hong Kong's international competitiveness even though exports were booming. Cowperthwaite refused to intervene. 'Our inflation is not the bad kind', he declared, 'but a reflection of high economic activity'.[76] The Governor joined the debate, attributing 'cost inflation' to 'high export demand'

and interpreting it as 'a consequence of increasing prosperity rather than as a premonition of ruin'. He argued that, in the past, excessive competition among local manufacturers had kept export prices excessively low. 'It is a good thing, surely not a bad thing, that our [export] prices should be forced up to correct world competitive levels by the high tension of our economy'.[77]

The government's critics were not convinced, and, at the end of his career, Cowperthwaite was still trying to persuade the community that inflation was good for Hong Kong and that an active monetary policy would prove a mistake. In the last resort, he explained, the colony faced 'the familiar dilemma between rapid growth and stabilization'. The government would encounter widespread opposition within the community if it tried 'to reverse all our previous policies and choose stabilization rather than growth'. He also argued that rising wages were beneficial, both socially and in terms of economic efficiency.[78]

Financial secretary Sir Philip Haddon-Cave (1971–81)

The monetary challenges of the 1960s were to recur in the following decade under Cowperthwaite's successor, Sir Philip Haddon-Cave. Thanks to the same generous creation of liquidity by the banks that had led to the 1965 bank crisis, speculation drove share prices to unrealistic levels before collapsing abruptly in 1973.[79] The colonial administration was attacked for allowing the surge in bank lending that financed the stock market speculation and to which the foreign-owned banks were regarded – correctly – as making a major contribution. Haddon-Cave claimed – quite wrongly – that foreign banks were importing capital to fund their local operations when, in fact, they were exploiting on a grand scale the loophole in the legal definition of minimum liquidity ratios.[80] The banks' creation of liquidity became an even more worrying issue after the inadvertent abrogation of the currency board system in 1974 when Hong Kong adopted a floating rate. As a result, Haddon-Cave acknowledged, 'the banks are no longer completely constrained by their liquidity ratios'.[81] Nevertheless, when legislation was passed in 1975 allowing the minimum statutory liquidity to be altered, Haddon-Cave reassured bankers 'that it is not envisaged that the ratio would ever be varied for monetary control purposes'.[82]

Haddon-Cave refused to use statutory liquidity ratios to influence credit creation within the banking system for two reasons. First, he misunderstood the way in which foreign-owned banks could create liquidity regardless of the apparent legal constraints. He believed that as long as their head offices had designated adequate funds to meet demands for cash from their Hong Kong depositors, the mechanics of their liquidity ratios did not matter. In terms of monetary policy, the freedom of these banks to lend money in excess of their local deposits was, of course, highly significant.[83] Secondly, and more important still was the colonial administration's anxiety in the 1970s not to deter financial institutions from using Hong Kong as their Asian base through the imposition of controls on their business activities in the colony. Once the government had ruled out tax incentives to attract them to Hong Kong, the only significant inducement Haddon-Cave could offer was to minimise official regulation of foreign financial institutions, including the liquidity requirements imposed on them and their deposit-taking company (DTC) subsidiaries.[84]

Under the floating rate regime, control of the money supply deteriorated. Domestic consumption began to increase at what the government termed an unsustainable rate in 1977. Yet, officials still placed their trust in 'the inevitable mechanism of the market operating in this instance through the exchange rate, interest rates and the money supply'.[85] By 1979, the banks were pumping liquidity into the share and property markets on an alarming scale, and Haddon-Cave was talking openly of the need to find 'suitable constraints for Hong Kong's particular circumstances'. The weapon immediately to hand, he noted, was the banks' liquidity ratios but he still found it repugnant 'to impose any form of direct control on the supply of credit ... I would much prefer to leave matters to the banking system itself'. Nevertheless, he warned that he might be compelled to restrain credit creation through higher liquidity ratios which would also apply to DTCs.[86] Still, he continued to vacillate. He had now grasped that an increase in the current statutory liquidity ratio would only constrain HSBC and local banks, thus giving foreign-owned banks an unacceptable advantage. Eventually, with considerable reluctance, he took legal powers to vary statutory liquidity ratios to support the government's monetary policies.[87] He never used them, however.

In the end, Haddon-Cave blamed the colony's monetary woes on the floating exchange rate introduced in 1974 and argued that it had made inflation an insoluble problem.[88] In 1981 he stated:

> To the extent that our present floating exchange rate regime leads, from time to time, to an expansion of the money supply disproportionate to the economy's ability to absorb additional credit without inflation, awkward questions of monetary management will

continue to arise, but we are not the only government that find such questions awkward.

Inflation proved a serious issue in the 1970s, increasing at an annual rate of 9.5% compared with only 3.3% in the previous decade.[89] The colonial administration did not see monetary measures as the remedy, and the Governor claimed that 'the main contribution the Government can make towards containing inflationary trends is through its social policies'.[90] Haddon-Cave insisted that Hong Kong could not suffer from serious domestic inflation so long as public expenditure did not increase faster than GDP over a significant period. With the colony's open economy, there was no danger of wages and other production costs spiralling out of control, he declared.[91] He was still sticking to the Cowperthwaite line that the colony did not need active monetary policies because of the economy's automatic adjustment mechanism.[92] By the following year, however, Haddon-Cave came close to admitting that the era of automatic adjustment was over. Hong Kong was an emerging financial centre, he argued, and as such, was doomed to suffer unstable monetary conditions.[93]

The real source of inflation was the lack of any control over the money supply. The currency board system had regulated the currency in circulation as long as increases in the note issue were fully backed in foreign assets. When the link with sterling was abandoned in July 1972, the colonial administration ceased to automatically convert the funds backing new bank notes into assets held overseas. When the Hong Kong dollar began to float in 1974, officials decided to adopt a policy of backing the note issue in Hong Kong dollars, thus formalising the practice into which they had slipped two years earlier.[94] This policy seemed benign at first because the effective exchange rate strengthened by almost 11% over its 1971 level up to 1978, when it fell by 10%.[95] Not until 1979 did Haddon-Cave tell the public that by ending the currency board practice of total backing for the currency in foreign assets, 'the Government has involuntarily contributed to the undesirable growth rates of the money supply and bank advances'.[96] Now a desperate but fruitless search began for techniques to restore financial stability.[97]

Political postscript

In the 1980s, a heavy price had to be paid for the *laissez-faire* preconceptions of the past, and it was left to Haddon-Cave's successor, Sir John Bremridge, to deal with the crises that the mistaken policies of the 1970s had made inevitable. Real estate prices had surged from 1978 to 1981, and interest rates reached record heights. The property market collapsed in 1982, undermining the stock market and business sentiment generally.[98] Real estate speculation had been financed by banks and DTCs, which were now seriously over-exposed to the property sector. Between 1982 and 1986, seven licensed banks failed, and 94 DTCs closed.[99] As public and business confidence crumbled, the government was forced to spend HKD3.8 billion on rescuing and restructuring the insolvent banks.[100]

The financial crisis was aggravated by the collapse of the currency during 1983 as Sino-British negotiations over the future of Hong Kong became confrontational. The colonial administration decided that a return to the currency board system was the simplest and surest solution for the instability and indiscipline that had developed in the previous decade. The linked exchange rate of HKD7.80 = USD1 was introduced, and officials now took charge of the management of monetary affairs.[101] Not until 1988, however, did the colonial administration 'establish the principle of the banking sector holding its settlement reserves in central bank money' via the Exchange Fund to overcome the weakness of the traditional currency board system which regulated only the 'physical currency'.[102]

These drastic reversals of policy in the 1980s were a rational response to the severity of the shocks to the financial system, but officials did not find them particularly comfortable. It was hard to admit that 'the much-vaunted automatic adjustment process of the textbook currency board could not be entirely relied upon in practice', and they made a determined effort to conceal how extensively the government had to intervene in financial markets from 1983 and 1988.[103] But the colonial administration could no longer dictate policy free from serious challenge to its *laissez-faire* attitudes. Elections, albeit limited and indirect, were introduced in 1985 and the government's use of its reserves to bail out ailing financial institutions came under hostile scrutiny in a legislature whose membership no longer consisted exclusively of officials and government appointees.[104] Direct responsibility for monetary affairs could no longer be denied, and public accountability made non-interventionism a political liability.[105]

Notes

1   I prepared this chapter while a Research Fellow at the Hong Kong Institute for Monetary Research. The Institute has no responsibility for the analysis or the views which are presented here.

2 For the evidence on financing, see Leo F. Goodstadt (2006) 'Dangerous Business Models: Bankers, Bureaucrats & Hong Kong's Economic Transformation, 1948–86', *HKIMR Working Paper No. 8/2006*, pp. 4–8.

3 Christopher Howe (1983) 'Growth, Public Policy and Hong Kong's Economic Relationship with China', *China Quarterly*, 95, p. 512; Census and Statistics Department (2005), *2004 Gross Domestic Product* (Hong Kong: Government of the HKSAR), pp. 20–1.

4 Ronald Findlay and Stanislaw Wellisz (1993) 'Hong Kong', in R. Findlay and S. Wellisz (eds) *The Political Economy of Poverty, Equity, and Growth. Five Small Open Economies* (New York: Oxford University Press), p. 47; Henry Smith (1966) *John Stuart Mill's Other Island. A study of the economic development of Hong Kong* (London: Institute of Economic Affairs), pp. 18–21.

5 *Hong Kong Hansard* (*HH*, hereafter), 24 March 1954, p. 136.

6 *HH*, 1 March 1961, p. 46.

7 Ida Greaves (1955) 'Dollar Pooling in the Sterling Area: Comment', *American Economic Review*, 45, 4, p. 656.

8 *HH*, 26 February 1964, p. 47; 24 February 1966, p. 57.

9 *HH*, 7 April 1976, p. 802.

10 Trevor Clark (2004), *Good Second Class* (Stanhope: The Memoir Club), p. 156.

11 For details of this statistical void, see Leo F. Goodstadt (2006) 'Government without Statistics: Policy-making in Hong Kong 1925–85, with special reference to Economic and Financial Management', *HKIMR Working Paper No. 6/2006*.

12 One governor publicly lamented the wilful opposition of his officials to statistics. Sir Geoffry Northcote, *HH*, 13 October 1938, p. 117. On the lack of improvement twenty years later, see Statistician minutes to Director of Commerce and Industry, 15 December 1958. Hong Kong Public Records Office (HKRS hereafter) 22-1-96.

13 Cowperthwaite, *HH*, 25 March 1970, pp. 495–6.

14 Haddon-Cave, *HH*, 27 February 1980, p. 516.

15 On the connection between colonial political systems and the quality of government statistical information, see Lord Hailey's comments in F. Searle *et al.* (1950) 'Colonial Statistics', *Journal of the Royal Statistical Society. Series A (General)*, 13, 3, p. 291.

16 Cowperthwaite made a passing, historical reference to the term 'currency board', *HH*, 18 December 1963, p. 303. One elected legislator discussed the system at the end of British rule, Christine Loh, *HH*, 27 March 1996, p. 153. There was also an official comment during the committee stage of Banking (Amendment) Bill 1996. David Carse, Deputy Chief Executive, HKMA, 22 October 1996 (LegCo Paper No. CB(1) 659/96–97).

17 Contemporary observers remarked on the preference of colonial banks and Third World banking generally for low ratios of loans to deposits. e.g., G.L.M. Clauson (1944) 'The British Colonial Currency System', *Economic Journal*, 54, 213, p. 22; Arthur I. Bloomfield (1957) 'Some Problems of Central Banking in Underdeveloped Countries', *Journal of Finance*, 12, 2, p. 192.

18 G.L.M. Clauson (1937) 'Some Uses of Statistics in Colonial Administration', *Journal of the Royal African Society*, 36, 45, pp. 10–12.

19   Tony Latter (1994), 'The Currency Board Approach to Monetary Policy – from Africa to Argentina and Estonia, via Hong Kong', in *Proceedings of the Seminar on Monetary Management organized by the Hong Kong Monetary Authority on 18–19 October 1993* (Hong Kong: HKMA), p. 27.

20   Economists dealing with currency boards, both in the contemporary world and in the context of Hong Kong's experience, draw attention to the 'passive' nature of monetary policy under a currency board. e.g., Steve H. Hanke (2002) 'Currency Boards', *Annals,* 579, pp. 90, 91, 101; Tony Latter (2007) 'Rules versus Discretion in Managing the Hong Kong dollar, 1983–2006', *HKIMR Working Paper No. 2/2007*, pp. 3–6.

21   Clauson, 'Some Uses', p. 14.

22   Clarence B. Davis (1982) 'Financing Imperialism: British and American Bankers as Vectors of Imperial Expansion in China, 1908–1920', *Business History Review*, 56, 2, pp. 253, 258–60; David Mclean (1976) 'Finance and "Informal Empire" before the First World War', *Economic History Review*, 29, 2, pp. 301–4; John Atkin (1970) 'Official Regulation of British Overseas Investment', *Economic History Review*, 23, 2, pp. 329–30; Monopolies and Mergers Commission (1982) *The Hongkong and Shanghai Banking Corporation. Standard Chartered Bank Limited. The Royal Bank of Scotland Group Limited. A Report on the Proposed Mergers* (Cmnd 8472, HMSO), pp. 88, 90.

23   H.C. Reed (1980) 'The Ascent of Tokyo as an International Financial Center', *Journal of International Business Studies*, 11, 3, 'Table 3 Rankings of Asian International Bank Centers', p. 28; E. Stuart Kirby (1951) 'Hong Kong and the British Position in China', *Annals*, 277, pp. 199–200.

24   The first to perceive the difference between Hong Kong and other colonies appears to have been Clauson, 'The British Colonial Currency System', pp. 2, 22.

25   Note the analysis in J.O.W. Olakanpo (1961) 'Monetary Management in Dependent Economies', *Economica*, 28, 112, pp. 397–8.

26   H. Myint (1954) 'An Interpretation of Economic Backwardness', *Oxford Economic Papers*, 6, 2, p. 158; Ida Greaves (1957) 'Colonial Trade and Payments', *Economica*, 24, 93, pp. 48–9; Frank H.H. King (1966) 'Sterling Balances and the Colonial Monetary Systems', *Economic Journal*, 65, 260, pp. 719–20.

27   This point was made in the context of misunderstandings about how currency boards work in another part of the colonial empire. A.N.R. Robinson (2001) *The Mechanics of Independence: Patterns of Political and Economic Transformation in Trinidad and Tobago* (Barbados: University Press of the West Indies), p. 60.

28   There was also a failure to draw the obvious comparisons with the role of the banks under an exchange standard. See, for example, the passing reference to commercial banks under a colonial currency board and the important discussion of the same mechanism in the Dominions in Philip W. Bell (1956) *The Sterling Area in the Postwar World: International Mechanism and Cohesion, 1946–1952* (Oxford: Clarendon Press), pp. 5–6, 67–9. One exception who recognised the powerful influence of the banks was A.R. Prest (1963) *Public Finance in Underdeveloped Countries* (New York: Praeger), pp. 101–2.

29   This analysis summarises John Greenwood (1984) 'The Monetary Framework Underlying the Hong Kong Dollar Stabilization Scheme', *China Quarterly*, 99, pp. 631, 632.

30 Cowperthwaite, *HH*, 16 September 1964, p. 331; 24 February 1966, pp. 75–6.

31 *Report of the Commission ... to Enquire into the Causes and Effects of the Present Trade Recession...*(Hong Kong: Noronha & Co., 1935), pp. 71–2, 74, 79, 89–90, 93–4; Governor's minute to Colonial Secretary, 30 March 1940. HKRS58-1-190-10.

32 *Report of the Commission to enquire into the Causes and Effects of the Present Trade Recession*, p. 103; *Report on the Social & Economic Progress for the year 1939*, p. 45.

33 The problem was aggravated by the dysfunctional arrangements for the note issue which hindered the smooth expansion of the money supply to match economic growth. *Report of Currency Committee, 1930*, pp. 105–6.

34 J.J. Paterson (Jardine Matheson) letter to Financial Secretary, 17 February 1939. HKRS170-1-305.

35 *Report of the Commission ... to enquire into the Causes and Effects of the Present Trade Recession*, p. 104.

36 For example, proposals for legislation to improve the quality of banking standards were regarded as unlikely to be effective. *Ibid.*, p. 104.

37 C.F. Joseph Tom (1989) *Monetary Problems of an Entrepot: The Hong Kong Experience* (New York: Peter Lang), pp. 66–70.

38 These pre-war developments are explained in Tony Latter (2004) 'Hong Kong's Exchange Rate Regimes in the Twentieth Century: The Story of Three Regime Changes', *HKIMR Working Paper No. 17/2004*, pp. 7–11, 13, 15–16.

39 'Hong Kong Civil Affairs Policy Directives. Financial Policy', revised draft, 7 July 1944. HKRS211-2-20.

40 War Office secret telegram to Commander in Chief Hong Kong, 22 March 1946. HKRS 169-2-26; Commander in Chief telegram to War Office, 19 January 1946; War Office/Colonial Office telegram to Commander in Chief Hong Kong, 16 January 1946. HKRS169-2-53; Officer Administering the Government telegram to Secretary of State for the Colonies, no. 958, 6 June 1947; S. Caine (Colonial Office) telegram to D.M. MacDougall (Hong Kong), 21 June 1947. HKRS163-1-442.

41 For details of the unsuccessful efforts to influence the power companies' charges, see HKRS1631-602 'China Light & Power Co. Ltd. and Hong Kong Electric Co'. Where government approval was required for changes in utilities charges, officials refused consent. For example. Sir Charles Follows, Financial Secretary, *HH*, 29 March 1950, p. 109.

42 The severity of these problems is recorded in detail in HKRS41-1-3378 'Cotton textiles'.

43 *Appendix C Hong Kong Departmental Report (1946–1947) Department of Supplies, Trade and Industry* (Hong Kong), p. 11.

44 Alan Birch (1974) 'Control of Prices and Commodities in Hong Kong', *Hong Kong Law Journal*, 4, 2, pp. 133–50. Most controls were abolished during 1953. Director of Commerce and Industry memo to Financial Secretary, 30 March 1953; UK [Colonial Office] Circular 305/53, 'Price Controls', 2 April 1953. HKRS170-1-418(2).

45 Follows, *HH*, 8 March 1950, p. 46.

46 Financial Secretary minutes to Governor, 17 August 1949 and 27 December 1950. HKRS163-1-634; *Far Eastern Economic Review*: 'Cotton Spinning in

Hongkong', 21 September 1950; 'Commercial Reports', 9 November 1950; 'The Hongkong Cotton Mills Pool', 6 September 1951.

47 The background to these events is recorded in HKRS1017-2-6 'Committee to Review the Unemployment Situation in the Colony' and HKRS163-1-1376 'Industry and Production. Industrial Situation in Hong Kong'.

48 Lawrence Kadoorie note, 'Labour Conditions in Hong Kong as affected by the U.S. ban on raw materials', 30 December 1950. HKRS163-1-1376; Spinners Club letter to Commissioner of Labour, 6 January 1951; Notes on a meeting, Labour Department, 2 April 1952; Labour Officer memo to Commissioner of Labour, 2 May 1952; J. Keswick letter to Commissioner of Labour, 12 May 1952. HKRS1017-3-4.

49 Arthur Hazelwood (1953–54) 'Colonial External Finance Since the War', *Review of Economic Studies*, 21, 1, pp. 48–9.

50 Albert O. Hirschman (1957) 'Economic Policy in Underdeveloped Countries', *Economic Development and Cultural Change*, 5, 4, p. 366; Michael Havinden and David Meredith (1993) *Colonialism and Development: Britain and Its Tropical Colonies, 1850–1960* (London: Routledge), pp. 269–70.

51 Stephen W.K. Chiu *et al.* (1997) *City States in the Global Economy: Industrial Restructuring in Hong Kong and Singapore* (Boulder: Westview Press), pp. 34, 66.

52 The controversy and its protagonists are recorded in *HH*: Clarke, 2 March 1955, p. 52; 29 February 1956, pp. 91–2; 27 February 1957, p. 31; 6 March 1958, p. 47; Lo Man Wai, 21 March 1956, p. 118; Ngan Shing-kwan, 21 March 1956, pp. 118, 121; C.E.M. Terry, 20 March 1957, p. 61.

53 Letter to Colonial Office, 25 June 1959. HKRS 163-1-1943.

54 Clarke, *HH*, 29 February 1956, p. 77.

55 Ricardo, 'Development of Banking in Hongkong during 1955', *Far Eastern Economic Review*, 2 February 1956.

56 On the relationship between transfers of official reserves to and from sterling and the local money supply in the 1950s, see Frank H.H. King (1957) *Money in British East Asia* (London: HMSO), p. 120.

57 Frank H.H. King (1991) *The Hong Kong Bank in the Period of Development and Nationalism, 1941–1984. From Regional Bank to Multinational Group* (Cambridge: Cambridge University Press), p. 338.

58 *HH*, 27 March 1957, pp. 116–17.

59 P. Mardulyn, Manager Banque Belge, letter to Deputy Financial Secretary, 30 November 1960; Deputy Financial Secretary's reply to Mardulyn, 3 December 1960; Statistician memo to DES, 'Banking Statistics', 22 April 1961; M. 35 AS(E) to DES, 19 May 1961. HKRS163-1-625; Commissioner of Banking memo to Financial Secretary, 19 March 1965. HKRS163-1-3273.

60 Goodstadt, 'Dangerous Business Models', pp. 4–8.

61 Cowperthwaite, *HH*, 26 March 1969, p. 205.

62 Cowperthwaite, *HH*, 24 February 1966, pp. 75–6.

63 See Y.C. Jao (1988) 'Monetary system and banking structure', in H.C.Y. Ho and L.C. Chau (eds) *The Economic System of Hong Kong* (Hong Kong: Asian Research Service), p. 45.

64 For evidence that the government had ignored the growing signs of excessive bank liquidity, see the data cited by Cowperthwaite, *HH*, 24 February 1966, p. 54.

65　*HH*, 26 February 1964, p. 45.

66　*HH*, 26 March 1969, p. 206.

67　For a statement of the case for non-interventionism under current conditions, see Adam S. Posen (2006) 'Why Central Banks Should Not Burst Bubbles', *International Finance*, 9, 1.

68　*HH*, 8 October 1969, p. 85.

69　Commissioner of Banking memo to Financial Secretary, 'Bank Loans – Dao Heng Bank Ltd and Kwong On Bank Ltd', 23 March 1966. HKRS163-3-249; Commissioner of Banking to Financial Secretary, 2 September 1965. HKRS163-1-3273.

70　Cowperthwaite letter to Sir Frank Figgures (United Kingdom Treasury), 19 October 1970 and 'A Preliminary Note on the International Monetary Fund with reference to dependent territories (and with particular reference to Hong Kong)', p. 11. HKRS163-9-217.

71　*HH*, 26 March 1969, p. 205.

72　*HH*, 8 October 1965, p. 85.

73　'There have been several references in the debate to inflation. This is a rather imprecise term. We do not have it in its worst economic sense because our monetary system does not allow that to happen'. *HH*, 30 March 1962, p. 128.

74　*HH*, 17 January 1962, p. 6; C.B. Burgess, Colonial Secretary, *HH*, 26 September 1962, pp. 278–88.

75　For its final demise, see Housing Department (2003) *Consultation Paper: Landlord and Tenant (Consolidation) Ordinance (LTO) (Cap.7) Security of Tenure* (Hong Kong, Housing, Planning and Lands Bureau), p. 1.

76　*HH*, 27 February 1963, p. 41.

77　Sir Robert Black, Governor, *HH*, 26 February 1964, p. 37.

78　*HH*, 9 October 1970, pp. 112–15.

79　Frederick Ma, Secretary for Financial Services and the Treasury, *Government Information Services*, 18 November 2002.

80　*HH*, 29 November 1973, p. 229. On the misleading nature of this defence of the foreign-owned banks, see M. 11 Exchange Controller to DES, 23 August 1972. HKRS163-3-12. On the substantial role played by foreign-owned banks in this bubble market, see Goodstadt, 'Dangerous Business Models', pp. 15, 16–17.

81　*HH*, 2 March 1975, p. 807.

82　*HH*, 5 November 1975, p. 190.

83　*HH*, 11 April 1979, pp. 707, 709; 15 November 1979, p. 217.

84　*HH*, 28 February 1973, pp. 494–5.

85　Lord MacLehose, *HH*, 5 October 1977, p. 11.

86　*HH*, 28 February 1979, p. 554.

87　*HH*, 11 April 1979, pp. 709–10.

88　*HH*, 25 February 1981, p. 523.

89　Census and Statistics Department, *2004 Gross Domestic Product*, 'Table 2 Implicit Price Deflators', p. 23.

90　MacLehose, *HH*, 17 October 1973, p. 26. The government also pointed to its strict control of the rice trade to ensure adequate supplies. D.H. Jordan, Director of Commerce and Industry, *HH*, 27 March 1974, pp. 710–21.

91　*HH*, 29 November 1973, p. 239.

92   *HH*, 28 March 1973, p. 640.

93   *HH*, 14 November 1974, pp. 217–18.

94   *HH*, 25 February 1976, pp. 496, 517–18; 2 March 1977, pp. 578–80; 16 November 1978, p. 208.

95   Andrew F. Freris (1991) *The Financial Markets of Hong Kong* (London: Routledge), Table 6.1, p. 185.

96   *HH*, 28 February 1979, p. 550.

97   J. Greenwood 'Hong Kong: How to Rescue HK$: Three Practical Proposals', *Asian Monetary Monitor*, Vol. 6, No. 5 (September–October 1982), pp. 11–12.

98   Freris, *Financial Markets*, Tables 2.14, 2.15, p. 48

99   Jao, 'Monetary system and banking structure', p. 59; Freris, *Financial Markets*, Table 2.9, pp. 40–1. *Hong Kong Annual Digest of Statistics, 1988 Edition* (Hong Kong: Census and Statistics Department), pp. 125–8.

100   T.K. Ghose (1987) *The Banking System of Hong Kong* (Singapore: Butterworths), p. 96. The actual exposure of the Exchange Fund in supporting these banks was probably significantly higher at the height of the crisis.

101   John Gray (1994) 'Monetary Management in Hong Kong: The Role of the Hongkong and Shanghai Banking Corporation Limited', in *Proceedings of the Seminar on Monetary Management organized by the Hongkong Monetary Authority on 18–19 October 1993* (Hong Kong: HKMA), p. 60.

102   Latter, 'Rules versus Discretion', p. 10.

103   *Ibid.*, p. 9.

104   See Bremridge, *HH*, 9 April 1986, pp. 981–7.

105   For example, in introducing regulatory reforms, Bremridge was far franker about the management of monetary affairs than his predecessors. *HH*, 19 March 1986, p. 771.

5
Rules Versus Discretion in Managing the Hong Kong Dollar, 1983–2007

Tony Latter

Introduction[1]

This chapter is concerned with Hong Kong's exchange rate regime as it has functioned from 1983 to the present day. The regime has variously been described as a link, a peg, and a currency board. For convenience, this paper takes these terms to be synonymous, and therefore elects to call the regime a currency board throughout the period. It is acknowledged, however, that some purists would argue that the regime has not always fulfilled all necessary conditions to be classified as such. What is incontrovertible, from the evidence, is that the arrangements, however they may be described, have been remarkably successful in their primary objective of keeping the exchange rate stable at around US$1 = HK$7.80. Since July 1984, the rate has never diverged from 7.80 by more than 1%.

The focus of the chapter is the question of 'rules versus discretion'. In essence, how much of the observed exchange rate stability has been the result of the prevailing currency board rules themselves (as amended from time to time by the authorities, whether or not on a strictly statutory basis) and the automatic adjustment processes arising from them;[2] and how much has, by contrast, been achieved only by the instrument of discretionary official market interventions? Following on from that, the chapter considers whether the exercise of discretion has been a *necessary* factor in attaining that exchange rate stability.

Interest in this question has been motivated partly by remarks made on occasion over the years suggesting or asserting that Hong Kong does not have a proper currency board, that the purity of the concept has been threatened or actually compromised by the exercise of other central banking functions, that discretionary actions by the authorities can only serve to undermine monetary stability, and so forth. Greenwood, for instance, writing in 1988, just after the authorities had acquired the means to influence the liquidity of the banking system, said: 'Any shift from a system of rules to a system of discretionary intervention must be regarded with circumspection'; and, almost a year later:'...since July 1988 the Exchange Fund has been operating more like a central bank than a passive colonial currency board.' Then, commenting on the announcement of a programme of issuing Exchange Fund bills he said:

> It seems likely that Hong Kong will move to a system of regular discretionary intervention in the domestic money market and/or in the foreign exchange market. Once this is accomplished later this year it will no longer be possible to claim that Hong Kong does not have a central bank. Judged strictly from the standpoint of the conduct of monetary policy, this development will take Hong Kong even further down the path towards full-scale central banking.[3]

Milton Friedman contributed to this debate when, at a conference in 1993 to mark the tenth anniversary of the HKD link and the establishment of the Hong Kong Monetary Authority, he made a thinly veiled criticism of the creation of an institution looking more like a central bank than a currency board.[4] More recently, Hanke declared that the HKMA was not a currency board, in a tone suggesting that it was a sin not to be one.[5] In fact, no-one ever claimed that the HKMA was itself a currency board; the important feature of Hong Kong's arrangement is that the HKMA operates a currency board regime within a wider set of functions and responsibilities. These wider duties may, taken altogether, indeed brand the HKMA institutionally as a central bank, but that does not necessarily undermine its discrete currency board function.

Prompted by such considerations, the next section provides a discussion of the concept of a currency board and the delineation of rules from discretion. Section 3 notes briefly the evolution of the institutional infrastructure within which monetary policy operates. Section 4 divides the period 1983–2006 into five sub-periods, each covering a slightly different regime phase. For each sub-period it describes the significant additions or changes to the monetary regime which are relevant to the rules-versus-discretion debate and which characterise the phase, before reviewing the behaviour of the exchange rate and the strategy pursued by the authorities. Section 5 draws together some conclusions about the use of discretion and its consequences.

The concept and rules of a currency board

The modern currency board has its origins in British colonies. They came to adopt it quite widely in the nineteenth and twentieth centuries. It was an administratively simple and financially efficient mechanism for ensuring an adequate supply of local currency notes and coins in a colony, solidly backed against sterling (mostly invested in British government securities) at a fixed rate. By replacing the metropolitan currency with its own, the colony also benefited in three other ways:

(a) The arrangements ensured that the colony, rather than the metropolitan authority, was the financial beneficiary of any loss or accidental destruction of currency within the colony.
(b) They ensured that the colony did not have to wait months before receiving value for used notes, as they lay idle during transportation back to the issuer.
(c) They ensured that the colony earned the seigniorage on the issue, albeit after having to meet the production costs itself.[6]

In these historical cases, the physical currency was the sole monetary liability of the currency board. Most banking transactions were conducted in sterling, so there was seldom any compelling need to develop financial markets in the local currency, or therefore to set up clearing arrangements in the local currency which could, if settlement was conducted through accounts with the monetary authorities, give rise to an additional form of official reserve money. If an increasing amount of local business and banking came to be denominated in the local currency, as it certainly did in Hong Kong over the years, then a banking structure for the local currency would emerge. There was a natural tendency for the exchange rate between the local currency and the anchor currency to hold close to the fixed rate which had been set for notes and coin. In other words, the whole economy was seen to function at that fixed rate. Until the time came when a colony began to talk about monetary independence and establishing its own central bank, there was scarcely the slightest doubt that the colony's currency would remain at its fixed rate.

Because the currency board, as practised today in Hong Kong and a few other places, is somewhat different from the simple colonial version – most notably because the monetary base to which the convertibility rules apply now includes the reserve money of the banking system – there is some confusion as to what constitutes the strict or pure model. In fact, there is no unequivocal definition. One might be inclined to take an entry in Palgrave as authoritative, but even there Alan Walters, after noting the initial colonial cash-only model, tended to sidestep the matter of the current definition.[7]

Where do the definitional uncertainties arise? It may be sufficient to provide four examples.

(a) First, under the simple sterling-based arrangements referred to above, the question of the convertibility of banks' reserve money balances did not arise, essentially because the financial systems had not yet reached that stage of development. The currency board was based only on physical currency; it was not involved in interbank settlement; the metropolitan authorities were effectively in charge of wider monetary and economic issues. That leaves one in a quandary as to whether the 'pure' model should only embrace cash, or whether, because cash was in the early days equal to monetary base, and because monetary base now includes banks' balances, a currency board must necessarily adopt the wider coverage. This was a particularly relevant consideration in Hong Kong's experience post-1983, since for much of the time it operated the cash-only model.

(b) The second example is the stock-flow controversy. Does the pure model require only the stock of currency to be fully backed (in which case any excess foreign reserves provide scope for issuance of extra money at will), or does it require only that *changes* in the monetary base are matched exactly with *changes* in foreign reserves? Is one or other sufficient, or are both necessary? This does not seem to be an issue that was ever discussed in the early days of currency boards. Passing the stock test was all that was necessary to get the regime started, but the flow rule could have been a useful additional discipline, and perhaps a necessary one, for the sake of prudence, in a situation of surplus reserves (again of relevance in the Hong Kong context). The answer perhaps needs to be based more on pragmatism than on dogma.[8] Hong Kong has tended to adopt the stance that both conditions should apply; this was confirmed in the most formal sense in a letter from the Financial Secretary to the Monetary Authority in 2003.[9]

(c) The third example relates essentially to the institutional framework within which the currency board operates. The purists would argue that a currency board should be a stand-alone body with a balance sheet comprised solely of the monetary base and the foreign currency which backs it. In Hong Kong, however the Exchange Fund, which was the original balance sheet when the currency board was first introduced in 1935, had its ambit extended over the years – most significantly as the repository for budget surpluses. That did not preclude it from continuing to serve the currency board, provided that the stock and flow rules were observed in respect of the monetary base. In fact, since 1999 the balance sheet of the Exchange Fund has been presented on a segregated basis, with a currency board sub-account to demonstrate compliance with currency board principles.

(d) Finally, there is the question of sterilised intervention. A fundamental principle of the currency board is that the change in the monetary base arising from an official foreign exchange transaction in response to an external inflow or outflow must not be reversed by open market operations or interbank activities carried out by the central bank or currency board. In short, there must be no sterilisation in those particular circumstances. That does not preclude the government or its agencies from being involved in sterilised intervention from other sources, when foreign currency is exchanged independently of the monetary base or its backing. Particular confusion may arise if, as in the case of Hong Kong, the same agency or balance sheet is both the guardian of the currency board and the conduit for sterilised intervention. In fact, neither the regular investment or drawdown of fiscal reserves, which are held and managed by the Exchange Fund and frequently involve foreign exchange transactions, nor the purchases of shares on the stock market by the Exchange Fund during the 1998 crisis (and their subsequent sale), have impacted in any way on the currency board account. The strict rules have not been broken.

Thus, a disciplined currency board does not necessarily require a separate institution with a dedicated balance sheet. It does not require that the authorities, in the widest sense of the word, never conduct any sterilised intervention. However, the main delineations of a currency board – the fixed rate, the principle of foreign currency backing (even if the stock-flow issue has not been conclusively resolved), the ban on the central monetary authority lending money to the government or the banks unless properly secured by foreign assets, and so on – are all clear enough. It also seems logical that the convertibility rule should apply not just to cash but to all monetary liabilities of the monetary authorities, whatever they may include.

Monetary management in practice

Before discussing Hong Kong's monetary developments in detail, it is worth noting the unique institutional environment. Prior to 1988 no mechanism existed for direct official influence over the reserve money of the banking system. There was no central bank, in name or substance; commercial banks and government all held their ultimate liquidity in the form of commercial bank money – essentially as balances with HSBC which was the dominant bank and the settlement bank for the payments system. The Accounting Arrangements introduced in 1988 (see next section), enabled the authorities for the first time to influence bank liquidity through their own operations in the foreign exchange or money markets. However, at this stage HSBC was the sole settlement counterparty for official operations, so that HSBC's actions in response to official interventions were key to determining the overall impact of such interventions on the banking sector.

HSBC's pivotal role ended in 1996 when the requirement for all banks to maintain an account at the Exchange Fund was implemented. From that moment onwards there was a competitive set of counterparties and the HKMA possessed the full monetary capability common to central banks around the world. As to accounting arrangements, the Exchange Fund is the government account through which any monetary operations have always been conducted. It is also the account with which HSBC held its obligatory balance under the Accounting Arrangements in the period 1988–96 and with which the banks have held their settlement accounts since 1996. With regard to formal authority over monetary policy, all matters relating to the Exchange Fund have always been under the ultimate control of the Financial Secretary. Executive responsibility lay with the Secretary for Monetary Affairs until 1991, when it passed to the newly created post of Director of the Exchange Fund. In 1993 the Hong Kong Monetary Authority was established, to which that responsibility in turn passed.

Having operated a currency board based on the pound sterling in the years up to 1972, in October 1983 Hong Kong re-established a currency board, this time against the US dollar, at the rate of US$1 = HK$7.80.[10] That is the system which, with a number of subsequent refinements, endures to the present day. For the purposes of this chapter, the period can be conveniently broken down into five sub-periods, each reflecting a revised operating strategy.[11] The remainder of this section reviews the strategy and operational experience in each successive sub-period.

Table 5.1   Chronology of Significant Administrative Measures Since 1983

October 1983	Re-establishment of currency board in respect of certificates of indebtedness (the backing for the note issue) at rate of USD1 = HKD7.80. Note-issuing banks agree with other banks to supply or redeem notes to/from them also against US dollars at 7.80 (see Box D)
May 1984	Enactment of amendment to Exchange Fund Ordinance giving statutory backing to the above arrangement for certificates of indebtedness
July 1988	Introduction of the Accounting Arrangements, *inter alia* requiring HSBC to hold a balance with the Exchange Fund. Focus of policy becomes, in practice, the management of banking sector liquidity
March 1990	First issuance of Exchange Fund bills, to be supplemented by Exchange Fund notes in May 1993
June 1992	Launch of the Liquidity Adjustment Facility
March 1994	HKMA states that it is revising its mode of operation from targeting liquidity to targeting short-term interest rates
September 1998	HKMA announces its 'seven measures' to enhance the system, including a firm convertibility undertaking on the weak side for banks' balances at the Exchange Fund into US dollars (at 7.75, subsequently rising to 7.80), abolition of the LAF, and introduction of the discount window arrangements
January 1994	Note-issuing banks revert to supplying/redeeming notes to/from other banks against payments in HK dollars (see Box D)
May 2005	Introduction of symmetrical convertibility undertakings for banks' balances, at 7.75 on the strong side and 7.85 on the weak side

October 1983–July 1988
Within a few weeks of the reintroduction of currency board arrangements the exchange rate had settled down close to 7.80. Apart from a subsequent bout of pressure which drove the rate to 7.90 in July 1984, the rate was never significantly beyond 7.82 on the weak side. Strong-side variance was somewhat wider but, with rare exceptions, appeared to be capped at 7.75.

When the currency board system was reintroduced in October 1983, the arrangements were simple. Certificates of indebtedness (CoIs) (the obligatory backing for the commercial banks' banknote issue and therefore synonymous for most analytical purposes with the physical currency) would be bought and sold by the Exchange Fund only against payment in US dollars at the rate of HK$7.80. Beyond that, the authorities retained the capacity to intervene in the foreign exchange and money markets. But that capacity did not include unsterilised

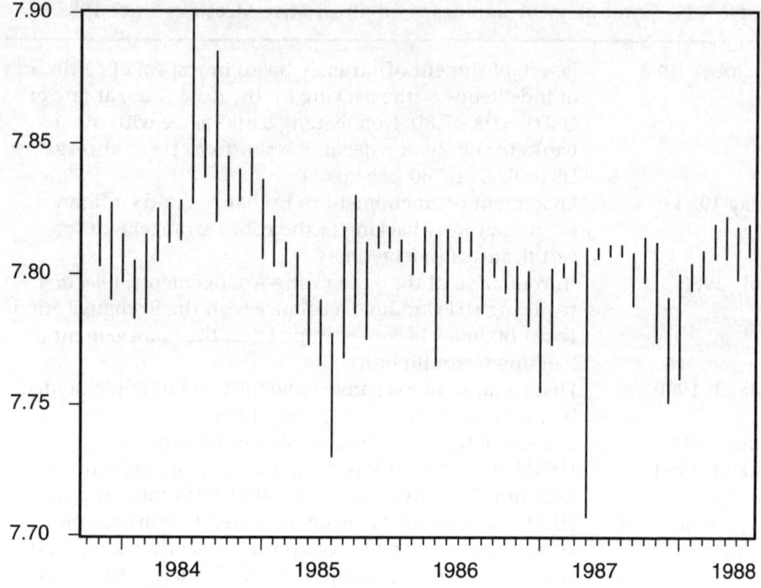

Figure 5.1 HK$–US$ Exchange Rate (lowest-highest spread per month) 17 October 1983 to 16 July 1988

intervention. This was because the Exchange Fund did its banking with the banks; it did not itself provide any banking services to the banks; and the payments system continued to function on the basis of settlement in commercial bank money. So, in this period the currency board was functioning in the most basic colonial format, applying to physical cash only. But the circumstances were quite different from those of the colonies further back in history. In those cases, no-one had ever experienced an independent currency, and the change encountered on adopting the currency board was simply the shift from use of metropolitan notes and coins to use of a separate physical currency, backed 100% by the metropolitan one.

By contrast, Hong Kong already had its own currency, which had been floating independently for a decade, and a relatively sophisticated banking and financial system based on that currency. The idea that the market exchange rate would dutifully fall in line with the rate for conversion of CoIs may be thought of as having been rather fanciful. Admittedly, in the period up to 1972 the market rate had kept to the conversion rate for CoIs without much trouble, but this was helped progressively by the psychological effect of the continuing sterling link itself, and by the underdevelopment, in comparison to later years, of financial markets. In those circumstances the durability of the rate had scarcely been challenged. In the 1980s, however, people were more familiar with the power of market sentiment, and with its prevailing (or, at least, recent) fragility in the Hong Kong context. The argument that arbitrage between banknotes and the wholesale foreign exchange market would bring about convergence of the two exchange rates was little more than an article of faith, given the high degree of segmentation between physical currency circulation and other monetary or financial transactions, and given that only two banks had direct access to the convertibility undertaking (CU).

If market exchange rates became significantly stronger than 7.80, the note-issuing banks would, given the likelihood of secular growth in currency demand, reap a profit (being able to purchase US dollars at, say, 7.75 in order to buy CoIs at 7.80). There would be no incentive for them to eliminate the discrepancy. If the market rate was persistently weaker than 7.80, the note-issuing banks might either accept the consequent exchange loss (as the price of retaining the undoubted status and publicity associated with being a note-issuer), or seek to contain that loss by rationing notes or imposing handling fees. This contrasts with the required adjustment process according to the currency board model, which would be to stem demand for physical currency by raising interest rates. Banks might have concluded, probably correctly, that raising interest rates would have rather little impact on currency demand, whereas it might cause some damage to other areas of their business.

At the inception of the arrangements in October 1983, the note-issuing banks agreed with the other banks that the former would supply (or take back) notes to (or from) the latter also only in exchange for US dollars at the rate of 7.80. There were some who believed that opening an additional channel for arbitrage (at the expense of the note-issuing banks) would assist the convergence process. However, such hopes again encountered the obstacle that, since there was no statutory obligation on the note-issuing banks to supply or redeem notes in unlimited quantities, they could simply ration the amounts in order to protect themselves from arbitrage losses.[12]

In view, consequently, of the probable stickiness of the arbitrage processes, some observers suggested that convergence of the market rate to 7.80 could be better assured if wider access was permitted to the 7.80 'window' – for instance, by allowing everybody access to the Exchange Fund for the purpose of switching between HK dollar banknotes and US dollars at the 7.80 rate.[13] This would, *a priori*, have assisted the arbitrage process and have led, for example, to a speedier upward adjustment of interbank rates in the event of currency weakness. If adverse speculation nevertheless persisted in the foreign exchange market, the situation would probably have induced the same ultimate defence by banks, of rationing notes, without achieving the desired convergence of the market rate to 7.80, and with the unwelcome side-effect that the stability of some smaller banks might have been threatened on the way.

That option was never pursued. In practice, the authorities needed to continue with active intervention. There are no statistics available on the scale of such intervention, but circumstantial and anecdotal evidence suggest that it was significant.[14] The authorities have never denied that intervention was in fact a key factor. The lack of transparency at the time, concerning official operations, was probably accounted for by the fact that the authorities did not wish to admit that the much-vaunted automatic adjustment process of the textbook currency board could not be entirely relied upon in practice. They preferred to give the impression that the rate was guided towards 7.80 by arbitrage.

During this phase, intervention was conducted mainly in the foreign exchange market but also, at least in the early stages, in the money market in accordance with a scheme agreed with HSBC back in 1981.[15] In the early months, intervention was needed to contain the rate from slipping too far on the weak side. Later in this period, upward pressure emerged and the authorities intervened to sell HK dollars. From the evidence of movements in the rate, it seems that in those days the authorities regarded 7.75 as the widest tolerable strong-side limit.

The only monetary liabilities of the Exchange Fund were CoIs, and there was no wider mechanism for unsterilized intervention in the true currency board style. Neither the authorities' intervention in the foreign exchange nor in the money market could have any direct impact on monetary or liquidity aggregates, since the Exchange Fund banked its HK dollars with the banking system. The process was automatically one of sterilization.

This does not mean that interventions were ineffective. There were at least four channels by which the intervention tactics may have influenced the exchange rate in the desired manner:

(a) The conventional portfolio effect, with pressure on the currency abating as agents' portfolios reached the desired rebalanced position.

(b) The fact that intervention generally took place only after the authorities had agreed a strategy with HSBC – ensuring that the two parties were not pulling against one another, and more likely that they were jointly operating in the same direction. With HSBC by far the most dominant player in HK dollar markets, their moves would be important both in substance and as a signal to the rest of the market.

(c) Given that potential pressure on the rate might come from a large order from a single player, the willingness of HSBC to contact the authorities and recommend responding to such a deal expeditiously before it sparked any significant move in the rate and provoked a snowballing effect. Such a tactic was especially helpful during periods of fragile sentiment.

(d) The ability of the authorities, not so much to intervene, as to abstain from intervening unhelpfully at particular times. Given habitual budget surpluses in this period, the Exchange Fund was receiving a steady stream of HK dollars from the government treasury to invest. In selecting the timing for any associated purchases of foreign currency, the authorities could exercise some influence over the exchange market.

In 1986–87, partly due to persistent weakness of the US dollar, there were periodic speculative flows into Hong Kong in anticipation of a possible revaluation. The authorities were concerned about the amount of exchange market intervention that might be needed to defend the 7.80 rate, and the adverse consequences for the local economy of a flood of liquidity into the banking system. Thus they established, via secondary legislation, a scheme which would enable them to charge negative interest rates on the banks, and allow the banks to pass those on to customers in the guise of 'deposit charges' on large HK dollar deposits. The scheme was formally authorised in December 1987, but was never in fact used.

In this period, therefore, the narrow currency board – based as it was only on physical currency – functioned just as it should in the immediate mechanical sense. That was insufficient to deliver broader currency stability, and consequently the authorities were active in the markets, outside the formal ambit of the currency board. This exercise of discretion to intervene in the markets plainly made a positive and crucial contribution to the goal of a stable exchange rate. With the passage of time, confidence in the fixed exchange rate grew, so that under normal circumstances there was less need for intervention (though the

gradual purchase of foreign exchange for investment purposes continued). Whenever a bout of unease re-emerged, the authorities still
found themselves with a role to play, and, when positive speculation
surged, they were even moved to put in place the negative interest
scheme as a reserve instrument.

July 1988 to March 1994
*For the first two years of this period the rate was mostly in the narrow range
7.78–7.82. From mid-1990, however, it tended to be persistently rather
stronger, hitting 7.714 in June 1991 and settling around 7.73 in the second
quarter of 1992; it moved between 7.72 and 7.76 for the rest of the period,
mostly in the stronger half of that range.*

This phase began with the instigation of the Accounting Arrangements in July 1988. HSBC, as the management bank of the clearing
house, was required to maintain an account with the Exchange Fund,
which would be determined by the HKMA and could only be altered
by transactions instigated or approved by the HKMA. A structure of
interest rate incentives and penalties was put in place to encourage

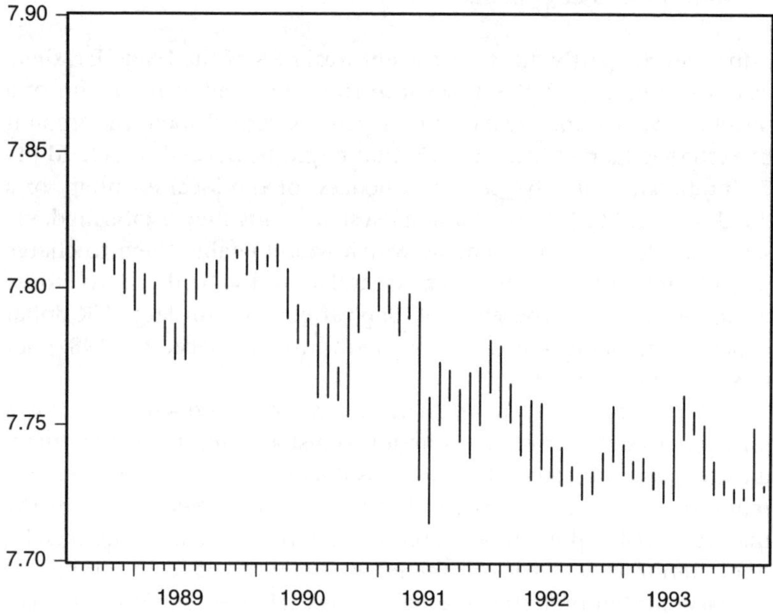

Figure 5.2   HK$–US$ Exchange Rate (lowest-highest spread per month) 18 July
1988 to 12 March 1994

HSBC to manage the net clearing balance of other banks with it to be at that same level. This, in effect, established the principle of the banking sector holding its settlement reserves in central bank money, although in practice not at a central bank. HSBC's balance at the Exchange Fund is referred to as the Balance. Subsequently, with the implementation of real-time gross settlement in December 1996, all banks became obliged to maintain settlement accounts directly with the Exchange Fund. Thus the intermediary role of HSBC came to an end. The Balance was thus superseded by what is known as the Aggregate Balance – the sum of all banks' balances at the Exchange Fund. In terms of the debate on discretion, it is the 1988 move which is important. The 1996 reform is best regarded as an operational refinement.

Now, for the first time, the authorities could undertake unsterilised foreign exchange intervention, by requiring the HK dollar leg of such transactions to be settled via the Balance. They could also settle money market interventions through this account. Yet the formal currency board convertibility rule continued to apply only to CoIs. The scope for arbitrage was as limited as it ever had been. The fact that the onus rested on the authorities to initiate any intervention implied a continuation of a significant element of discretion. Meanwhile, investment activities in connection with the fiscal reserve could continue to take place outside the monetary regime. In practice, the focus of intervention became the money market rather than the foreign exchange market.

Initially the market exchange rate was quite stable, but it later displayed persistent strength, sometimes at a margin of almost 1% beyond the 7.80 point. This might be interpreted to mean that the revised regime was unable to improve exchange rate convergence. More probably it reflects the fact that the authorities deliberately tried to intervene less often, and that they were not averse to the currency exhibiting some underlying strength by staying comfortably on the strong side of 7.80.

March 1990 saw the first issue of Exchange Fund bills – to be supplemented by the longer dated Exchange Fund notes from May 1993. The programme was partly motivated by the desire to develop a debt market in Hong Kong, but it could also serve as an additional instrument of liquidity management. Once the market became established it would be preferable, from a prudential point of view, for the authorities to inject liquidity to the banks by buying back these securities for the account of the Exchange Fund, or by entering into sale and repurchase agreements in these securities, rather than by lending unsecured.

Exchange Fund paper was for a while regarded as an active intervention tool of that sort, but, going forward in time, with the advent of real-time gross settlement in December 1996 the paper came to be seen principally as a collateral device in the payments system. The subsequent measures of September 1998 limited the overall issuance of such paper and assured the banks of unrestrained convertibility for their holdings of Exchange Fund paper into settlement balances (albeit at a discount rate, which might be penal).[16] The introduction of Exchange Fund paper appeared to presage more frequent interventions, but in the money market rather than the foreign exchange market. Thus it was announced that:

> 'With the launching of the Exchange Fund bills programme in mid-March, the Exchange Fund will operate more frequently in the money market. Under normal circumstances, the operations are either for the purpose of relieving a shortage of liquidity arising from a take-up of Exchange Fund bills, or to mop up surplus liquidity arising from the redemption of these bills. But, if the need arises, the Exchange Fund may, through under- or over-compensating the effect of the issue or redemption of Exchange Fund bills, or through buying or selling bills in the secondary market, produce a level of interbank liquidity necessary to ensure exchange rate stability.'[17]

It was tactics of that sort which were the main source of changes in HSBC's Balance, as shown in Table 5.2. By contrast, during this period the Exchange Fund did not appear to intervene in the foreign exchange market for settlement through the Balance.

June 1992 marked the inception of the liquidity adjustment facility (LAF). This provided, in effect, for HKMA to serve as residual lender and borrower in the HK dollar short-term money market at announced floor and ceiling interest rates. These were fixed by reference to US rates and were set 2% apart for most of the period – expanded to 3% in October 1997. Operationally, the authorities continued, subject to the exchange rate performing satisfactorily, to focus on the level of liquidity, fixing the Balance at what was deemed an appropriate level, which was not expected to be altered very often.

Despite the suggestion in the passage quoted above that the authorities might have been quite active from March 1990 onwards, they elected to alter the Balance on only seventeen occasions in the ensuing four years (making a total of only thirty during the entire period July 1988 to March 1994).[18] Available details are shown in Table 5.2. In this

Table 5.2 Action by the Authorities to Alter the Level of Interbank Liquidity, Mid-July 1988 to Mid-March 1994 (HK$ million)

	Injection (+)/ Withdrawal (–)	Closing level of HSBC's Balance with the Exchange Fund
18 July 1988	accounting arrangements initiated	1,250
7 Sept 1998	–150	1,100
11 Oct 1988	–150	950
12 Oct 1988	–70	880
30 Nov 1988	–20	860
6 Dec 1988	+200	1,060
7 Dec 1988	–200	860
5 Jan 1989	–132	728
5 June 1989	+194	922
7 Aug 1989	–194	728
30 Dec 1989	+150	978
1 Jan 1990 to mid-March 1990	two interventions, amounts not known	not known
late-March 1990	withdrawal, amount not known	510
4 July 1990	–30	480
25 May 1991	–100	380
28 June 1991	+100	480
17 July 1991	+60	540
30 July 1991	+60	600
1 Nov 1991	–100	500
24 Jan 1992	+100	600
16 March 1992	+100	700
28 April 1992	+150	850
29 April 1992	+138	988
6 Aug 1992	+512	1,500
10 Feb 1993	+650	2,150
31 May 1993	+650	2,800
20 July 1993	–800	2,000
13 Oct 1993	+1,000	3,000
7 Dec 1993	+1,000	4,000

The intervention figures refer only to operations initiated by the authorities to influence the level of interbank liquidity. They exclude overnight liquidity assistance provided to banks at their initiative (whether before or after the process was formalised under the LAF), and any deposits made by banks under the LAF. The figures for HSBC's Balance correspondingly exclude any effect of such transactions.

Sources: Successive editions of the government's *Economic Background* and *Economic Report*, *Asian Monetary Monitor*, May–June 1989, for figures for 1988.

period, interventions were mainly undertaken with the aim of smoothing the money market. For example:

(a) Around the time of the Hong Kong Telecom share issue in December 1988, there was intervention first to inject and subsequently to withdraw liquidity.
(b) When some China-related banks found their liquidity under pressure immediately following the Tiananmen incident of 4 June 1989, the authorities injected funds into the system.
(c) The withdrawal of liquidity in May 1991 was said to be in order to contain inflationary pressures.
(d) In July 1991 liquidity was injected to pre-empt possible tightness that might ensue from the collapse of Bank of Credit and Commerce International.
(e) In March 1992 the injection was to ease a squeeze arising from share issuance activity.
(f) The heavy injections listed at times in 1993 were also motivated by share issuance activity.
(g) The withdrawal of liquidity in July 1993 was, however, sparked by some negative pressure on the exchange rate rather than by liquidity concerns *per se*.

For the sake of completeness, it is also relevant to record that:

(a) Prior to the establishment of the LAF in June 1992, banks which needed help to square their clearing accounts after the close of the interbank market could request so-called late assistance from the Exchange Fund. This facility was used in 15 instances during 1991 and a further 34 instances in 1992 up to the time that the LAF was launched in June.
(b) Late assistance was then superseded by the LAF lending facility, accompanied by the creation of the LAF deposit facility. Available statistics for utilisation of the two sides of the LAF are shown in Table 5.3.

Both those facilities were, however, initiated at the discretion of the banks, not the authorities. In the context of the debate about rules and discretion on the official side, the notable feature of this period was that the authorities saw it as their role to deliberately manage the money market, almost as an end in itself. Of course, the overriding aim was still the stability of the Hong Kong dollar against the US dollar, but

Table 5.3   Number of Instances of Usage of LAF Facilities by Banks

Period	Lending to banks by Exchange Fund	Placing of deposits by banks with Exchange Fund
8 June 1992 to 31 Dec 1992	90	52
Year 1993	92	789
First quarter 1994	25	314

Source: Hong Kong Government, *Economic Report*.

that rate was allowed to drift into the strong side and was left there, apparently with official approval, while the authorities busied themselves with deciding the appropriate level of liquidity in the banking system.

Although there is no evidence that this tactic actually caused any damage, one may wonder whether it was strictly necessary or optimal. An alternative would have been to intervene in the foreign exchange market, more in the tradition of a currency board, holding the rate closer to 7.80 and then, by allowing the deals to affect the aggregate balance, flooding the market with extra liquidity (in the case of upward pressure on the currency) which would have forced interest rates down and set in motion the classical currency board adjustment mechanism. Moreover, on the occasion of major share offerings, it is possible that the banks, if left to their own devices, could have sorted out the attendant liquidity problems themselves. It may only have been because the authorities were visibly so anxious to help, that the banks did not feel obliged to do more for themselves.

In seeking an explanation for the authorities' apparent fixation on money market conditions, one should note that the market was dominated by a single commercial bank, HSBC, and there was always a suspicion that HSBC dictated market conditions to its own advantage, even after the Accounting Arrangements were put in place. This was the principal consideration behind the creation of a deposit facility for banks under the LAF, and it helps explain why the authorities felt the need to monitor closely and exert influence over the money market.

In sum, the authorities began this period by arming themselves with the framework which would allow the currency board mechanism to operate on a wider and more effective definition of the monetary base – cash plus banks' reserve money instead of just cash alone. In practice, however, they largely rejected that opportunity, preferring to concentrate, in day-to-day terms, on looking after the liquidity of the banking system. They would not, of course, do this in a manner that was ultimately inconsistent with broad stability of the exchange rate, but one is left wondering whether they needed to do it at all, or for so long a period, and whether they would not have been better advised to move more quickly to the sort of reforms which were eventually introduced in 1998.

March 1994 to September 1998

Apart from breaking out to 7.77 at one point in January 1995, the rate stayed in the range 7.72–7.75, and mostly 7.73–7.75. As the period progressed, 7.75, rather than 7.80, became established as the de facto *weak-side limit.*

This phase was in most respects a continuation of the preceding one, except for the fact that in March 1994 HKMA announced that it had revised its mode of operation from targeting the level of liquidity, to targeting short-term interest rates in order to prevent the Hong Kong interbank offer rate (HIBOR) going outside the LAF range.[19] Since the very existence of the LAF would tend to prevent HIBOR moving outside the range (but did not prevent it entirely), the intended

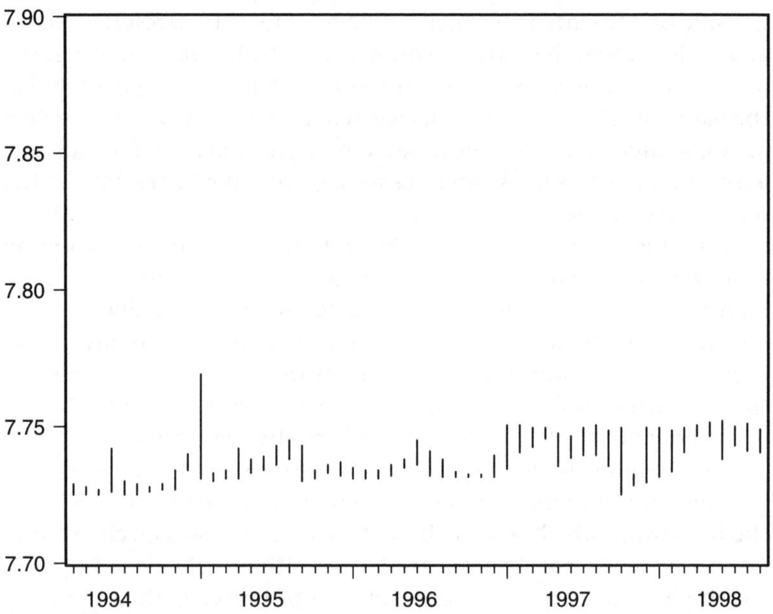

Figure 5.3   HK$–US$ Exchange Rate (lowest-highest spread per month) 13 March 1994 to 5 September 1998

message seems to have been that the Aggregate Balance (of the banking system at the Exchange Fund) might be varied more often in order to steer HIBOR closer to the middle of the band, rather than allowing it to hit the extremes – occurrences which would have triggered more intensive use of the LAF and perhaps have also aroused concerns about interest rate volatility in the broader macroeconomic context.

In its limited objective, the change of approach appeared to have some success. In the remaining months of 1994, for example, overnight HIBOR kept within the LAF band, whereas it had broken out occasionally under the previous approach. The HKMA was indeed adjusting the level of liquidity somewhat more frequently and aggressively. The HKMA for instance records that it injected $3.8 billion in late March to smoothen end-quarter effects, and reversed that in early April; towards the end of June it was again active on a more frequent basis than before; on 30 August and 2 September it injected $1,500m and $2,690m respectively, and then took it back shortly afterwards.[20]

There was, however, an inherent ambiguity in the HKMA's approach. It hoped that, 'by thus containing the volatility of the interbank rate, the LAF mechanism helps to reduce the volatility of the exchange rate'. But 'HKMA normally adjusts the LAF rates with close reference to movements of US interest rates' (in practice it was not so much 'normally' as 'always').[21] However, the whole basis of the currency board approach is that interest rates should be free to move sharply in response to any change in sentiment about the currency, and should certainly be allowed to open up a sizeable differential, in whichever direction, relative to rates of the anchor currency. Thus there was little sense in priding oneself on keeping interest rates stable *vis-à-vis* US rates. This could frustrate rather than promote exchange rate stability.

This inconsistency between exchange rate policy combined with interest rate policy (albeit with the latter ultimately subservient) was tolerated probably due to two factors. First, there was a continuing concern about market domination by a single bank. Second, as noted earlier, the role of the Aggregate Balance in terms of the currency board had not yet been specified. Although it could be readily demonstrated that the balance was amply backed by foreign exchange, there was no convertibility undertaking in respect of it. The HKMA still described its objective as simply to ensure that money market conditions were consistent with exchange rate stability. Paradoxically, its actual tactics may have weakened rather than strengthened that consistency. The inconsistency was finally exposed during the Asian financial turmoil of 1997 when the HKMA felt impelled to ration access to the LAF window. This caused consternation. Recognition of the problem led eventually to widespread reform in 1998.

The true objective of monetary management at this time could perhaps have better been described as to maintain maximum stability in interest rates, relative to US rates, consistent with the exchange rate being within an acceptable range on the strong side of 7.80. That objective – if one could set aside the issue of currency board discipline for a moment – would have sounded very reasonable to many economic agents in Hong Kong, for whom interest rates were probably of greater concern than the exchange rate. In fact, the exchange rate strengthened to almost 1% stronger than 7.80 in the summer of 1994. This, while seen by some as a symbol of virility, caused doubts in other minds as to the authenticity and hence durability of Hong Kong's currency board system. When the rate momentarily weakened quite sharply in January 1995 – albeit only to 7.7725 – the HKMA intervened significantly in the foreign exchange market to arrest the decline.

In May 1995 the HKMA claimed that Hong Kong's regime was indeed an authentic currency board because the monetary base was 100% backed by foreign exchange (this seemed to mean the stock basis, but did not exclude the flow too), and because the Exchange Fund did not lend to government or business, while any lending to banks was fully secured by Exchange Fund paper which was in turn backed by foreign exchange. Oddly, and in contradiction to textbook teaching on currency boards, the HKMA also claimed that its capacity to conduct open market operations to smooth interest rates strengthened rather than weakened the system.[22]

The HKMA had also veered away from, rather than towards, currency board authenticity when, in March 1994, it began to allow banks to submit certain Hong Kong debt securities other than Exchange Fund paper as collateral for borrowing under the LAF. Exchange Fund paper could be demonstrated to be fully backed by foreign reserves, so that any expansion of bank liquidity which might result would comply with the backing rule. The same could not be said of the alternative instruments now being admitted.[23]

In the continuing absence of any formal convertibility undertaking for banks' balances (individual banks since December 1996 held accounts at the Exchange Fund), the Chief Executive of the HKMA defended 'constructive ambiguity' in a speech in March 1998,[24] declaring 'I am not in favour of showing my cards to speculators'. Interestingly, he also made it explicit that the HKMA might 'in exceptional circumstances' alter the aggregate balance without a corresponding change in US dollar holdings; he cited the example of wishing to smooth the money market at the time of a big public share offering. However, the market was already becoming adept at coping with such events without much official assistance. He also emphasised how fiscal transfers (e.g. of surpluses to the Exchange Fund for investment, but equally applicable to drawdowns in the event of a deficit) were sterilised so as to be entirely neutral to monetary policy. In terms of the rules-versus-discretion debate, however, this phase of operation, despite the declared greater focus on interest rates than on liquidity, was not significantly different from the preceding one. The HKMA, as it now was, was continuing to exercise a great deal of discretion in its money market interventions.

Close to the end of this period, in August 1998, the HKMA intervened heavily in the foreign exchange and stock markets to thwart market manipulation by certain dominant market players. The action was justified because the free play of market forces, which includes speculation of a price-taking nature, was being swamped by actions to manipulate prices in an anti-competitive manner. The bulk of HKMA interventions were conducted on a sterilised basis, outside the currency board system.[25] This episode well illustrates the point that official bodies are capable of conducting sterilised interventions, and entitled to do so, even if the core monetary policy regime is a currency board. The episode is not therefore relevant to the question of rules versus discretion within the currency board operation.

September 1998 to May 2005
Mirroring the new convertibility undertaking, the rate moved to just under 7.80, and was steady there until September-October 2003 when it strengthened sharply to 7.71. This was short-lived and the rate was in the range 7.76–7.80 for most of the rest of the period, being at or close to 7.80, but never weaker, for much of the time.

As part of a package of measures in September 1998, HKMA introduced a firm convertibility undertaking for banks' balances at the Exchange Fund, on the weak side.[26] This was initially set at 7.75 (i.e. the Exchange Fund stood ready to sell US dollars to banks at that rate), but was raised during the course of 1999 to 7.80. There was, however, no corresponding undertaking on the strong side. Also, the LAF was abolished. On one side this was replaced by the discount window facility, which was different in the significant respect that the ceiling rate at which the HKMA would provide funds would ultimately be set by reference to peak local interbank rates and not by a pre-announced rate

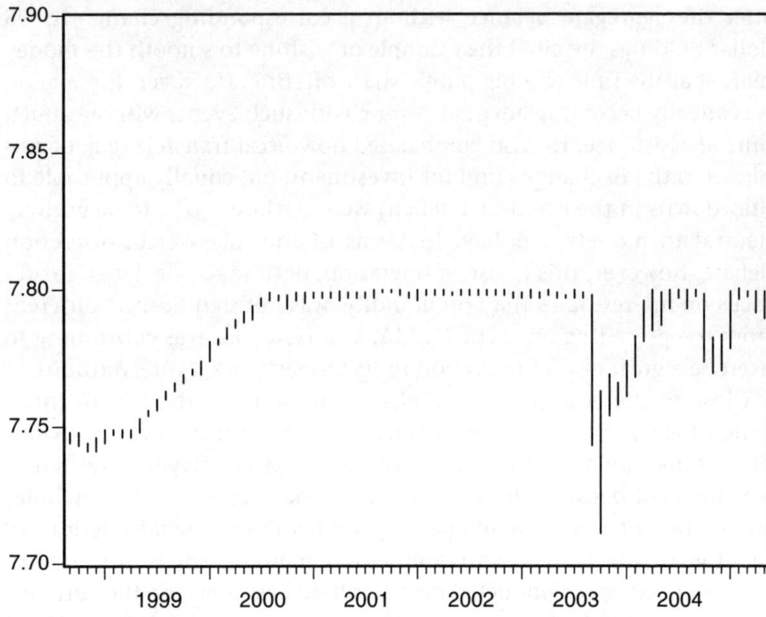

Figure 5.4   HK$–US$ Exchange Rate (lowest-highest spread per month) September 1998 to 18 May 2005

based on US rates. On the other side, the LAF floor rate and the associated facility for banks to place surplus funds with the Exchange Fund at that rate were discontinued altogether. This package, and the accompanying changes in operational strategy, stripped HKMA of a considerable amount of the discretion which it had hitherto exercised. Most obviously, the introduction of weak-side convertibility for banks' balances at 7.80 and the subsequent practice of never intervening on that side unless the 7.80 promise was triggered, brought an end to the exercise of discretion on that side. However, HKMA continued to exercise discretion in intervening on the strong side.

At the same time, with the abolition of the LAF bid rate and conversion of the offer rate to the discount window arrangement where the discount rate would be permitted, if necessary, to be driven to any height in response to market pressures, the HKMA effectively withdrew from proactive involvement in the money market. It no longer sought to intervene to keep interest rates in a particular corridor. Clarification of issuance procedures for Exchange Fund paper also removed any possibility that they might be used to massage the money market. From then until May 2005, the sole area of controversy concerning

Table 5.4   Discretionary Sales of HK Dollars by HKMA on the Strong Side, 5 Sept 1998 to 18 May 2005

	Number of days on which HKMA intervened	Gross amount sold during period, HK$ billion
1998, 5 Sept–Dec	1	0.2
1999	26	26.8
2000	20	17.7
2001	4	3.0
2002	2	1.0
2003	18	31.9
2004	18	34.8
2005: 1 Jan–18 May	Nil	Nil

Source: Report on Currency Board Operations, as reprinted in successive *Quarterly Bulletins* of the HKMA.

discretion was intervention on the strong side. The amounts of discretionary intervention over this period are shown in the Table 5.4.

The topic of strong-side discretion clearly created a certain amount of angst, as it was repeatedly reconsidered by the Exchange Fund Advisory Committee (EFAC) Sub-committee. Thus:

(a) The matter was reviewed by the sub-committee in October 1999. It recommended leaving things alone and retaining flexibility. Two particular reasons were cited: the possibility of 'year 2000' problems at the turn of the year, and the desirability of allowing time for any after-effects of the transition of the weak side convertibility rate from 7.75 to 7.80, which had been completed in August, to settle down.

(b) The topic was considered again in July 2000. While recognising the advantages of an explicit undertaking in terms of transparency, tidiness and predictability, arguments on the other side again prevailed. These arguments included the notion that too rigid a structure would play into the hands of speculators, that if the announced spread was too narrow it would have the effect of disintermediating the banks, and that too wide a spread might bring undesirable volatility to the market.

(c) This advice was reaffirmed at the meeting in August 2000; it was agreed that the HKMA should continue to practise discretion, taking three factors into account: the position of the exchange rate, the level of interest rates, and banking liquidity as evidenced by the Aggregate Balance.

(d) In November 2003 the sub-committee again reviewed the policy
and recommended maintenance of the status quo.

The reluctance of the HKMA to set a clear strong-side limit was interpreted by some market participants as vacillation on the question of a
possible formal revaluation, given that upward pressures on the
Renminbi, from economic forces as well as political argument, were
washing over into fairly persistent pressure of inflows into the HK
dollar. At its meeting on 13 May 2005, therefore, having rejected the
idea on four preceding occasions, the sub-committee at last decided
that the time was ripe to introduce a formal strong side convertibility
undertaking, as well as symmetry around 7.80.

May 2005 to March 2007
*The rate remained within the 7.75–7.85 convertibility band, and in the
stronger half until early 2007.*
The HKMA announced that the weak side convertibility promise
would be moved to 7.85 (by steps over the ensuing month), and a new

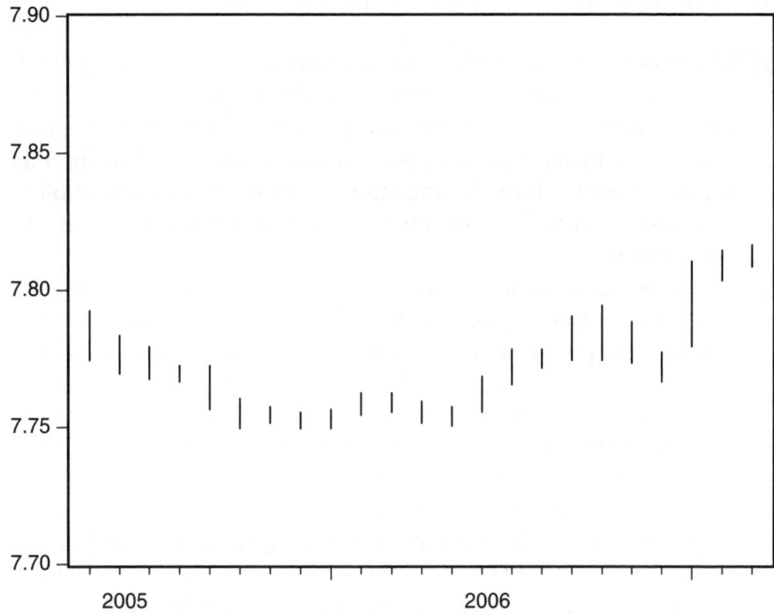

Figure 5.5 HK$–US$ Exchange Rate (lowest-highest spread per month) 19 May
2005 to 31 March 2007

strong side convertibility undertaking was established at 7.75. The HKMA would retain discretion to intervene within the band. This new regime, with its symmetrical two-way convertibility undertaking, came into effect on 19 May 2005.

Previously HKMA had not exercised any discretion on the weak side – only ever intervening when the 7.80 promise was triggered. In approving discretionary interventions in either direction within the bounds of the zone, the sub-committee felt that this might at times be appropriate, aimed at 'promoting the smooth functioning of the linked exchange rate system, for example, by removing any market anomalies that might arise from time to time'. No clue was offered as to what such anomalies might be, but on 25 May, one week after the new arrangements had begun, the HKMA did intervene inside the band with a sale of HK$544m. The official explanation was that this intervention was needed to avoid a sharp rise in interest rates on account of share issuance activity. Once again, however, one may query whether the financial system was not perfectly capable of dealing with such a situation on its own in an adequately efficient manner. If it could, then any disturbance to interest rates would be too short-lived to create any problems in the real world.

However, at least part of the reason behind the 25 May intervention may have been HKMA's wish to put down an early marker to the effect that it could and would make use of its discretion. Yet, fundamentally, there seems to be no convincing reason for leaving this residual scrap of discretion with the HKMA. It is possible that the authorities felt it desirable to retain some means of surprising speculators or inflicting some pain on them. However, in the strict context of HKMA's mandate to achieve exchange rate stability it is not obvious that intervention before the band limits of 7.75–7.85 are actually reached makes any significant contribution to the goal. Since the May 2005 action, up to the time of writing (March 2007), there has be no further intrazone intervention.

Conclusions

When Hong Kong restored a currency board in 1983 it was, through force of circumstances, based only on the physical currency. The authorities were active in the foreign exchange market and, at least in the initial stages, in the money market, to ensure that the market exchange rate held close to 7.80. Without such intervention, divergences would almost certainly have been larger, belief in the ability of the arrangement to deliver exchange rate stability would have faded, and Hong Kong might have been left with a segmented system; an essentially floating market exchange rate operating in parallel with a restricted market in banknotes. In that event, the 7.80 rate for currency might reasonably have been abandoned as serving little useful purpose, and Hong Kong would have been back at square one. Thus, it seems that the discretionary interventions of the initial currency board period were both necessary and successful.

One might argue that, given such dependence on intervention in apparent contravention of currency board principles, the authorities should have been quicker to introduce the reform which eventually came in 1988, when the Accounting Arrangements were introduced. However, this matter did not receive immediate attention in the period following October 1983 because there was a lingering hope that arbitrage might somehow deliver convergence. And even when that hope faded, it required time to negotiate the new arrangement, since it involved a substantial upheaval to the traditional position and role of the leading commercial bank.

The following decade, 1988–98, can be characterised as one during which the basic framework was in place to allow bank reserve money to play its proper role in the currency board process, in terms of convertibility on an unsterilised basis. Yet the authorities chose to leave that mechanism in limbo, and instead concentrated on managing interbank liquidity or short-term interest rates. This choice was partly motivated by the belief that the money market, if left to itself, would not function fully in accordance with free market principles because of the dominance of a single bank. Although this strategy was fundamentally at odds with currency board principles, the authorities held firm to the overriding objective of keeping the market exchange rate within close range of 7.80, and they therefore only operated in the money market within the scope allowed by that objective. As a result, it would be wrong to say that the use of discretion detracted significantly from the goal of exchange rate stability, but at the same time it seems that the discretionary money market interventions might not have been necessary had the authorities been more willing simply to allow the classical currency board mechanism to be triggered by automatic foreign exchange intervention once the rate reached the limits of some declared tolerable range.

The authorities waited until the shortcomings of this regime phase became starkly apparent before proceeding, in 1998, with reforms which took the exchange rate regime significantly closer to the concept of a tightly rules-based currency board. Thus, the 1998 measures brought the system much further into line than hitherto with the principle of the entire monetary base being convertible on the basis of fixed rates, through unsterilised intervention; but not the whole way: discretion was retained in respect of foreign exchange intervention on the strong side. Meanwhile, discretionary money market intervention was discarded, and interest rates were freed up. Although, over the ensuing years, this remaining strong-side discretion may sometimes have been exploited profitably by the HKMA at the expense of speculators, there is no evidence that, on balance, it assisted underlying exchange rate stability. On the contrary, the absence of an announced intervention point occasionally gave rise to unhelpful rumours about revaluing the peg or abandoning it.

Eventually, in 2005, a strong-side convertibility undertaking was introduced, and the weak-side peg adjusted to provide symmetry around 7.80. This was the penultimate step towards what could be a fully rule-based system in accordance with the purist textbook model of a currency board. However, it will only be possible to claim complete adherence to that model if the HKMA takes the ultimate step of surrendering the discretion which it has kept for itself to intervene within the band. It is far from clear why the HKMA needs to retain that intra-zone discretion, although once again it is difficult to argue that it will be damaging. If nothing else, the HKMA is providing a target at which the purists can continue to snipe.

In sum, discretionary intervention was necessary and effective in the early years from 1983. As the years passed, although retention of discretion was not obviously damaging, the authorities may have clung on to it rather longer than they needed to. Indeed, whatever, the excuses or explanations for its retention – which might even include an instinctive reluctance of HKMA to write itself out of the script – twenty-one years seems an inordinate length of time for the authorities to have taken in moving from the rudimentary arrangements of 1983 to the almost entirely rule-based regime reached in 2005. With such a set of rules now in place, it is doubtful whether HKMA needs to hold on to its modest remaining discretionary capability. Stepping back from the nitty-gritty of the regime, one must remind oneself of the overall stability of the exchange rate at close to 7.80 for over 23 years. This is proof enough of success in meeting the declared monetary policy objective. In the final analysis, it may not matter very much that, in meeting their objective, the authorities did not always adhere to currency board 'best practice', or that they were rather slow in moving towards it.

Notes

1 This paper has been adapted from Hong Kong Institute of Monetary Research Working Paper 2/2007. Parts of the paper are incorporated in Latter (2007) *Hong Kong's Money: the history, logic and operation of the currency peg* (Hong Kong: Hong Kong University Press). The author is grateful to the Hong Kong Institute for Monetary Research for the award of a research fellowship to work on this paper. He is grateful to John Greenwood for helpful comments; to Kitty Lai, Grace Lau and James Lau for their recollections of events covered in the paper; and to Dickson Tam for preparing the charts. The author remains responsible for any errors of fact. The views expressed here are those of the author; in particular, they do not necessarily represent the views of the HKIMR, or its advisers or directors.

2 Thus, although the backing rate of HK$7.80/US$1 for certificates of indebtedness set in October 1983 was a voluntary agreement between government and the note-issuing banks, and was only given statutory force when the Exchange Fund Ordinance was amended in May 1984, it is considered here to have been a 'rule' throughout. Similarly, the Accounting Arrangements which operated from 1988–1996 were a non-statutory agreement between the authorities and HSBC, but are regarded here as a 'rule'. The convertibility undertakings for banks' balances are classed as 'rules' even though the Monetary Authority could, theoretically, alter these undertakings at will, provided that any such action was in furtherance of the instruction from the Financial Secretary to aim for stability of the exchange rate at around 7.80.

3 *Asian Monetary Monitor*, July–August 1988 and May–June 1989. These are contemporary quotes which should be seen in the context of the mood of the times. Greenwood's recent reflections on this and other issues are collected in J. Greenwood (2008) *Hong Kong's Link to the US Dollar; Origins and Evolution* (Hong Kong: Hong Kong University Press).

4 M Friedman (1993) 'Do We Need Central Banks?' *Monetary Management in Hong Kong* (Hong Kong: HKMA).

5 S. Hanke (2002) 'On dollarisation and currency boards: error and deception', *Policy Reform*, 5(4).

6 If sterling notes were used in a colony, they had to be bought from the Issue Department of the Bank of England with funds which would then be invested to earn a profit for the Bank of England. When a colony issued its own notes, the local colonial administration earned the profit from the sterling investments which it held as backing. Such a profit is known as seigniorage.

7 A. Walters (1992) 'Currency Board' *The New Palgrave Dictionary of Economics* (London: Palgrave Macmillan).

8 For a fuller discussion see Corrinne Ho (2002) 'A survey of the institutional and operational aspects of modern-day currency boards', BIS working paper 110.

9 The letter dated 25 June 2003, clarifying the demarcation of a range of responsibilities between the Financial Secretary and the Monetary Authority, can be found on the HKMA website (www.hkma.gov.hk).

10 For the full historical background, see T. Latter (2004) 'Hong Kong's exchange rate regimes in the twentieth century: the story of three regime changes', Hong Kong Institute for Monetary Research working paper 17.

11 The scope of the commentaries which follow is constrained by the limited availability of information. Prior to July 1988 no regular statistics on monetary operations were released, and even after that the information was for many years somewhat sporadic and incomplete. Before the HKMA began its *Quarterly Bulletin* in November 1994 the main source of information was the government's *Economic Reports*. Since 1994 the HKMA *Quarterly Bulletin* includes regular chapters on monetary operations. In more recent years the minutes of the Exchange Fund Advisory Committee's sub-committee on the currency board have been published in the *Quarterly Bulletin*, together with the monthly review of currency board operations prepared for that committee. This is available on the HKMA website.

12 For a fuller account of the initial note-issuing arrangements after October 1983, see Annex F in Latter (2007) *Hong Kong's Money*.

13 See 'Why the HK$/US$ linked rate system should not be changed', *Asian Monetary Monitor* Nov–Dec 1984.

14 Within this period the author was intimately involved in Hong Kong's monetary management until April 1985.

15 The money market intervention scheme was introduced in November 1981 in collaboration with HSBC. HSBC withdrew funds from the money market on behalf of the government and at the government's expense (in terms of interest), and then refrained from re-lending them into the market. This was intended to have the effect of tightening interest rates as a result of the withdrawal of liquidity. In practice, although the mechanism could prop up interbank rates on a particular day, the impact faded thereafter since banks and others could draw on facilities with HSBC to replenish liquidity, and the government's presence as a ready bidder merely encouraged round-tripping. The effect could be sustained only by borrowing ever-cumulating amounts, at rising cost. Despite its shortcomings, the scheme could be effective in the short term. It continued to be employed after the re-introduction of the currency board in 1983 to assist the convergence of the market exchange rate. The scheme became formally redundant when the Accounting Arrangements were introduced in 1988.

16 As part of the September 1998 measures it was decided that, other than to absorb payments of interest, net additions to the total of Exchange Fund paper would in future only be made in the event of a sustained inflow of funds to the HK$. However, when the question has since been raised in the Currency Board Sub-committee of the Exchange Fund Advisory Committee as to whether additional paper should be issued to mop up excess liquidity in the money market (see minutes of meetings of 7 May 1999 and 5 March 2004), the decision has gone against such issuance. This seems to be the correct decision, since any attempt to reward the holders of surplus, non-interest-bearing balances with interchangeable interest-bearing instruments would merely weaken the currency board adjustment mechanism. In that sense, the strategy announced in 1998 was probably mistaken. The upshot is that the stock of Exchange Fund paper was in practice frozen, apart from the additions which mirrored interest payments. Thus, Exchange Fund paper is no longer seen as an instrument for influencing the macro-monetary situation and is no longer a material topic in the rules-versus-discretion debate.

17 *First Quarter Economic Report* 1990.
18 HKMA *Quarterly Bulletin*, November 1994.
19 'Management of interbank liquidity', HKMA *Quarterly Bulletin*, November 1994.
20 As reported in the section 'Operation of Monetary Policy' in successive *Quarterly Bulletins*.
21 'The interest rate structure in Hong Kong', HKMA *Quarterly Bulletin*, November 1994.
22 HKMA *Quarterly Bulletin*, May 1995.
23 This loophole was later closed by the measures of September 1998.
24 Reproduced in the *Quarterly Bulletin*, May 1998.
25 For an account of these events, see 'Operation of monetary policy' and 'Why we intervened', HKMA *Quarterly Bulletin*, November 1998.
26 For a full account of these measures, see 'Strengthening of currency board arrangements in Hong Kong', HKMA *Quarterly Bulletin*, November 1998.

6
The Origin and the Evolution of Hong Kong's Currency Board I[1]

John Greenwood

At the time of the restoration of the Currency Board system in October 1983 the author was the editor of, and a leading contributor to, Asian Monetary Monitor (AMM), a Hong Kong-based bi-monthly publication that was published between 1977 and 1996. In addition to analysing monetary systems elsewhere in Asia, the journal carried numerous articles aimed at explaining and critiquing Hong Kong's monetary system. The *AMM* was influential within government and among the banking community during this crucial period when the case for reforming Hong Kong's monetary system was strengthening. Greenwood's suggestions through AMM that a currency board be re-established, therefore, played a key part in the policy choices made at the time. The key articles from *AMM* referred to in this chapter are reproduced, with later commentary, in J. Greenwood (2008) *Hong Kong's Link to the US Dollar: Origins and Evolution* (Hong Kong: Hong Kong University Press).

Initial approaches to the problem of monetary instability (mid 1970s to July–August 1981)

In the late 1970s the HK$ began a prolonged decline against the US$ as well as other currencies. By 1981 there could now be no escaping the conclusion that there was something seriously amiss with Hong Kong's monetary arrangements. Using AMM as a platform, I had begun to publish a number of articles that tried to analyse the source of this weakness. But, far from addressing the causes of the problem, the authorities appeared to be tackling only the symptoms by intervening in the foreign exchange markets to support the local currency. Normally such intervention ought to have succeeded if it was supported by other policy measures, but it was quite clear to me that – given Hong Kong's institutional structure – such measures could not possibly succeed in halting the slide in the currency. It was therefore time to 'blow the whistle' on Hong Kong's monetary arrangements, pointing out as forcefully as possible the inherent weaknesses of the prevailing structure, and to insist again (as had been done in earlier issues of AMM) that reforms were necessary if the currency slide was to be stopped and inflation was to be avoided.

In articles published in *AMM* in 1979 and 1980 I had advanced the argument that, in the Hong Kong banking system of that era, the monetary authority lacked the capability to impose a policy of monetary restraint or ease. The reason was that instead of the commercial banks holding accounts with the monetary authority, the normal accounting relationship was reversed: the monetary authority at this time held accounts with the commercial banks. The effect of these arrangements was to undermine completely the ability of the Hong Kong monetary authorities to contract or expand the monetary base either by open market operations or by intervention in the foreign exchange market. The result was that there could be no consequent multiple contraction or expansion of bank balance sheets or the monetary aggregates flowing from such central banking operations, even if they were attempted. In other words, the monetary authority was reduced to the same status, in terms of its ability to expand or contract the volume of funds in the system, as any other private sector commercial company. I had therefore argued consistently in several issues of *AMM* that these monetary arrangements should be reformed, and replaced with a central bank where all the commercial banks would maintain reserve accounts – as in any other orthodox banking system.

In an article dated July–August 1981 ('Time to Blow the Whistle') I offered a comprehensive restatement of these previous ideas and proposals, but the article also contained two critical additions to previous arguments which considerably sharpened the critique – (1) a list of the steps that the authorities had taken in 1972 that had undermined their ability to hold the exchange rate steady at some specified nominal rate against the US$, and (2) a tabular presentation of a series of transactions from the T-form balance sheets of the Exchange Fund, the commercial banks and the non-bank public. These proved conclusively that foreign exchange intervention by the authorities under existing arrangements was futile.

It should be noted that at this time I was still thinking in terms of a central bank as the only feasible alternative to Hong Kong's prevailing monetary arrangements – not a reformed currency board system. In this connection the July–August 1981 article contained a 'box' which critiqued the government's case for maintaining the status quo, pointing out key differences between the accounting arrangements of Hong Kong's monetary system versus other monetary systems. A second 'box' explained how a monetary authority could operate without government debt since the absence of government debt in the territory was often cited as a reason why Hong Kong could not introduce a central bank. An interesting sub-plot was that the government, by adopting mistaken remedies to deal with symptoms resulting from monetary problems, threatened to damage the wider economy of Hong Kong, for example imposing rent controls to suppress rising rents.

If the authorities were to continue to hold out against the arguments in *AMM* they would now have to prove that the principles demonstrated in 'Time to Blow the Whistle' were incorrect in logic. It was not long before they showed their cards. As author of the article I received a call requesting that I attend a meeting with the Financial Secretary, John Bremridge, at 4.30 pm on Monday October 12th 1981. Also present was Douglas Blye, Secretary of Monetary Affairs, who did most of the talking. He said that the article was destabilizing to Hong Kong, and contained serious mistakes. When asked for specifics he pointed out a couple of factual errors (subsequently corrected), but when asked if the principles underlying the relationship between the Exchange Fund and the banking system were wrong, he gave no answer. The stand-off was to continue for two more years.

Improved understanding of how the credit cycle operated

There were two sides to the problem of analysing Hong Kong's monetary system. One was the challenge of showing what was wrong with existing arrangements. The other side of the problem was to explain how the existing system operated, and how and why asset prices, business activity, and inflation behaved under existing arrangements.

Between 1980 and 1982 the developed world experienced two back-to-back recessions, with the US having recessions from January 1980 to July 1980, followed by another from July 1981 to November 1982 according to the National Bureau of Economic Research. Not surprisingly this led to a sharp downturn in Hong Kong's external trade. Of more significance, perhaps, from the standpoint of elucidating the monetary mechanism at work in Hong Kong was that the trade downturn was accompanied by an abrupt slowdown in monetary growth. This provided an opportunity to prove my contention that Hong Kong's monetary system had a tendency to exacerbate cyclical upswings and downswings, or alternatively to devise a more robust hypothesis that was consistent with the empirical data.

The hypothesis I proposed in *AMM* in May–June 1982 (*Hypothesis for the Hong Kong Trade Cycle*, in 'Monetary Downturn Compounds Trade Woes') in the face of this new situation was essentially an application of the real bills doctrine. This is the proposition advanced in the 18th century by Adam Smith (among others) that money and credit should expand and contract to meet the needs of trade. It featured prominently in the bullionist controversy of the early 19th century, when it was repudiated by Henry Thornton and David Ricardo, who argued that controlling the volume of bills discounted (i.e. the quantity of high-powered money) was more important to overall economic stability than allowing flexibility of supply since there was no other limit to the depreciation of the currency 'than the will of the issuers'.[2] The real bills doctrine appeared again in the Federal Reserve Act of 1913 and in the deliberations of the Fed in its first two decades. It was one of intellectual factors contributing to the Great Depression of 1931–33.[3]

At the time I was continuously grappling with the problem of how, in the absence of a central bank in Hong Kong, one could explain the accelerations and decelerations of the money supply. In view of the global economic slowdown of 1980–82 it was natural for Hong Kong's external trade to slow down, and this could be extended to explain the behaviour of money and credit. The additional twist to the hypothesis was the idea that, since the banks in Hong Kong set their deposit rates through the Hong Kong Association of Banks (HKAB) and lending rates were derived from these regulated rates, money growth and bank credit growth could in turn be viewed as a result of whether interest rates were set too high or too low by the HKAB cartel. If rates were set too low, or lower than equilibrium levels, this would generate excess money growth, whereas if rates were set too high this would generate inadequate money growth.

The global recession and the downturn in Hong Kong's trade, together with the delayed adjustments in HKAB interest rates, produced exactly the set of conditions that could explain the sharp downswing in Hong Kong's money growth in 1982. Moreover, the temporary stabilisation of the exchange rate during the global recession was also consistent with the idea that Hong Kong's monetary system was subject to a real bills mechanism. Although nothing can ever be conclusively proved in the real world from economic theory, it would be hard to replicate a situation that more closely conformed to a textbook case of the real bills doctrine than that in Hong Kong between 1974 and 1983.

The analysis placed strong emphasis on the desirability of monetary base control, or at least a quantitative approach to monetary control. In part this approach was designed to highlight the defects of the Hong Kong monetary framework in an era when the authorities had no direct means of managing expansions or contractions in the system; in part it reflected the academic spirit of the times which featured Paul Volcker at the Federal Reserve System attempting to implement monetary base control, and Margaret Thatcher's first government in the UK attempting to control the broader monetary aggregates. An updated analysis would be more sympathetic to the use of interest rates as a means of indirectly achieving monetary stability, but it would still home in on the lack of suitable monetary instruments available in Hong Kong at the time, and the inappropriate structural or accounting relationship prevailing between the Hong Kong authorities and the banking system.

The link between monetary analysis and the automatic adjustment mechanism

In September 1982 Margaret Thatcher made her infamous visit to Beijing to discuss with Deng Xiaoping and other Chinese leaders the future of Hong Kong after June 30th 1997, when the British government's lease over Hong Kong's New Territories was due to expire. From the viewpoint of the people of Hong Kong the visit went badly. Not only had Margaret Thatcher tripped and fallen on the steps of the Great Hall of the People in Tiananmen Square – an ill omen in Chinese eyes – but following these discussions Sir Geoffrey Howe, the British Foreign Secretary, had confirmed in Hong Kong that it would not be possible for Britain to maintain sovereignty in Hong Kong beyond June 1997. At this stage there was no official indication of the terms on which Hong Kong might be handed back, and therefore Hong Kong people were left to fear the worst – that there might be a complete transfer to communist rule. In this atmosphere a capital flight from Hong Kong started, causing the currency to tumble again. Between June and November 1982 it fell from an average of HK$5.86 per US$ to HK$6.67, a depreciation of 13.8%.

Having made it clear by means of the T-form balance sheets why the Hong Kong authorities could not stop the currency slide through intervention in the foreign exchange markets, and having been brushed aside by government officials in August 1981, the only course of action that seemed open to me was to offer a comprehensive restatement of the entire range of monetary problems facing Hong Kong. This was the role of an extended *AMM* article entitled 'Hong Kong's Financial Crisis: History, Analysis, Prescription' (69 pages in the original *AMM*) in November–December 1982.

The broad-brush argument was that the Hong Kong authorities had been treating the symptoms of the territory's monetary and financial problems instead of dealing with the underlying causes. An example of this is the authorities treatment of bank and DTC insolvencies only by introducing increased regulation and supervision. Similarly, they dealt with stock market booms and slumps by tightening securities regulation, whereas in *AMM*'s view it was monetary instability that was causing both banking and DTC problems, as well as stock market and property market booms and busts. Furthermore the wide cyclical fluctuations in the economy, and a growing problem of inflation since 1974 were also evidence of underlying monetary problems. Because the Hong Kong government and banking circles at the time focused almost exclusively on 'prudential' solutions to Hong Kong's problems, much of my analysis was necessarily focused on these topics, attempting to offer corrective analysis of the true nature of the problems facing Hong Kong. The article exhaustively presented the four supposed major instruments of monetary policy (liquid assets, interest rates, a government borrowing scheme, and intervention in the foreign exchange market), and explained why each of them did not work.

The new contribution of the article was an attempt to deal with the widespread misunderstanding in Hong Kong at the time of how the business cycle worked. One particular feature of business cycle analysis as presented in the government's budgetary statements of this period was the complete separation of developments in the real economy from monetary developments. Whereas monetary economists view fluctuations in financial markets and in economic activity and inflation as part and parcel of the transmission process of monetary policy, Hong Kong government officials at the time had developed a view of the business cycle that entirely omitted money and its impact on the economy.

The two concluding proposals for reforming the monetary system had appeared previously in earlier issues of *AMM* – either to control the quantity of money by converting the Exchange Fund, Hong Kong's monetary authority, into a central bank (e.g. by requiring the banks to hold reserve accounts at the Exchange Fund), or to manage the exchange rate with a central bank or modified Exchange Fund. Both proposals would have required a fundamental change in the relationship between the existing Exchange Fund and the banking system, a change that the authorities were not ready to consider at this stage. Moreover, it was clear that a return to orthodox currency board arrangements was not considered one of the leading contenders for reforming Hong Kong's monetary system. In effect, of the three possible solutions that were to be offered by *AMM* in September 1983, none was regarded as remotely relevant in December 1982.

Alternative solutions offered at the time

In contrast to the monetary analysis offered by *AMM*, the two main sets of proposals offered by other economists at the time were (1) a reform of banks' liquidity ratios, and (2) variations on the existing scheme for Exchange Fund (EF) borrowing in the money market. There is no space here for an extensive treatment of this subject. However, the various liquid asset ratio reform proposals generally amounted to shifting the composition of banks' assets in the hope that this would reduce their lending and hence money growth. None of these schemes grasped the key point that it is only when the monetary authority becomes the source of liquidity in the system that the government could start to control the overall growth of banks' balance sheets. This in turn would have required banks to maintain reserve accounts with the Exchange Fund, a proposal that was far from acceptable in the Hong Kong of the early 1980s.

The second set of proposals involved some degree of enhancement of the existing scheme for Exchange Fund or government borrowing in the money markets.[4] Perhaps the most important of the revised schemes was that proposed by Tony Latter in an internal Monetary Affairs Branch memorandum dated 4th August 1983, that remained confidential. In it he argued that the existing scheme was not working 'because its operation is not wholly under government's control.' His proposals were 'intended to overcome this deficiency by putting government firmly in the driving seat.'

His scheme envisaged the creation of a HK$ account for HSBC at the Exchange Fund, which HSBC would add to by selling foreign exchange to the Exchange Fund or by selling eligible HK$ paper to the Exchange Fund at market rates. The Fund would not accept any assets for the HSBC account that could readily be created by the banking system – such as HK$ deposits. In other words, there was a recognition here that, in its role as manager of the clearing system, HSBC had the power to create new assets or new liquidity that could undermine any intention of the authorities to tighten monetary conditions, although this was not made explicit in the memorandum. It was intended that the Exchange Fund would announce a penal rate, and this would be followed by two sets of actions: fund borrowing to enforce the new rate, and HSBC actions to build up its account at the Fund. The scheme did not propose any return to a fixed exchange rate. While there are similarities with the scheme ultimately proposed and implemented in July 1988, this scheme was not activated in 1983.

The restoration of the currency board, October 1983

At the height of the HK$ currency crisis in September 1983 I wrote another article in *AMM* that formed the basis for the government's return to a currency board mechanism in October 1983.[5] As a development of the arguments previously put forward in *AMM* for a reform of Hong Kong's monetary system, the main innovation was the fuller treatment of the case for a currency board arrangement.

From my monetary studies of the United States, Japan and China I was aware of the possibility of operating a monetary system without a central bank, provided the underlying monetary standard was sound and credible. During 1982 and early 1983 I had met with various Hong Kong government officials on an informal basis, and these encounters had conveyed the message that any proposals to introduce a central bank along with a far-reaching restructuring of the institutional framework of the banking system would not be seriously considered. The main innovation in the August–September article of 1983 was the idea that Hong Kong's monetary problems could be solved almost in one fell swoop and without any institutional upheaval if the 1972 changes could be reversed and a price for issuing and redeeming Certificates of Indebtedness (CoIs) (the HK$-denominated permits that gave banks the right to issue bank notes) could be fixed in US$. The article therefore presented a three-part proposal: (1) a central bank to manage the money supply (2A) a central bank to manage the exchange rate, or (2B) a return to the traditional currency board arrangement with no central bank. If the adoption of a central bank (under schemes 1 and 2A) was not acceptable for institutional or other reasons, then the exchange rate could in effect be controlled by the re-introduction of a currency board system (scheme 2B) without far-reaching institutional changes.

The presentation of scheme 2B focused on some issues that perhaps would generate little interest today, such as the stability of the monetary determinant ratios, and how cash arbitrage would work under the restored currency board. In retrospect both these points derived from my understanding of the gold and silver standard mechanisms, and my view at the time that, just as arbitrage between gold and currency notes under the gold standard was critical to the automatic corrective features of the gold standard, a similar kind of arbitrage would be critical to the currency board mechanism. In fact this turned out to be a mistake and a blind alley. It was not until the Asian Financial Crisis of 1997–98 that Hong Kong learned the need for the currency board to offer not only a fixed rate for currency note issues, but also a more or less fixed US$ rate to banks for the conversion of their reserves or HK$ settlement balances. In practice, the wholesale transactions of banks in the foreign exchange market and through the inter-bank settlement system were the fulcrum of the system, not the transactions of the public in banknotes.

Two appendices to the August-September 1983 article applied familiar academic theories of the time to the particular circumstances of Hong Kong. Appendix 1 explained why interest rates were a bad tool for monetary control. It should again be remembered that in the early 1980s monetary base control (MBC) was a monetary remedy proposed both by a number of leading academic economists and by a number of market practitioners both in the US and in the UK, and hence the emphasis on the quantitative aspects of monetary control. In practice few if any central banks ever adopted monetary base control. In the US the Federal Reserve adopted a modified version of MBC from October 1979 until September 1982. According to Charles Goodhart, the volatility of short-term interest rates in the US increased fourfold during this period, while the experiment also resulted in greater volatility of the targeted aggregate, M1.[6] In the UK, despite toying with the idea, the authorities formally rejected MBC and only ever targeted M3, and that only for a while.

Although there are some interesting theoretical points made in the original article, especially in the context of Hong Kong, some of those arguments could not be used today. In practical terms the distinction between money and credit is even more difficult to pinpoint nowadays, and the current consensus (in 2006) is that, aside from exceptional cases such as Japan's episode of deflation between the late 1990s and 2006, managing short-term interest rates is regarded as the only practical way for central banks to conduct monetary policy. By raising or lowering short-term rates, not only does a central bank influence the incentives to borrow and lend (which in turn affects the quantity of money at the same time), but it also influences the prices of a whole range of securities (e.g. bonds, equities and derivatives), currencies and other assets (e.g. commodities, real estate etc) in a way that reinforces the effect of the initial interest rate change. In this way the central bank's changes in interest rates percolate outwards to influence financial asset prices, economic activity, and the overall price level. Changes in the quantity of money are nowadays regarded as simply one step in the transmission process rather than an immediate or intermediate objective of monetary policy.

Appendix 2 showed how amending the liquid asset ratios would have failed to bring any long-term solution to Hong Kong's monetary problems. While this issue has less significance today because the distinction between matters of prudential supervision and matters of monetary control are better understood, the fact that it merited a separate appendix shows how central the topic was in the debates over Hong Kong's money and banking systems at the time.

I subsequently learned that there were two officials within the government – the Deputy Secretary for Monetary Affairs, Tony Latter, and the Government Economist, Dr Alan McLean – who, recognizing that a central bank was a non-starter, began to lend their support to the *AMM* idea of a return to a pre-1972 style currency board. At one stage Tony Latter showed me his internal memorandum that had been circulated within the Monetary Affairs Branch diagnosing the problems of Hong Kong's monetary system, although it was nowhere near as radical or outspoken as the *AMM* article. Had it not been for pressure from these two individuals within the administration, action might have been delayed significantly longer. Another point to note is that in a formal sense the British government left Hong Kong to run its own economic policy and would not have wished to be seen to interfere (especially while the British were arguing in Beijing for a high degree of autonomy for Hong Kong), still less to dictate to the local administration, notwithstanding the acute circumstances. It was greatly preferable that any initiative for change should be seen to come from the Hong Kong authorities – as it ultimately did – and not from London.

On October 6th and 7th a delegation of two (Charles Goodhart from the Bank and David Peretz from HM Treasury) visited Hong Kong to vet the scheme and give Hong Kong officials the necessary seal of approval. The new arrangements were announced on Saturday October 15th 1983, and implemented from the following Monday. As announced by the Financial Secretary, John Bremridge, there were two elements in the plan.

First, the new scheme would operate by restoring a fixed rate against the US$ for the issue and redemption of CoIs, equivalent to Hong Kong dollar banknotes, at HK$7.80 per US dollar. This meant that the two note-issuing banks would in future pay the Government's Exchange Fund for additional CoIs, which they were required to hold as backing for any increase in their note issues, in foreign exchange at a fixed rate of HK$7.80 equals US$1. Conversely, when notes were to be withdrawn from circulation by the note-issuing banks surrendering CoIs, the Exchange Fund would henceforth pay them the equivalent foreign exchange at the same fixed rate. The Financial Secretary said that it was his intention to hold this rate unchanged.

The expected effects of these arrangements on the wider economy were only very briefly spelled out. Bremridge reassured the public that the rates of exchange which a bank customer would obtain, whether exchanging bank notes or making any other foreign currency trans-actions, would continue to be determined by market forces, but would in practice be close to the fixed rate of HK$7.80 equals US$1.00. This would be the case because market forces of competition and arbitrage would operate against the background of the fixed rate for Certificates of Indebtedness. In the short term there might be some upward pres-sures on Hong Kong dollar interest rates, Bremridge said, but once the stability of the exchange rate became evident and accepted, interest rates should fall below present levels – which indeed they did. Looking further ahead, changes in the exchange rate would no longer be an element in Hong Kong's adjustment process. Factors such as interest rates and money supply would adjust to balance of payments pressures automatically without Government intervention.

The second change was the abolition of the prevailing interest tax on Hong Kong dollar deposits. This meant that there would no longer be a tax advantage in holding foreign currency deposits or in holding Hong Kong dollar deposits offshore. Although the measure had adverse revenue implications for the government, it was a sensible move designed to maximize the expected arbitrage between Hong Kong dollar deposits and US dollar deposits, and thus improve the operation of the new monetary stabilization scheme.

The HSBC account at the Exchange Fund, July 1988

In the early years of the restored currency board from October 1983 until mid-1988 the scheme operated tolerably well, but it was not entirely automatic. Occasional shocks and political crises caused the spot exchange rate to deviate considerably from the fixed rate for the conversion of CoIs. Moreover, despite sharp upward spikes in interest rates, arbitrage and competition did not seem to bring about an automatic convergence of the spot rate with the official parity of HK$7.80. This therefore required intervention in the foreign exchange market from time to time by both the Exchange Fund as well as by HSBC operating in conjunction with the authorities.

The problem related to the fact, hinted at in Tony Latter's 1983 internal memorandum mentioned above, that as manager of the clearing system, HSBC had the power to create credit for other banks that either wished to borrow from HSBC, or were overdrawn on their clearing accounts. This could at times negate any intervention by the authorities intended to tighten credit or strengthen the Hong Kong dollar exchange rate. Consequently in July 1988 the authorities devised and implemented a mechanism to overcome this shortcoming in the 1983 currency board scheme.

The July 1988 package of new accounting arrangements for the Hong Kong monetary system represented the first major change in the design of the system since 1983. The measures required HSBC to maintain an Account with the Exchange Fund, with the level of the balance in the Account to be set by the monetary authorities. If the authorities wished to ease monetary conditions they could purchase US currency and thereby expand the Account, effectively adding funds to the monetary system and lowering interest rates. Conversely, to tighten monetary conditions they could sell US currency for HK dollars, effectively reducing the amount of funds in the system.

However, the July 1988 measures also set a new direction. In retrospect *AMM* had paid insufficient attention to one of the key problems that the July package sought to address – namely the potential leakage of funds into the system from the inter-bank clearing arrangements. In effect the *AMM* design had concentrated on only one element of the monetary base, namely the banknote issue and its backing. As mentioned earlier, this was based on the idea – derived from the operation of gold and silver specie standards – that if banknotes and deposits were interchangeable, then market arbitrage could be relied upon to bring the convertibility rate for banknotes and the exchange rate for wholesale funds into line. In practice this never happened, and the July 1988 package of measures was the first step to tackling this problem by moving in a different direction.

Looking back on these events from the perspective of 2006 one can see that the new direction implied, but not articulated, by the July

1988 measures was to start to extend gradually the authorities' control over all the elements in the monetary base, not simply the currency issue. Only then would any tightening or easing, whether market-induced or deliberately induced by the authorities, be transmitted to all parts of the system in such a way that interest rate movements reinforced the tendency of the market exchange rate to appreciate or depreciate.

It had been obvious that Hong Kong's banks did not maintain reserves at the monetary authority, but the fact that Hong Kong's banks had maintained a private clearing and settlement system had obscured the fact that the ultimate settlement bank (HSBC) in fact had the power to operate like a central bank in the sense of granting credit to any bank in the system that might become overdrawn on its settlement account. Such credits were equivalent to the creation of high-powered or base money, and therefore undermined the ability of either the authorities or any auto-pilot mechanism in the currency board to exercise monetary control. In essence this means that currency boards in the modern world must incorporate banks' reserve deposits in the books of the monetary authority. A simple, standard currency board limited to currency notes issued and redeemed by the monetary authority is not a viable system.

It is important that students of the Hong Kong monetary system understand the significance of this shift, and see that this was a first logical step on the way to the 'seven technical measures' of September 1998 that finally made the system much more robust. My *AMM* article of July–August 1988 provided a full explanation of the new measures, including two pages of T-form balance sheets setting out the mechanics of the new arrangements, together with the press release announcing the new measures and their effect. At the end of the article there is some mild criticism of the measures, though it is more suspicion of the authorities' motives than any view that the measures would not work.

The central contribution of the article is a detailed explanation of how any mandated changes in the size of the account to be held by HSBC at the Exchange Fund would enable interest rates to support desired changes in the market exchange rate. This mechanism remained the core of the system from July 1988 until December 1996 when a new clearing system (real time gross settlement, or RTGS) was introduced, and all licensed banks were required to maintain clearing accounts with the Exchange Fund or the Hong Kong Monetary Authority (HKMA) as it became known following its merger with the Office of the Commissioner of Banking in April 1993.

Developments in the 1990s

By the end of the 1980s the Hong Kong monetary system had been reformed to the point where the convertibility of banknotes at a fixed rate provided some sort of anchor for the currency, but there was no assurance of convergence between the wholesale market exchange rate and the convertibility rate for banknotes. As a result, the authorities had brought in several measures, primarily the Account of HSBC at the Exchange Fund, to enable them to steer interest rates in a direction that would assist that convergence. Although *AMM* continued to argue (mistakenly in retrospect) for cash arbitrage to be given a greater opportunity to work, the authorities shifted to a different tack. Most of the 1990s was spent developing mechanisms that would (a) give the authorities greater control over money market rates, and (b) enable the banks to resolve any overdrafts or surpluses in their settlement or reserve accounts through a discount window or deposit facility, while providing the requisite instruments to enable the banks to conduct such transactions without the Exchange Fund being put at risk. The former would achieve adequate convergence, while the latter was intended to prevent sudden, sharp movements in interest rates that could threaten the stability of the system. The system was still far from operating on autopilot.

Over much of the next decade until 1998 developments in Hong Kong's monetary system were mainly aimed at the creation of a more efficient short-term debt market, and the simultaneous development of mechanisms for smoothing out day-to-day imbalances in the interbank market. Although *AMM* continued to monitor these developments and a number of articles were written on these issues during these years, I moved from Hong Kong to San Francisco at the end of 1993. My focus on monetary developments in Asia became less intense, and ultimately *AMM* ceased publication at the end of 1995.

Having created a mechanism for managing the money market through The Account of HSBC at the Exchange Fund, the Hong Kong authorities viewed the next set of priorities as the orderly development of a deeper and more active money market. Moreover, given that cash arbitrage was not working to achieve exchange rate convergence, the money markets needed to be managed to ensure the proper outcome. Hong Kong prided itself on its role as an international financial centre in Asia, but it had always felt handicapped by the fact that with continuous budget surpluses and hardly any government borrowing, there was essentially no government debt market in Hong Kong. This would inevitably impose constraints on the range of instruments the Exchange Fund could deal in when conducting transactions to influence liquidity in the local market via the level of HSBC's Account, but it also meant that there was no satisfactory array of high quality debt issues that could serve as a benchmark for market participants. The solution was for the Exchange Fund to create some liabilities on its own balance sheet, and issue these to the market with enough maturities to build a quasi-Hong Kong government yield curve.

On the eve of the handover of Hong Kong to China on July 1st 1997 and immediately ahead of the onset of the Asian Financial Crisis the monetary system in Hong Kong appeared stronger than it had been at any time since 1972. The note issue was now not only fully backed by US$, but incremental issues had to be paid for with US$ at the official HK$7.80 rate per US$, and could be redeemed on the same terms. Insofar as there was a lack of convergence between the market rate and the official conversion rate for banknotes or CoIs, there were now several mechanisms for the HKMA to nudge interest rates up or down to achieve closer exchange rate convergence, together with a range of new instruments, Exchange Fund Bills and Notes (EFBN), that the banks could use to adjust their own positions, thus reducing the risk of interest rates unexpectedly spiking up or down. Moreover, the authority had ample foreign exchange reserves to ensure full cover for all its new liabilities.

In spite of this seemingly solid framework, there remained some concerns. One clue to these unspoken fears was the authorities' preference for keeping the exchange rate at a premium to the official conversion rate from 1991 onwards. If they had been entirely confident about the robustness of the system, they could have allowed the exchange rate to trade much closer to the official conversion rate, and even fall below it, but after 1990 this never happened. Throughout the years 1990–1998 the free market rate remained at a persistent premium, typically around HK$7.73–7.75 to the US unit. This was the canary in the coalmine that told the market that there was an inherent vulnerability in the system. The maintenance of the market rate at this elevated level seemed to indicate that the authorities needed a protective buffer between the market rate and the official rate – just in case something serious happened, which it inevitably did.

Onset of the Asian financial crisis and post-crisis reforms

The Asian financial crisis exposed the fundamental vulnerability of the monetary edifice that had been constructed in the 1980s and 1990s in two important respects. First it showed clearly that no matter how high rates rose, there was little if any convergence between the market exchange rate and the official parity. Second, it showed that the system was built on altogether too narrow a base – a few hundreds of millions of HK$ held by banks in the Aggregate Balance (the newly established reserve accounts of banks at the HKMA). This amount could easily prove too little in the case of sudden shifts in investor attitudes towards Hong Kong.

After several waves of speculative attacks on Hong Kong's currency and stock market the government responded by intervening in the stock market to purchase nearly HK$120 billion of equities. Simultaneously with the intervention in the stock market, moves were already in preparation to solve the problems of the currency board. A Sub-Committee of the Exchange Fund Advisory Committee (EFAC) was formed, including a number of outsiders, to enhance the transparency of currency board operations, and to draw on the expertise of members of the banking and academic communities in Hong Kong. Then on 5th September 1998 the HKMA announced a package of measures designed to strengthen the mechanism even further and make it less susceptible to the disruptions of the preceding year. The Seven Technical Measures, which included a weak-side convertibility undertaking (CU) for banks' balances at the HKMA (initially set at 7.75) and a mechanism for banks to discount EFBN in order to make good any overdrafts in their clearing accounts, demonstrated the government's resolute commitment to maintaining the fixed rate currency board system. The CU meant that banks now had greater certainty about future levels of the HK$ spot rate and would therefore be more willing to conduct interest rate arbitrage transactions. The discounting mechanism effectively provided a shock absorber that would prevent sudden large outflows from having such a drastic impact on interest rates as had been experienced in the past year.

Seven months after the successful introduction of the weak side CU, the Currency Board Sub-Committee proposed moving the rate upwards in steps of 1 pip per day (1/10000 of a HK$) from 7.7500 to 7.8000 (or 500 pips), starting in April and ending in July the following year. This finally removed the anomaly that the CU (or previously the HKMA's intervention point) differed arbitrarily from the conversion rate for banknotes. However, the question of whether this was the optimum strategy repeatedly came up at meetings of the Currency Board Sub-Committee between October 1999 and May 2005 because the existence of a weak side CU meant that there was still uncertainty about the upper limit for the HK$/US$ rate, and scope for discretionary intervention by the HKMA.

Discussion centred on two issues. Should there be a strong side CU? If so, at what level should it be set? For several years executives of the HKMA maintained the view that there should be no strong side CU, and that some "constructive ambiguity" was desirable because this would enable the authorities to impose costly surprises on speculators. Sometimes there was a transitional reason to maintain the status quo, as for example following the completion of the shift of the lower side CU from 7.75 to 7.80. However, most expressed the view that if a strong side CU was set too close to the market rate, then this would undercut the operations of private foreign exchange operators, and that it was an explicit requirement of the Basic Law that Hong Kong maintain an active international foreign exchange market (Article 112).

It was not until active speculation on a revaluation of the RMB in 2003–04 that the HKMA was compelled to take action, once again by market developments rather than by its own choice. Against a background of widening Chinese trade surpluses and strong capital inflows into the Mainland, many market participants, unable to purchase RMB currency directly, began to view the HK$ currency as a substitute for the Mainland's currency. Perhaps not understanding the autonomy of Hong Kong in financial matters, they expected the HK$ to appreciate in line with the RMB if that currency were to be revalued. The effect of such speculative spot and forward purchases of the HK$ was to drive down HK$ interest rates, encouraging strong upward movements in Hong Kong equities and real estate prices. Between October 2003 and 17th May 2005 the HK$ one-year forward premium averaged 682 pips, or a premium to the spot rate of some 8.75%, while the Hang Seng Index of Hong Kong equities rose from 11,000 to 14,000, some 27%. Over the same period the Centa-City Leading Index of transaction prices in the secondary market for selected housing estates increased 76%.

Between November 2004 and January 2005 the three-month interbank interest rate differential with US rates had risen to over 200 basis points, and although it narrowed in February and March, it widened again in April as speculation about a revaluation of the RMB resumed, pushing down HK$ interest rates again. Concerned by the risk that another extended bubble in asset prices might develop, the Currency Board Sub-Committee reviewed again the question of the indeterminate upper limit to fluctuations in the HK$/US$ spot rate. In view of the prolonged upward pressure on the RMB that seemed likely in coming years and the persistent knock-on effect that this was likely to have on the HK$ and asset prices in Hong Kong, the Committee this time decided that it was preferable to end the adverse effects of strong-side speculation by introducing a strong-side Convertibility Undertaking.

Consistent with previous discussions about not restricting the activity of the local foreign exchange market, the new strong-side CU (where the HKMA would buy US dollars from licensed banks) was set at 7.75, and the weak-side CU was to be shifted from 7.80 to 7.85. The shifting of the existing weak-side CU (where the HKMA would sell US dollars to licensed banks) was to be achieved in a gradual manner over five weeks by moving the weak-side CU by 100 pips every Monday starting with 7.81 on 23 May 2005 until it reached 7.85 on 20 June 2005. The end result would be a symmetric band of 5 cents on either side of the 7.80 conversion rate for banknotes. However, the authorities retained the right 'to conduct market operations consistent with Currency Board principles' i.e. to make discretionary interventions *within* the band between the two CU points. The announcement was made on May 18th 2005, and within days interest rates in Hong Kong returned to rough parity with US rates.

An obvious result of the modified framework for the currency board regime in Hong Kong was that it was now far more transparent and automatic, and less subject to discretionary intervention. Equally important, the need for the Hong Kong authorities to use a variety of instruments to steer interest rates upward or downward in order to maintain the spot exchange rate within some undefined range disappeared altogether. There were now clear limits to the fluctuation of the spot rate on either side of the 7.80 conversion rate for banknotes. Purchases of US$ at the strong-side CU or sales of US$ at the weak-side CU would be triggered by the banks, not by the authority. Moreover, by limiting the possible range of exchange rate fluctuation, the strong-side and weak-side CU points would in turn indicate the limits of any potential loss to a bank or private investor who wished to conduct interest rate arbitrage transactions between HK$ and US$ interest rates. In combination, the implementation of these refinements in May 2005 meant that, after 22 years of experimentation, an auto-pilot was finally installed.

Conclusions

The long period of nearly 22 years between the restoration of the currency board system in October 1983 and the adoption of a two-sided, symmetric CU in May 2005 which finally enabled the system to operate with virtual automaticity reflects the innate cautiousness of officials and bankers in Hong Kong about making radical institutional changes when the existing arrangements were – for the most part – consistent with a high degree of economic success. This dilemma – the need for systemic monetary reforms while maintaining intact Hong Kong's broader formula for past financial and economic successes – finds echoes in the sometimes ambivalent official treatment of two issues that spanned most of the 22-year period: the role of HSBC and the whole approach to interest rate management. Given a currency board mechanism that was pre-disposed to return to equilibrium at or close to the 7.80 rate, there would have been no need for back-up measures involving interest rates. However, until the convertibility undertaking for bank reserves came into operation in September 1998 there was always likely to be a nagging worry that disturbances to the exchange rate would not be truly self-correcting, and hence the authorities' need for additional lines of defence.

The combination of currency board features in force after May 2005 – a fixed rate for CoIs, symmetrical CU bands on either side of it, and intra-day or overnight discounting of EFBNs by banks to smooth liquidity imbalances – are compatible *both* with a number of characteristic features of Hong Kong (such as the issue of bank notes by private commercial banks, the encouragement of free capital flows and the absence of foreign exchange controls, and the existence of a vibrant foreign exchange market etc) *and* with the desirable theoretical features of a modern currency board system. Having been subject to careful and incremental reforms over the past two decades, the currency board system of Hong Kong has now reached a state of development where the key features of its monetary aspects – as opposed to technological developments affecting (say) bank clearing or fund transfers – can be expected to pause for some years.

The challenges facing the Hong Kong monetary authorities in future years are (a) whether the fixed rate currency board link to the US dollar alone continues to be the optimum monetary policy choice for Hong Kong (b) whether pegging to an alternative currency such as the RMB would represent an improvement over the current US\$ peg, and (c) whether a variable rate system with the currency either linked to a basket or independently managed would be superior. In the longer term it may be necessary to consider whether Hong Kong should participate in an Asian monetary union.

In my view, none of the exit options from Hong Kong's present-day currency board are especially attractive compared with maintenance of the *status quo*. Although it took 22 years since the initial resumption of the currency board system in 1983 to evolve to a stage where the system works automatically and without regular discretionary intervention by the authorities, the system as it stands now is uniquely appropriate both to Hong Kong's status as an international financial centre that encourages the free flow of capital, and to Hong Kong's special position as a highly open trading economy, both as a direct trader with the rest of the world and as an intermediary serving as a major gateway to China.

Notes

1   This chapter draws heavily on the narrative text from my book, J. Greenwood (2008) *Hong Kong's Link to the US Dollar: Origins and Evolution* (Hong Kong: Hong Kong University Press).
2   David Ricardo, see J. Eatwell, M. Milgate and P. Newman (eds) (1987) *The New Palgrave: A Dictionary of Economics* (London: Palgrave).
3   Allan Meltzer (2003) *A History of the Federal Reserve System* (Chicago: University of Chicago).
4   For details of the existing scheme, see *AMM* November–December 1982, The Exchange Fund's Borrowing Scheme: A Twist on Operation Twist pp. 20–2.
5   In a short letter I received from the Financial Secretary, Sir John Bremridge, he says: 'Many thanks for all your advice – some of which as you know we have taken.' (Letter in author's possession dated 17th October 1983.)
6   For details see 'Monetary Base' in Eatwell *et al.*, *The New Palgrave: A Dictionary of Economics* (London: Palgrave).

7
The Origin and Evolution of Hong Kong's Currency Board II[1]

Joseph Yam

Introduction

This article presents a brief history of the reforms to Hong Kong's monetary framework over the past two and a half decades, drawing on my own personal involvement in the process and internal correspondence, as well as commentary from leading experts at the time. It covers the background to the present currency board system, and traces the key technical changes to it since its introduction, including the assumption and development of official control over the monetary base, measures to create deeper and more liquid money markets in Hong Kong, and, more recently, technical refinements to the system following the Asian financial crisis. The article concludes that the Hong Kong currency board system has served Hong Kong well over the past quarter of a century, notwithstanding the economic and political challenges during this time. However, the way in which the system operates has effectively changed beyond recognition.

Background

It is worth noting at the outset that there is a general consensus in Hong Kong that the main objective of monetary policy should be exchange rate stability, even though the way that this has been achieved has changed over time. This reflects the fact that Hong Kong is a small, open economy and therefore dependent on external trade and – increasingly in recent decades – global capital flows. Thus, apart from a period of floating between 1974 and 1983, prior to the setting up of the present system, the Hong Kong dollar exchange rate has been fixed. Between 1863 and 1935, the exchange rate was on a silver standard, moving to a sterling-based currency board between 1935 and 1972, and then to a US dollar-based currency board from October 1983.

A natural starting point to understanding the present arrangements is the early to mid-1970s, when the Hong Kong dollar was de-linked from sterling and was allowed to float from November 1974. The end of a fixed exchange rate for the Hong Kong dollar, combined with the lack of a mechanism for official control over the supply or the price of money effectively meant that there was no anchor for ensuring currency stability.

The determination of the money supply and therefore interest and exchange rates was largely left to the market. Specifically, the HSBC managed the interbank clearing system and, therefore, was in a position to create money – a privilege that is normally that of a central bank. The HSBC was, and still is, a commercial bank – the largest in Hong Kong – but somehow it managed to balance the pri-vate interests of a large, commercial bank with the public interest of monetary and currency stability – or whatever happened to be the focus of economic policy at any particular point in time.

There was little serious discussion in official circles about the need for monetary control. This may seem astonishing to the central banking community nowadays. However, in the 1970s and early 1980s, there was no agreement on the need for official monetary targets, for example, for the money supply. In fact, in official documents in Hong Kong it is difficult to find any reference at all to the monetary base, let alone arguments for control. There was instead a general feeling that the system worked well, supporting a *laissez-faire* attitude to issues sur-rounding the control of the monetary base and monetary conditions more generally.

Some commentators were pressing for more monetary control by the authorities, especially as economic problems appeared, but there was little support in the administration. By the end of the 1970s, the lack of control had manifested itself in a depreciating Hong Kong dollar and rising inflation, putting pressure on the authorities for some kind of monetary reform. In 1981 John Greenwood published "Time to blow the whistle" in his publication, the *Asian Monetary Monitor* (AMM), urging the Government to introduce monetary reforms to stop the slide of the Hong Kong dollar and to avoid inflation. However, there remained a general reluctance among administrators to engage in any proper debate about monetary policy. In response to the AMM article, for example one senior civil servant who, for the usual reasons of confidentiality, shall remain anonymous, wrote

> What the article lacks is any serious attempt to tell us why whistles have to be blown. He strikes me as a confirmed regulator for whom regulation is a worthy end.

And, in response to internal suggestions for a meeting with John to discuss the *AMM* article, that

> I am not having any discussion with the gentleman concerned. I suppose I did not persuade you not to waste your time.

So we had this interesting situation in which the administration clearly did not want to do anything, but the private sector was pushing for action by the administration to put its house in order.

The pressures for reform increased during the early 1980s, but there was still a reluctance to take control of monetary affairs. One official, writing in July 1983, near the height of the currency crisis in September 1983, when the Hong Kong dollar depreciated sharply, did argue that

> I do not believe that any worthwhile improvement to our monetary armoury can be achieved without first establishing a mechanism to give government some control over the Hong Kong dollar resources of the banking system and hence leverage over its balance sheet.

But there were many who argued that there was no need for action, notwithstanding the on-going crisis. The following comment from that period is by an outside academic commentator, but is interesting because it pretty much reflects mainstream official thinking at that time. Rejecting the arguments of those who claimed that the system was grossly ineffective, he said

> If money at all matters, then few can deny that our present system possesses rather definite merits ... I, for one, have been enormously impressed that, in spite of the current difficulties, the economy is still very much afloat. We are hurting indeed, but far from dead.

Meanwhile, the economy was in turmoil. As the newspaper cuttings show, there was a serious run on the Hang Lung Bank on the weekend of the 23rd of September 1983, and panic-buying in the supermarkets.

7.1   Bank Run in Hang Lung Bank, *Hong Kong Standard*, 28 September 1983

SIGN here says: All rice sold out. One of the supermarkets all over the colony yesterday besieged by housewives and their family members as they raided the shops for groceries in fear of prices going up as a result of the plunging Hongkong dollar in the currency exchange market. Below left, trolley-ful of foodstuffs queue up with others to be taken out. Right, a lad lugging his share of rice bags helped to deplete rice stocks all over.

7.2　Panic Buying in the Supermarket, *Hong Kong Standard*, 28 September 1983

South China Morning Po

Vol. XXXIX No. 265   HONGKONG, SUNDAY, SEPTEMBER 25, 1983

$9.50!

No relief as dollar dives

HONGKONG DOLLAR VERSUS US DOLLAR

SEPTEMBER 1983

Market has gone 'wild'

GOLD TAELS

SEPTEMBER 1983

Have confidence in yourselves: Luce

7.3   Headline from *South China Morning Post*, 25 September 1983

The Chinese characters in Figure 7.2 translate as 'all rice had been sold out' and, at the bottom, you see the little boy with his sacks of rice going home. So while it was true that the economy was far from dead, it was not far off! Further headlines from the *South China Morning*

Post were 'no relief as dollar dives', 'market has gone wild', and the then Foreign Office minister, Richard Lewes, urging the general public to 'have confidence in yourself'. In the end the deteriorating economic situation forced a reluctant administration to take action.

The 1983 reform

The present arrangement of a US dollar-based currency board was introduced in October 1983. For the first time since 1974, the issue and redemption of Certificates of Indebtedness issued for the account of the Exchange Fund to note-issuing banks for backing the issue of local currency notes was conducted at a fixed rate, of HK\$ 7.80 per US dollar. The idea was that the fixed exchange rate for bank notes would open any arbitrage activities that would force convergence of the foreign exchange rate for the Hong Kong dollar in financial markets with the official rate.

The issue of whether or not there should be official control over the supply or price of money, however defined, and how this should be done, continued to be divisive. Meanwhile, although there was full US Dollar backing for the amount of bank notes in circulation and changes in it, the HSBC continued to be the management bank of the interbank clearing house and endowed with the powers of money creation. Some commentators and external advisors argued for more radical monetary reform, through the setting up of a central bank with direct control over the money supply. One advisor cautioned that circumstances could be envisaged when an adjustment or even a reversion to a managed float might be desirable, with the Exchange Fund adopting more of the features of a central bank.

It soon became clear that banknote arbitrage was not working effectively to align the foreign exchange rate in the open market with the official rate. The note-issuing banks, being obliged to issue and redeem bank notes, considered potential profits from banknote arbitrage as potential losses for them. Arbitrage was condemned as 'round-tripping' that hurt the profitability of the note issuing banks. Thus the note-issuing banks took action to frustrate the transferability between bank balances and the bank notes – which is important for arbitrage to work effectively – by imposing cash-handling charges on large amounts of bank notes.

Though the market exchange rate proved fairly stable over this period, there was an increasing sense of frustration at what were perceived to be flaws in the system. Again, quoting from internal correspondence at that time, one exasperated official exclaimed that:

> The link has succeeded probably as much because of as in spite of it being imperfectly understood by the majority in whose hands its fate rests.

And, further:

> I hope I have made clear my belief that monetary framework could be and should be enhanced, but like others before, and I fear after me, I bow down with my fingers crossed with the job hardly begun.

Despite growing frustration, there were several hurdles to immediate reform of the monetary framework in the mid-1980s. First and foremost, it was a politically sensitive period with the signing of the Sino-British joint declaration. Internal correspondence at that time suggests that this did not completely rule out reform of the monetary system:

> The evolution of the Exchange Fund into a more fully-fledged monetary authority would appear not to be inconsistent with the Sino-British agreement, which implies monetary autonomy for the HKSAR, although the Agreement also speaks of unchanged monetary arrangements.

However, there was a general perception that reform could involve a lot of down-side risk, and the chances were that nobody would agree to it. Any reforms had to be agreed between Beijing and Whitehall. The HSBC also needed to be consulted, given its central role in existing monetary arrangements.

Secondly, the drafting of the Basic Law diverted quite a lot of attention away from what needed to be done on the monetary framework. At the same time, there was a lot of change of personnel within government. Thirdly, there were problems with the economy, characterised by a series of banking crises in Hong Kong involving seven bank rescues, and, financial market turmoil arising from the 1987 global stock market crash. Thus, during the five years to 1987, it felt very much as if the financial authorities were fire-fighting one crisis after another, against a backdrop of unsettling political and external developments.

The real turning point came in May 1987. The pressures for reform culminated in high-level talks between the Financial Secretary and Secretary for Monetary Affairs and Beijing (for which I prepared the papers) to address the issue of whether or not the administration was in a position to maintain monetary and financial stability during a period of political transition and beyond. Simply asking that question, and generating interest, marked a turning point in attempts to reform monetary arrangements.

The 1988 reforms

The key change, announced in July 1988, was official, indirect control of the clearing balance used to settle interbank transactions in the banking system. Two options were, in fact, discussed. The first, which was adopted – and what I called the 'umbilical cord approach' – was for HSBC to operate an account with the Exchange Fund. Crucially, the balance of that account was used to cap the net clearing balance that other commercial banks held with the HSBC, thus giving the Exchange Fund indirect control over the amount of liquidity in the banking system. The second option was for all banks to open and operate clearing accounts with the Exchange Fund, but this was more complex and would have necessitated a more fundamental overhaul of the clearing system. It proved hard enough to reach agreement between the parties involved – Beijing, Whitehall, the HSBC and Hong Kong's Executive Council – on the first option. Once Beijing and Whitehall had agreed, there were lengthy negotiations with the Chairman of the HSBC who eventually signed up to the reforms, saying that: 'What is good for Hong Kong must be good for the Hongkong Bank. Let's do it.'

The overall aim of the above 'accounting arrangements', as they were described then, was the assumption of more official control over money for the purpose of more effectively achieving exchange rate stability. With the benefit of hindsight, however, it is clear that insufficient consideration was given to the precise way in which monetary control for this specific purpose was to be exercised. The key issue concerned the control of the amount of liquidity in the interbank system, represented by the balance in the account that HSBC was operating with the Exchange Fund. Should such control be rule-based or left to the discretion of the asset crisis? If it was to be rule-based, what rules should be followed and what instruments used? If discretion was to be exercised, what parameters and instruments were appropriate to guide the taking of discretionary decisions?

The next set of reforms during the early 1990s were, in essence, aimed at creating deeper and more liquid money markets in Hong Kong, in part, to try to smooth out the volatility in domestic interest rates arising from exchange rate stabilisation efforts. These are well documented elsewhere and so are only listed briefly. The Exchange Fund Bills Programme was launched in March 1990 to create a domestic debt market and, also, to provide the monetary authorities with an instrument for adjusting liquidity in the money markets. In 1991 the Office of the Exchange Fund (OEF) was established, which was the forerunner of the Hong Kong Monetary Authority (HKMA) set up in April 1993. A liquidity adjustment facility (LAF) was introduced in June 1992, which set up a discount window aimed at dampening interest rate volatility, for instance in the face of a large initial public offering in the stock market. In May 1994 the Bank of China became the third note-issuing bank. In December 1996 a real time gross settlement system was introduced to the Hong Kong dollar payment system and the opportunity was used to require all banks to operate clearing accounts with the HKMA instead of the HSBC. Thus the HKMA assumed direct control over interbank liquidity, in the form of the sum of balances in those clearing accounts – the so-called Aggregate Balance. An intra-day repurchase agreement (repo) arrangement and a proper discount window were also introduced for Exchange Fund paper to provide additional liquidity within the banking system when needed. These reforms, aimed at creating a better-functioning money market, were on the whole judged to be successful.

The Asian financial crisis

The first big test of the new arrangements came with the Asian financial crisis, which hit Hong Kong financial markets in 1997–1998. Much has been written about the so-called 'double-play' by speculators seeking to exploit the sensitivity between Hong Kong interest rates and capital flows, on the one hand, and Hong Kong interest rates and asset prices, on the other. The HKMA intervened heavily in the foreign exchange and – more unusually – the stock market in a successful bid to defend the currency board. Following that episode, there was further discussion on how to make the system more robust, which led to a further set of reforms to refine the currency board framework – the so-called seven technical measures.

Seven technical measures

The next set of reforms brought the currency board closer to a rules-based system in an attempt to keep the exchange rate closer to its target rate. In September 1998, after the stock market intervention, a convertibility undertaking was introduced, which commits the HKMA to purchase Hong Kong dollars in exchange for US dollars at a predetermined rate (initially set at 7.75 and subsequently moved from 7.75 to 7.8 by 1 pip per calendar day starting from 1 April 1999) to anchor expectation on the exchange rate on the weak side. Around the same time, the definition of the monetary base was expanded to include all Exchange Fund paper issued, which were allowed to be offered for discount through the discount window, and the base rate – the interest rate that the HKMA charges for repo liquidity assistance through the Discount Windows – was set at a penal level over the Fed Funds target rate. The HKMA also moved to publish a transparent account of currency board transactions and set up a currency board sub-committee of the exchange fund advisory committee.

Three refinements

In 2003 the currency board started to face with pressures in the opposite (strong) direction as a result of substantial capital inflows into the Hong Kong dollar following financial market speculation of a revaluation of the Renminbi. This suggested a need also to anchor exchange rate expectations on the strong side, prompting further reform in May 2005, just ahead of exchange rate reform on the Mainland in July of that year. Three refinements were introduced. First, a strong-side convertibility undertaking was introduced, which commits the HKMA to sell Hong Kong dollars in exchange for US dollars at a rate of HK\$7.75 per US dollar. Secondly, to ensure symmetry, the weak-side convertibility undertaking was gradually shifted to HK\$7.85 per US dollar, from its previous level of HK\$7.80 per US dollar. This opened up a convertibility zone, between HK\$7.75 and HK\$7.85, within which the exchange rate could fluctuate in response to market forces. Thirdly the authorities reserved the right to intervene in the money and foreign exchange markets within the convertibility zone and announced that any intervention within the convertibility zone would be undertaken in a manner consistent with currency board principles.

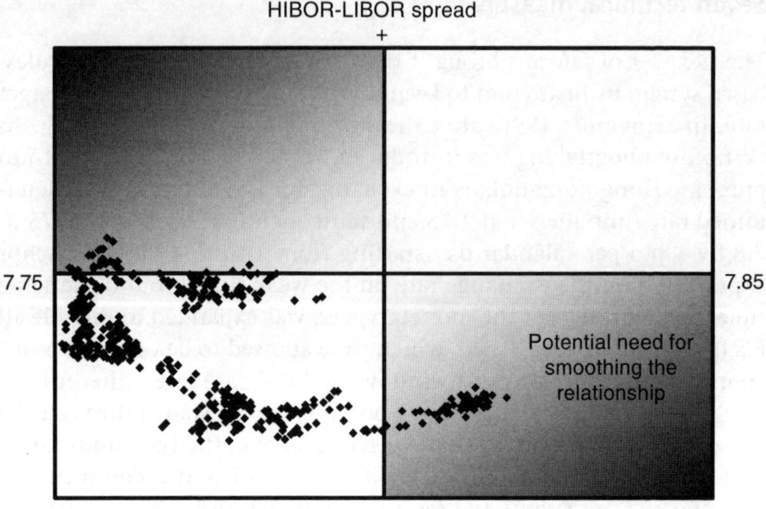

7.4   HIBOR-LIBOR Spread

On the whole, the technical refinements to the currency board system appear to have worked well. To illustrate this, Figure 7.4 plots the HKD/USD exchange rate against the corresponding interest rate differential, the HIBOR/LIBOR spread. As expected, during periods when the exchange rate is weaker than HK$7.80 per US dollar there is a positive interest rate differential, that is, HIBOR is above LIBOR, and when the exchange rate is stronger than HK$7.80 the interest rate differential is negative. In other words, one would expect most of the observations to be in the white boxes in the chart, instead of the grey ones. The chart provides some element of comfort that the refined system is indeed working well, but more observations are needed before we can come to a firm view on whether or not there is a need for a more active stance for the authorities within the convertibility zone to ensure exchange rate stability and monetary conditions consistent with that objective.

Future issues

This leads neatly on to outstanding issues for the future. The first is the question of the monetary policy stance when the exchange rate is within the convertibility zone. Should the monetary authorities do more to smooth out fluctuations in the exchange rate and in monetary conditions within the zone? Secondly, the present system has two sets of convertibility undertakings, one for banks' clearing balances, and the other for the certificates of indebtedness backing the bank notes. Is this necessary, or should there be transferability between bank notes and the banking balance given that there is now official control over the latter? Alternatively, is it possible to have a convertibility undertaking with regard to the banks' clearing balances only, and allow the note-issuing banks to issue and redeem bank notes against their balance with the Exchange Fund? Finally, should the authorities do more to smooth out interest rate volatility, arising from a fixed supply of money in the inter-bank market and varying demand arising from, for instance, Initial Public Offerings (IPOs)? These are all issues for future discussion and potential further reform of the system.

In conclusion, the currency board system in Hong Kong has undergone substantial reform since its introduction in 1983. These have moved the system closer to a rule-based one, although the authorities retain discretion about how they operate within the convertibility zone. The reforms to the money markets during the 1990s have been chiefly aimed at reducing interest-rate volatility that stems from efforts to constrain exchange rate fluctuations, but have also helped to generate deeper and more liquid financial markets in Hong Kong. The broad currency board framework has remained in place despite some large economic shocks over the past two decades or so. However, the reforms during the 1980s and 1990s have been crucial in maintaining the robustness of the system – particularly in the face of the pressures that arise from the increase in global capital flows – and have changed the original currency board as established in 1983 almost beyond recognition.

Note

1 This chapter is based on a transcript of a slide-presentation by Joseph Yam during the final session of the conference.

Part III

The Future of the International Financial Centre

8
Hong Kong's Transformation as a Financial Centre

David R. Meyer

Introduction

Over the past century Hong Kong's status as an international financial centre (IFC) seemingly ebbed and flowed as wars, a world depression, economic booms, and geopolitical restructurings of imperialism and the end of colonialism swept across Asia. Even as the political status of Hong Kong was resolved during the years leading up to its return to Chinese sovereignty in 1997, fears about the strength of its financial sector increased, but these worries abated prior to the handover. Then the Asian financial crisis hit in 1997, the economy of Hong Kong shrank drastically, and the financial sector retrenched, raising anew the concern that the city's rank as a financial centre rested on weak foundations. As financial activity expands, questions about the resilience of this recovery lurk behind many statements of financial officials and other observers.[1]

Ebbs and flows in Hong Kong's status as an IFC, however, send misleading signals about the roots of the city's financial strength and its future prospects. These roots reach far back into its history, and they remain salient determinants of its prospects. Hong Kong's standing extends beyond customary measures of IFCs which focus on characteristics such as numbers of international banks, sizes of these organizations, and scale of financial activities (e.g., trading, volumes of stocks, bonds, currencies, and derivatives) and on competitiveness factors such as availability of skilled personnel, regulatory environment, and corporate tax regime.[2]

Traditional assessments of IFCs offer little explanation of the behaviour of decision makers who control exchanges of financial capital – broadly defined to include financial assets and commodities – among individuals, firms, organizations, and governments. An evaluation of Hong Kong as a decision making centre of capital demonstrates that it became the leading IFC for Asia during the late nineteenth century, maintained that position throughout the 20th century, and is positioned as the world's third greatest IFC after London and New York. Before presenting this alternative interpretation of Hong Kong as an IFC, a previous analysis of its rank using standard financial indicators provides a benchmark.

Hong Kong's fluctuations as an IFC

Figure 8.1 shows that from 1900 to 1980, Hong Kong's status among the top-ten international financial centres fluctuated between a high ranking of 8 out of 10 and the lowest rank of one.

This evidence rests on a systematic set of banking indicators such as local international bank headquarters, presence of foreign banks, and foreign bank links which cover the entire period. During this time

Figure 8.1   Rank of Hong Kong, Shanghai, and Tokyo (Yokohama before 1935) as International Financial Centres, 1900–1980

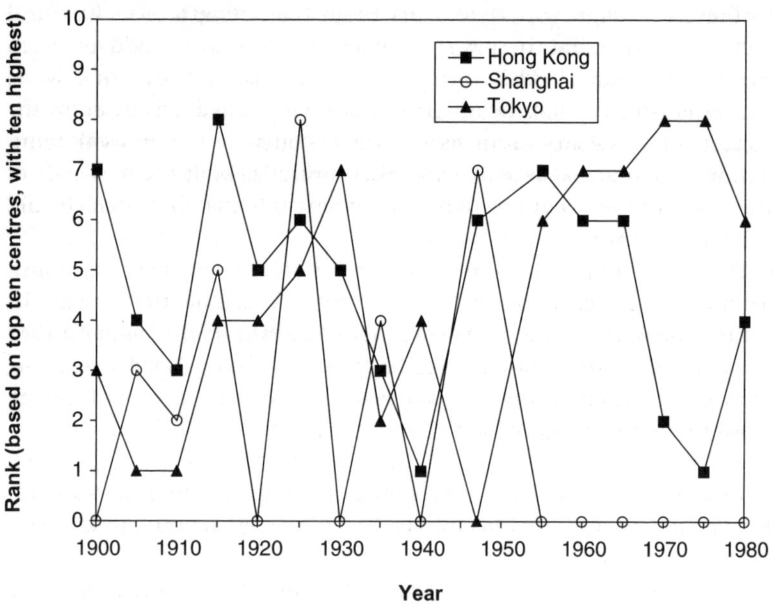

Source: Reed, *Preeminence*, Table A.11, pp. 131–8. A rank of zero means a centre is not in the top ten.

London and New York always ranked in the top positions of nine or ten. Although differences in rank among the top-ten centres sometimes reflected small variations in scale of importance as an IFC, the overall trends for Hong Kong have plausible bases. Its lower rank for 1905 and 1910 reflect idiosyncrasies; St. Petersburg Russia, and Montreal Canada, briefly moved higher in rank. Nonetheless, Hong Kong's Asian trade remained robust during that time, indicating that its financial sector likewise was strong. The severe impact of the depression on Asia and the turmoil of the Second World War contributed to decline in its rank after 1930.[3]

Economic recovery in Asia following 1945 underpinned Hong Kong's improved banking position over the subsequent two decades. An influx of foreign banks led to an increasing sophistication of the exchange market in cash and securities for Asia, as well as strengthening Hong Kong's integration with global markets. Other international financial sectors grew, including gold trading both in Asia and globally, the modest beginning of the stock exchange, and an influx of foreign insurance companies. The decline in rank after 1965 did not indicate a reduced role for Hong Kong in Asian finance. Instead, temporary moves into the top ten by financial centres from Germany (Hamburg) and the United States (San Francisco and Chicago), combined with small differences in significance among these centres below London and New York exaggerated the seeming decline of Hong Kong.[4]

Debate over Hong Kong's status as an IFC inevitably turns to its putative Asian competitors. Shanghai holds a special place because it was China's leading IFC prior to 1949, however, it surpassed Hong Kong's rank only a few times between 1900 and 1980. Shanghai first entered the top-ten IFCs in 1905 and did not outstrip Hong Kong until 1925, exceeding Hong Kong's rank twice more, in 1935 and 1947. It could be argued that turmoil which swept over China during the first half of the twentieth century occasionally caused Shanghai to plunge out of the top ranks of IFCs. This temporary condition was quickly rectified, and it regained its rightful status, according to this argument. Foreign banks shrank their exposure to China during the Boxer rebellion around 1900 then they re-entered, boosting Shanghai into the top-10 financial centres. During the First World War foreign banks retrenched yet again. The city's recovery to new heights as an IFC in the 1920s, when it reached eight out of ten – just below London and New York, seemed to validate Shanghai's significance. Nonetheless, conflict between the Guomintang (Nationalists) and the Communists, coupled with Japanese pressure on China, eroded the enthusiasm of foreign banks. Shanghai dropped out of the top-ten in 1930, regaining its position briefly in the mid-1930s. The quick post-World War II recovery of Shanghai to a top rank in 1947 above Hong Kong, seems to validate the claim that Shanghai was a leading IFC.[5]

Nonetheless, the large number of foreign banks which flocked to Shanghai at any sign of reduced turmoil in China exaggerated its status as a sophisticated decision making centre of international financial capital. With few exceptions, they consisted of branch offices of banks in European countries, along with those in the United States and Japan, who saw opportunity in financing their home country's trading firms which handled China's diverse commodity output. They also lent capital in China through their ties with Shanghai's native banks, and they funded infrastructure developments; a few of the larger banks participated in loans to the Chinese government. However, these foreign banks did not make key decisions about reallocating capital within Asia and with the global economy.[6] Thus, recent journalistic claims that Shanghai's current resurgence as an IFC reclaims its former financial glory misreads that past. It was a domestic financial centre for central and north China, and foreign financial firms mostly linked these parts of China to their home countries.[7]

Financial observers also point to Tokyo as another presumed competitor of Hong Kong. Its status as a leading IFC appears self-evident. Most contemporary rankings list it right below London and New York, and some even place Tokyo on par with them. Viewed from a longer perspective, Yokohama was the leading IFC of Japan prior to 1935. It outranked Hong Kong for the first time in 1930, but Tokyo did not continually surpass Hong Kong until after 1955. Nonetheless, Tokyo's high ranking overstates it as an IFC because most of the indicators measure size of financial activity. Japan's large economy attracts foreign banks who want to do business in that country, and its domestic banks carry out extensive international financial transactions for the wealthy Japanese population and for its numerous large and small corporations engaged in export markets. Few of the foreign international banks, however, use Tokyo as their base for Asia-Pacific finance; Hong Kong is that base.[8]

Singapore also has been identified as a potential Asian competitor of Hong Kong. In contrast to Tokyo, Singapore entered the top-ten IFCs between 1900 and 1980 only in 1947, when it ranked fifth, and that year Hong Kong was one rank higher. This limited role of Singapore has not stopped the debate in Asian newspapers and in comments by government officials in both cities about which IFC is more significant.

Likewise, researchers have taken up the challenge of comparing their relative standing as IFCs based on traditional measures, as well as on indicators such as regional headquarters for foreign firms. Results are consistent: Singapore ranks significantly below Hong Kong as an IFC on most financial measures, although occasionally it has ranked higher in selected sectors such as foreign exchange trading or funds under management. Since the late-nineteenth century, Singapore has been the regional finance and trade center for southeast Asia, broadly defined to include the nearby countries of Thailand, Indonesia, and Malaysia. Hong Kong, however, has been both the finance and trade centre for that region as well as for the rest of Asia-Pacific.[9]

Based on standard financial indicators, therefore, Hong Kong has maintained a solid position within the top-ten IFCs, albeit with fluctuations in rank. Government and business leaders in most IFCs would envy Hong Kong's status, yet its leaders aspire to the top of that ranking. This probably contributes to their anxiety about whether or not the goal can be achieved. I argue that such a goal has solid foundations, but it is necessary to broaden the conceptualization of an IFC to see why this is so.

A broader conceptualization of IFCs

Financial intermediaries make decisions about the control and coordination of the exchange of capital in both money and commodity form.[10] This focus on decision making shifts attention to individuals, organizations, firms, and governments which have the greatest say in the exchange of capital. The intermediaries' power to implement exchanges of capital, in part, derives from the amount of capital they control (or their firm, organization, and so on); standard measures of IFCs partially pick up this power.

However, other sources of strength are of equal, if not more, consequence. Financial intermediaries occupy different positions in the networks of decision making. They may have greater access to capital through participation in networks that bridge to other social networks of capital, but their competitors do not have as great a degree of access to that capital. These network bridges supply confidential or expert knowledge which gives well-positioned intermediaries the capacity to make more strategic decisions than competitors. Intermediaries share this knowledge through social networks, and these networks in a local agglomeration permit the greatest amount of knowledge exchange at the most sophisticated level. In this setting, intermediaries build trust and have a wide range of venues for checking on each others' expertise and veracity.

This attention to social networks of capital also provides a perspective on the consequences of advances in transportation, telecommunications, information processing and media, all of which permit exchanges of capital at larger volumes, over greater distances, and at higher speeds. In effect, the pure physical movement of capital in financial form reduces to its most primitive feature as exchanges of ones and zeros over digital networks. Physical nodes and lines of that digital exchange do not need to coincide with the location of the decision makers; for example, currency and derivative trading can be done electronically through servers. Similarly, control over the physical exchange of commodities such as raw materials and manufactured goods need not coincide with the nodes of transportation such as ports or air cargo hubs. Consequently, these physical movements of capital do not adequately measure the social networks of capital; the latter are the most consequential.

Thus IFCs are pivotal nodes in social networks of capital. All decision makers of capital are important: this includes not only standard firms and institutions (and their employees) such as commercial and investment banks, insurance firms, stock exchanges, and fund management, but it also includes each new specialized financial intermediary that emerges such as private equity firms, hedge funds, and so on. Other actors who make decisions about the exchange of capital also fall into this group. Thus global and world regional corporate headquarters of non-financial firms are pivotal participants in social networks of capital. At an even wider scale, key business services which work closely with decision makers of capital, such as international law and accounting firms and management consultancy, are constituents of these networks. This wider array of actors has been recognized in studies of global cities, but the social network bases of these agglomerations as decision making centres of capital have been underplayed.

Roots of the Hong Kong pivot

From the standpoint of Hong Kong as an IFC, this argument about networks translates into the following analysis. Hong Kong is the pivotal meeting place in Asia of the Chinese and foreign (non-Chinese) social networks of capital. Individuals, firms, and organizations in the city are the most highly specialized and capitalized decision makers who control the exchange of capital over much of Asia and link that region to the global economy. Hong Kong quickly became the pivot of these networks of capital in Asia after the leading British trading firms flocked to the new city in the 1840s, and other foreign firms followed. As prominent Chinese trading firms joined this agglomeration from the 1840s to the 1860s, Hong Kong's dominance in Asia became assured. Consequently, the city housed the firms and decision makers with the greatest expertise in finance and trade in Asia, and their networks reached into most of the countries of Asia, as well as outside to other regions of the world economy. This expertise and knowledge was exchanged within the Hong Kong agglomeration. The formation of the Hongkong and Shanghai Bank (HSBC) by the leading trading firms of Asia in 1864/65 ratified Hong Kong as the pivotal business centre of Asia with control over the exchange of capital.[11]

The trading firms which organized HSBC supplied links to all of the key economies of Asia, Latin America, North America, and Europe. As the bank expanded, it developed a branch office network in Asia that gave it an organizational entrée to the demand for and the supply of financial and commodity capital across the region. Similarly, Chinese trading firms who agglomerated in Hong Kong developed trading ties across much of Asia and to countries outside of Asia, with the exception of Europe, in ways that mirrored the HSBC's branch office network. Other financial institutions located in Hong Kong over the late nineteenth and early twentieth centuries, solidifying it as the pivot of the social networks of capital of Asia. These financial and trading firms with their Asia-Pacific focus placed their senior decision makers in Hong Kong. This did not preclude cities such as Shanghai or Singapore from becoming major financial and trade centres, but in each case their decision makers generally had more restricted responsibilities. In Shanghai's case the individuals and firms focused on China, and in Singapore's case their focus was on the nearby countries of Thailand, Indonesia, and Malaysia, or what became these nations.

The social networks of capital in the Hong Kong pivot retained their resilience through the turmoil of the first half of the twentieth century, including the First World War, the depression of the 1930s, the Second World War, and the emergence of the People's Republic of China following 1949. As Hong Kong added a large industrial sector during the 1950s, the city's finance and trade sectors stood ready to move manufactures into world markets, and these sectors expanded accordingly. The late-twentieth century witnessed an explosive growth of Hong Kong as a decision making centre of capital, but the alteration of that trajectory beginning around the mid-1990s raises questions about the capacity of Hong Kong to be Asia's leading IFC.

Hong Kong's altered trajectory as an IFC

The economic base

The economy of Hong Kong passed through wrenching changes during the 1980s as the share of manufacturing in gross domestic product (GDP) began to plummet after 1984 from about 24% to 9% a decade later, after which its share drifted below 4% by 2004 as is shown in Figure 8.2.

The shift of manufacturing to Guangdong Province and beyond lay behind that transformation, converting the city into a management and redistribution centre for manufacturing in China and elsewhere in Asia. These economic functions are partially identified in the rising share of GDP consisting of wholesale, retail, and import/export during the 1980s to a level of about 25%, albeit with a dip during the recession following the Asian financial crisis of 1997. The changing share of finance, insurance, real estate, and business services in GDP, however, raises potential alarms about Hong Kong's status as an IFC. This sector's rising share tracked manufacturing's declining portion during the decade after 1984, reaching a peak of 27% of GDP. Yet, in contrast to the reinvigoration in wholesale, retail, and import/export, the finance and other components showed little evidence of recovery from their plunge to 21% following the crisis of 1997.

Figure 8.2   Sectoral Shares of Total Gross Domestic Product (GDP) in Hong Kong, 1980–2004

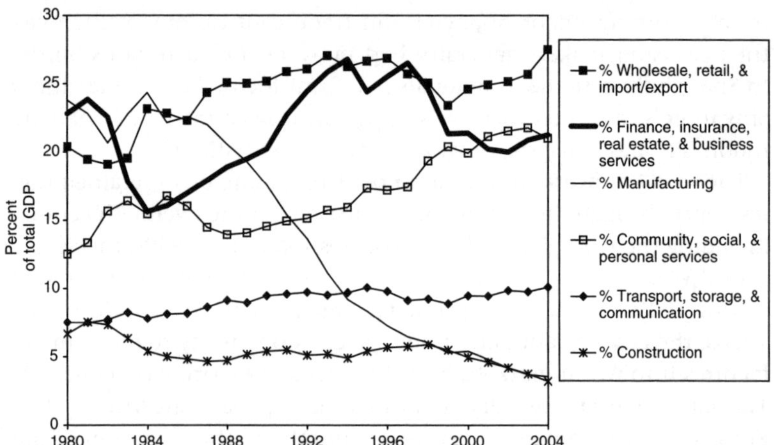

Source: Hong Kong Census and Statistics Department, *Annual Digest of Statistics* (Hong Kong: Hong Kong Special Administrative Region).

Although the wholesale, retail, and import/export sector has exhibited resilience since the 1990s, signs of change in the core import/export sector are evident, and this has consequences for Hong Kong's status as an IFC. Over the past century this sector's firms, which control and coordinate trade in Asia and between it and the global economy, contributed to making Hong Kong the pivot of the social networks of capital in Asia. Figure 8.3 shows how the trade sector, measured by the real value of domestic exports and total re-exports, experienced explosive growth beginning in the early 1960s as Asian economic development took off. The opening of China to Asian trade following the reforms of Deng Xiaoping in 1978 and the subsequent relocation of Hong Kong's manufacturing to Guangdong Province powered the acceleration in the growth of re-exports beginning in the 1980s. Nonetheless, the pace of growth of re-exports began a sharp retardation during the 1990s, and the pace of the recovery after the late-1990s recession has not returned to the growth rates of the 1980s.

Asian trade as a whole is soaring so the question for Hong Kong is whether its physical commodity trade can keep pace. The booming

Figure 8.3 Real Value of Domestic Exports and Re-exports of Hong Kong and of Re-exports To and From Mainland China Involving Outward Processing, 1961–2005 (2000=100)

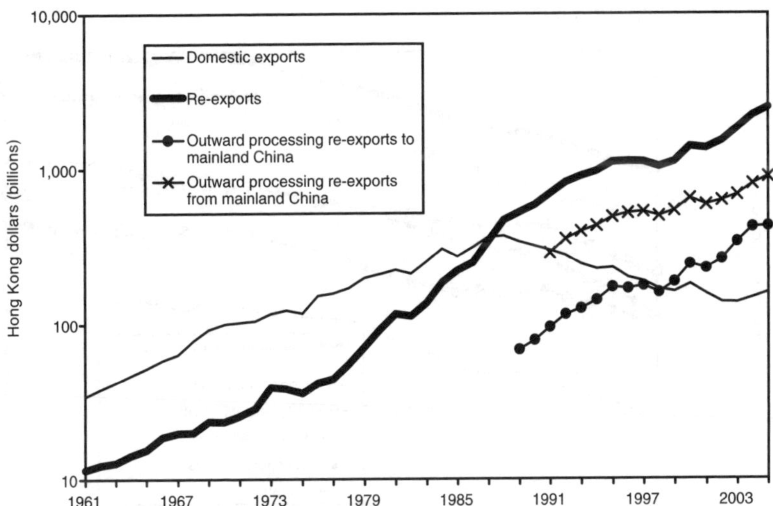

Sources: Hong Kong Census and Statistics Department, *Annual Digest of Statistics*; Hong Kong Census and Statistics Department, *Gross Domestic Product, 2006* (Hong Kong: Hong Kong Special Administrative Region, 2007).

Shanghai region trades directly with other countries of Asia, and other parts of the world are developing direct trade ties to that port. Hong Kong's re-exports related to outward processing in Mainland China are growing, but the trajectories of inward and outward processing re-exports exhibit signs of adjusting to a slower rate of increase. Other ports in the Pearl River Delta provide increasing competition for Hong Kong in physically moving goods. The government recognizes that efficiencies of these other ports benefit Hong Kong as it shifts to providing trading and logistics services for goods that do not touch its port. The amount of Hong Kong's re-exports which do not involve processing in China has more than tripled in real terms from the early 1990s to 2005. This share of total re-exports has risen from the low 40% range to the mid-40% range, hinting at a possible restructuring of Hong Kong's trade towards greater importance of goods unrelated to inward/outward processing manufacturing in China.[12]

The shift to trade services and logistic services comprises part of the growth of the broader intermediary businesses and their support services in Hong Kong evident in Figure 8.4.

Total employment in these sectors expanded at a compound annual rate of about 9% between 1976 and 1996, but since that time employ-

Figure 8.4 Employment in Intermediary Businesses and their Support Services in Hong Kong, 1976–2005

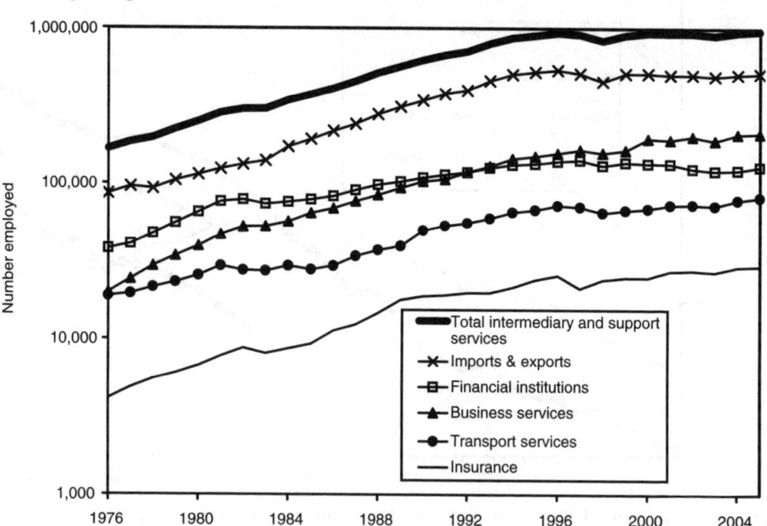

Source: Hong Kong Census and Statistics Department, *Annual Digest of Statistics*.

ment has stagnated. The smaller sectors of insurance and transport services have continued to grow modestly from the mid-1990s to 2005, and the sizeable sector of business services also has grown. The largest employment sector, imports and exports, has stagnated since the mid-1990s, and employment in financial institutions, formerly the second largest sector of the group, has declined. Its 2005 employment fell 13,000 below the peak of 141,000 reached in 1997, the start of the Asian financial crisis. Although employment in financial institutions has started to recover, this decade-long failure to grow points to a transformation in Hong Kong's role as an IFC.

Change in traditional banking

The banking sector has been the customary indicator of IFC status in most rankings of these centres. Based on several core measures of banking, this sector in Hong Kong has ceased to be a leader. Figure 8.5 shows that the forty-year long (1955–1995) increase in the number of licensed banks has ended, and the number declined precipitously from the peak of 185 in 1995 to 138 in 2006. These banks offer the full

Figure 8.5   Number of Licensed Banks in Hong Kong, 1955–2006

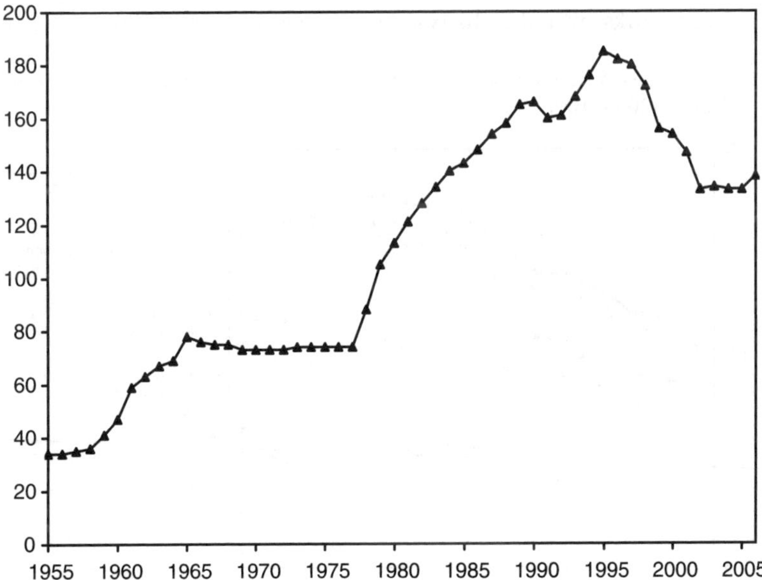

Sources: Hong Kong Government Information Services, *Hong Kong*; Hong Kong Census and Statistics Department, *Annual Digest of Statistics*; HKMA, *Annual Report*.

range of domestic and international banking services. Thus the decline suggests that many global banks no longer see the need to open a full licensed bank in Hong Kong. Part of the decline results from mergers and acquisitions which have taken place among the world's largest banks. Consequently, the remaining licensed banks are huge global banks and virtually all of the world's top fifty banks operate in Hong Kong as licensed banks.[13]

Many traditional activities of banks in Hong Kong, however, are no longer growing. In fact, most have either stagnated or declined, some precipitously. The change in the real value of loans and advances of licensed banks over the period from 1973 to 2005, shown in Figure 8.6 exemplifies the reduced role of the banking sector. Total loans and advances soared at a compound annual rate of 15% from 1973 to their peak in 1995, but from that date until 2005 the aggregate amount plunged 25%. Symptomatic of the alteration in operations of these licensed banks in Asia, they reduced the aggregate amount of loans and advances for use outside Hong Kong by almost 90% since the 1995 peak. Loans and advances for use in Hong Kong constitute the main area of resilience. These borrowings by households, firms, and government for domestic use track the robustness of the local economy.

Changes in selected indicators of the real value of balance sheets of licensed banks over the thirty-five year period since 1970 shown in

Figure 8.6   Real Value of Loans and Advances of Licensed Banks in Hong Kong, 1973–2005 (2000=100)

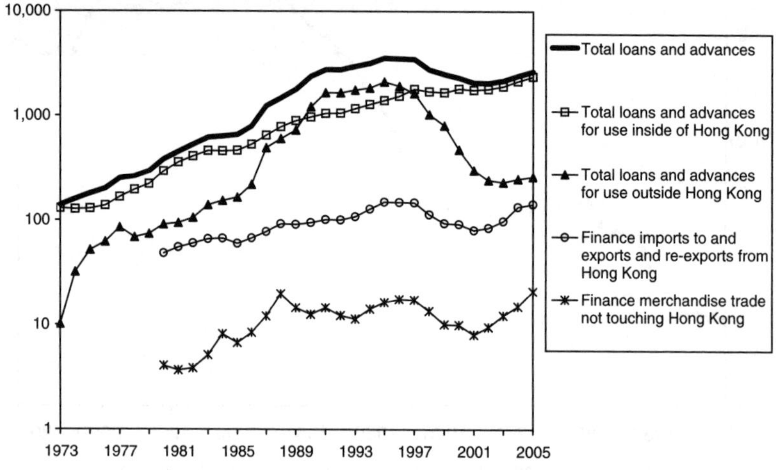

Sources: As for Figure 8.3.

Figure 8.7 Real Value of Balance Sheets of Licensed Banks in Hong Kong, 1970–2005 (2000=100)

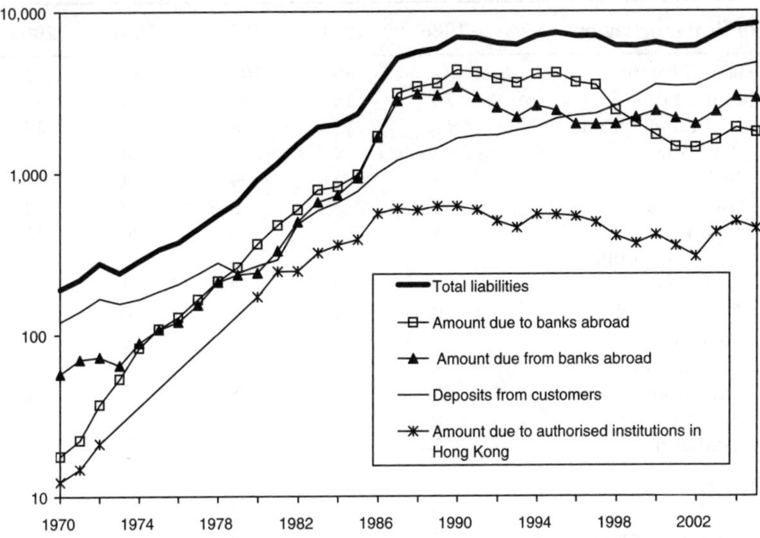

Sources: As for Figure 8.3.

Figure 8.7 reveal alterations that have occurred in their macro capital positions. Except for deposits from customers (an indicator of growth of assets held by local individuals, firms, and organizations) every key measure of the capital positions of licensed banks peaked between the late 1980s and mid-1990s. The aggregate measure of total liabilities has stagnated since the mid-1990s. Inflows of capital to the banks from outside Hong Kong (amount due to banks abroad) for either local use or recirculation in Asia has plunged by over half, and capital sent from licensed banks to other banks around the world (amount due from banks abroad) has levelled off.

To the extent that Hong Kong's rank as an IFC rests on time-honored banking paths of licensed banks, its status has declined since the mid-1990s. Nonetheless, these banks are repositories of expertise in allocating capital, and they provide other services to clients in Hong Kong and Asia through their specialized banking services and advisory activities. From this standpoint, even as the number of licensed banks has declined, the representation of them from around the world in Hong Kong shown in Table 8.1 indirectly portrays the social networks of capital in which the city is embedded. Since the mid-1980s these networks have possessed consistent components. Banks from across Asia

Table 8.1 Number of Licensed Banks in Hong Kong by Political Unit of
Beneficial Ownership, 1986–2005

Political unit/region	1986	1991	1997	2001	2005
Asia and Pacific	84	89	108	85	75
Hong Kong	20	15	16	14	12
Mainland China	15	15	18	19	12
Australia	4	4	4	4	4
India	4	4	4	4	5
Indonesia	2	3	3	2	1
Japan	25	33	44	20	12
Korea, Republic	3	3	3	3	3
Malaysia	2	2	3	1	3
New Zealand	0	1	0	0	0
Pakistan	1	1	1	1	1
Philippines	2	2	2	2	2
Singapore	5	5	5	7	4
Taiwan	0	0	4	7	15
Thailand	1	1	1	1	1
Europe	37	48	50	44	40
Austria	0	2	2	2	1
Belgium/Luxembourg	3	3	4	4	2
Denmark	0	2	2	0	0
France	8	8	8	5	5
Germany	8	8	10	9	8
Italy	4	7	6	6	6
Netherlands	3	3	3	3	3
Republic of Ireland	0	1	0	0	0
Spain	1	3	3	1	1
Sweden	0	3	2	1	1
Switzerland	3	3	3	3	3
United Kingdom	7	5	7	10	10
North America	28	24	20	15	15
Canada	6	6	6	5	5
United States	22	18	14	10	10
Middle East	2	2	2	2	2
Bahrain	1	1	1	1	0
Iran	1	1	1	1	2
South Africa	0	0	0	1	1
Total licensed banks	151	163	180	147	133

Sources: Office of the Commissioner of Banking, *Annual Report of the Commissioner of
Banking for 1989* (Hong Kong, 1989), table 1.5, pp. 57–8; HKMA, *Annual Report 1995*,
table 4, pp. 94–5; HKMA, *Annual Report 1997*, table 3, pp. 120–1; HKMA, *Annual Report
2005*, table D, p. 197.

use Hong Kong as a major base of operations, signifying that they value participation in the hub of the networks of capital of Asia. European banks maintain a strong presence in Hong Kong, testifying to the importance of Asia to their home country's businesses, and the major economies (United Kingdom, Germany, France, and Italy) retain the largest representation. Canada and the United States also remain large players in Hong Kong banking. The big drop in the number of United States banks results from mergers and acquisitions among its large domestic banks.

Indicators of transformation

Foreign headquarters and offices

The decline of traditional banking activities has coincided with the growing importance of long-standing intermediary sectors and their support services, and these businesses point to increased strength of Hong Kong as an IFC. Decisions by international firms from outside Hong Kong to choose it as their regional headquarters or regional office for operating in Asia or in parts of the region have been a

Figure 8.8 Number of Regional Headquarters and Regional Offices in Hong Kong and Total Number of Companies Incorporated Outside Hong Kong, 1979–2006

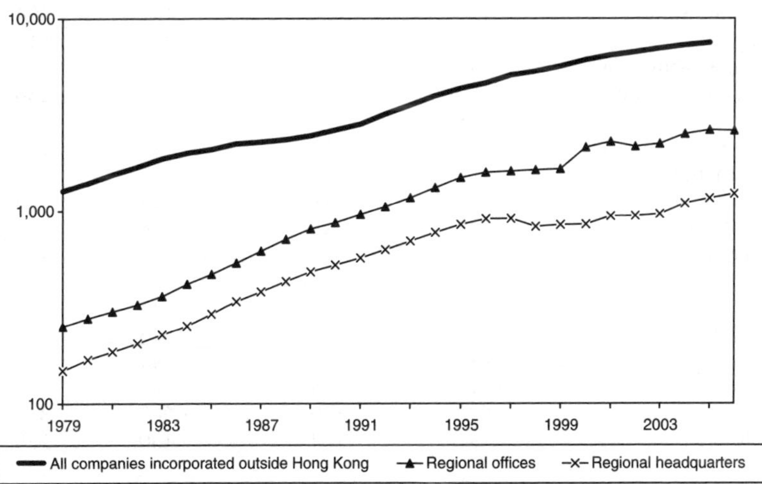

Source: Hong Kong Census and Statistics Department, *Report on Annual Survey of Companies in Hong Kong Representing Parent Companies Located outside Hong Kong.*

foundation of the city's social networks of capital since the mid-nineteenth century. Regional headquarters supervise offices outside Hong Kong, whereas regional offices have managerial control outside Hong Kong, but do not supervise other offices.

Figure 8.8 shows that the rate of growth of the number of regional headquarters and regional offices continued at an almost constant rate from the late 1970s to the mid-1990s, when a dip occurred in the number of regional headquarters while the pace of increase in regional offices slackened somewhat. The rate of growth in regional headquarters has regained traction, though at a reduced pace from earlier decades. Still, their numbers in 2006 are 34% higher than their peak in 1997, a dramatic recovery to new heights. The total number of companies in Hong Kong which are incorporated outside the territory has maintained an almost unbroken compound annual rate of increase of about 7%, reaching almost 7,500 by 2005.

Intraorganizational links between the global headquarters of foreign firms and their regional headquarters, regional offices, and offices

Table 8.2   Number of Regional Headquarters and Regional Offices in Hong Kong by Political Unit of Parent Company, 1994 and 2006

Political unit of parent	Regional headquarters		Regional offices	
	1994	2006	1994	2006
United States	178	295	193	594
Japan	91	212	257	519
United Kingdom	91	114	107	223
Mainland China	62	112	69	156
Germany	35	76	52	136
France	26	55	25	117
Netherlands	22	48	46	47
Singapore	6	44	25	106
Switzerland	34	42	38	68
Taiwan	14	28	39	149
Italy	11	23	25	52
Australia	14	21	31	65
Sweden	13	19	26	34
South Korea	12	16	45	62
Canada	11	15	24	31
Selected total	620	1,120	1,002	2,359
Other	94	108	130	258
Total	714	1,228	1,132	2,617

Source: Census and Statistics Department, Hong Kong Special Administrative Region.

(without supervisory oversight elsewhere in Asia) in Hong Kong serve as conduits to transfer expert knowledge about capital investment opportunities and decisions about the exchange of capital. Regional headquarters and regional offices in Hong Kong shown in Table 8.2 provide tight integration with the world's leading economies. They account for about 90% of these managerial units in the city, and this has remained stable between 1994 and 2006 with the United States housing the greatest share.

Corporations in the wealthiest Asian economies, including Japan, Singapore, Taiwan, and South Korea, have determined that they must participate in the networks of capital in Hong Kong. After the USA, the second rank of Japanese firms testifies to the superiority of Hong Kong's networks for participating in the exchange of capital in Asia compared to those in Tokyo, which predominantly provide access to its domestic economy. Singapore's businesses dramatically increased their number of regional headquarters and regional offices in Hong Kong, indicating that they do not view their global headquarters' city as a viable alternative to Hong Kong for participating in Asian capital networks. Likewise, foreign firms have the same perspective on Singapore; they housed only 330 regional headquarters in that city whereas they placed 1,228 in Hong Kong as of 2006.[14]

European corporations increasingly cast their lot with Hong Kong as a base for accessing Asian networks. For reasons that date back to colonialism, the United Kingdom continues to be among the top three economies with regional headquarters and regional offices, as was seen in Table 8.2. At the same time, Germany, France, the Netherlands, and Italy have more than doubled their numbers of headquarters and of offices between 1994 and 2006. Mainland China maintains the fourth rank position. Its corporations see Hong Kong as a place from which to access Asian business networks; their corporate headquarters city cannot adequately serve that purpose. The Mainland's firms, with 18% of all offices, account for the most local offices in Hong Kong.[15]

The decision by leading global commercial and investment banks to house their Asia-Pacific regional headquarters in Hong Kong supports its status as an IFC. These banks include Citigroup, Credit Suisse, Deutsche Bank, Goldman Sachs, HSBC, ING, JP Morgan Chase, Merrill Lynch, and Morgan Stanley. Typically these firms have huge offices which oversee India, Southeast Asia, China, Northeast Asia, and Australia, although occasionally these offices do not cover Japan. The senior financiers supervise branch offices throughout Asia-Pacific, and these top people frequently travel across the region to meet with clients, government officials, and employees in branch offices. In sum, the decision of foreign firms to operate from Hong Kong confirms that participants (individuals and firms) in its networks continue to occupy a pivotal position in the global control and coordination of the exchange of capital.[16]

Specialized financial services

Published surveys by Hong Kong's government imperfectly measure the financial services that are transforming the city as an IFC. Changes in the organizational structures of financial firms contribute to the measurement difficulties. Sometimes businesses such as private equity are internalized into more diversified firms, while at other times they are spun off or started as specialized firms. With these qualifications, indicators of financial specialization provide some clues about the transformation of Hong Kong as an IFC. It is clear from Table 8.3 that from the mid-1980s to the mid-1990s, the numbers of firms and of employees surged across areas as disparate as investment and holding companies, stock and share companies, and other financial institutions and services, especially mutual funds. Over the subsequent decade ending in 2005, however, the numbers of firms and of employees levelled off in investment and holding companies and in stock and share companies. These specialized financial services seem to be undergoing a restructuring which has similarities to changes in intermediary businesses and in traditional banking seen in Figures 8.4 to 8.7. On the other hand, the category 'other financial institutions and services'

Table 8.3   Specialized Financial Services in Hong Kong, 1984 to 2005

	Number of establishments			Number employed		
	1984	1995	2005	1984	1995	2005
Investment & holding companies	642	3,202	2,777	6,041	21,289	19,832
Stock & share companies	777	855	719	5,412	10,031	11,509
Other financial institutions & services	133	986	1,357	1,733	7,597	12,700
Stock, bullion, & commodity exchanges	6	3	2	190	587	792
Commodity futures & gold bullion brokers/ dealers	161	260	82	1,578	2,049	547

Source: Hong Kong Census and Statistics Department, *Employment and Vacancies Statistics, Series A (Services Sectors)*.

which includes specialized firms and mutual funds continued to surge, hinting at the expanding sectors of the Hong Kong IFC.

Producer services

Changes in the broad category of selected producer services shown in Table 8.4, which provide specialized support to businesses indirectly confirm the strengthening of Hong Kong as an IFC over the two decades since 1984. The dramatic expansion of air and sea cargo forwarding services demonstrates that even as the physical commodity trade passing through Hong Kong grows at slower rates, the city's firms maintain control over global decision making about the logistics of this trade such as chartering transport vehicles, insurance, warehousing, and so on, although these service firms and their workers do not physically handle commodities. Collectively, with almost 3,000 firms and 35,000 employees, these business services are one key to the city's position as an IFC.

Services such as legal, accounting, and advertising expanded significantly between 1984 and 1995, after which the expansion of their

Table 8.4 Producer Services in Hong Kong, 1984 to 2005

	Number of establishments			Number employed		
	1984	1995	2005	1984	1995	2005
Air cargo forwarding	269	606	750	4,840	9,571	14,208
Sea cargo forwarding	332	1,456	2,126	3,640	12,505	20,369
Ship brokerage	29	134	55	177	649	226
Solicitors	285	572	786	6,878	14,743	15,433
Barristers	213	468	800	393	725	1,073
Accounting & auditing	454	1,181	1,937	6,645	14,461	14,082
Bookkeeping & general accounting	271	1,518	1,829	896	4,122	6,689
Advertising cost & agencies	608	787	944	4,158	6,744	5,504
Other advertising services	502	2,537	3,045	1,743	8,273	7,925
Public relations	29	168	274	206	1,070	1,451
Market research	58	114	95	563	1,099	762
Business management & consultants	312	3,240	3,732	2,094	16,908	24,407
Selected total	3,362	12,781	16,373	32,233	90,870	112,129
Other business services	2,320	7,892	12,219	24,536	55,519	92,430
Total business services	5,682	20,673	28,592	56,769	146,389	204,559

Sources: Hong Kong Census and Statistics Department, *Annual Digest of Statistics*; Hong Kong Census and Statistics Department, *Employment and Vacancies Statistics*, Series A (Services Sectors).

total numbers of firms and of employees slowed or leveled off. The exact international component of these services cannot be separated from the large domestic part. In contrast, the business management and consultancy group, which includes many services that international firms demand, soared about tenfold between 1984 and 1995. Over the next decade the number of firms rose another 15% from a large base and the number of employees jumped 44%, reaching over 24,000 by 2005. The total number of employees in the selected producer services which have ties to Hong Kong's business as an IFC almost tripled between 1984 and 1995. Then this number increased another 23% over the next decade which included the downturn during and after the Asian financial crisis.

The growth in real value of net exports of services shown in Figure 8.9 confirms that they now constitute another key component of Hong Kong's status as an IFC. Over the twenty-six year period from 1979 to 2005 these net exports rose at an extraordinary compound annual rate of 9%. The pace of growth varied from a slow rate of increase in the early 1980s, then a rapid increase during the period of China's opening to Hong Kong manufacturers, followed by an erratic sideways movement during the 1990s. From a low point reached in 1998, at the height of the Asian financial crisis, the real net export of services accelerated to a pace similar to the early 1980s, but on a far larger base. This rate of

Figure 8.9　Real Value of Net Exports of Services from Hong Kong, 1979–2005 (2000=100)

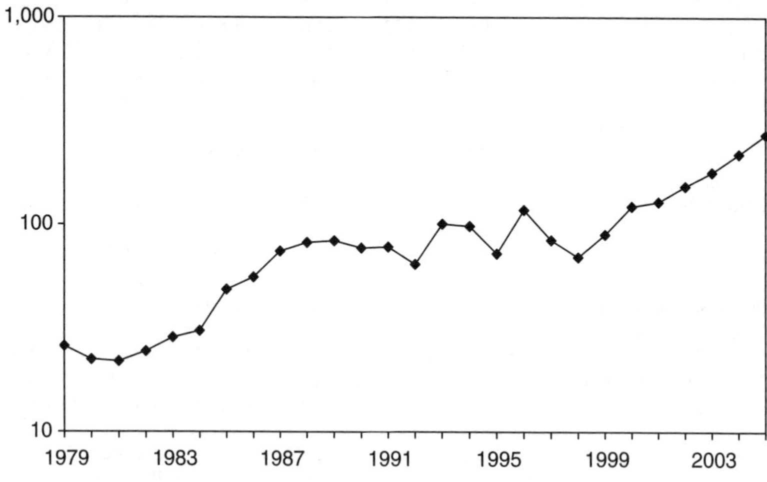

Sources: As for Figure 8.3.

growth during the 1998–2005 period reached the astounding pace of 19% compounded annually, and over the seven-year span the aggregate net exports almost quadrupled. The 2005 amount of HK$272 billion, translates into a US$35 billion net gain to the economy.

These indicators of Hong Kong's transformation point to the increasing importance of sophisticated financial services which control and coordinate exchanges of capital and of specialized producer services that support them. Together, they strengthen Hong Kong as an IFC. Nonetheless, the stagnation or even outright decline of some financial intermediary services seen in Figure 8.4 seems to call this interpretation into question. If this apparent stagnation/decline in the face of increasing specialization in financial services can be explained, the trajectory of Hong Kong's financial sector will be apparent.

Outsourcing of routine financial services

The return of Hong Kong to Chinese sovereignty in 1997 made increased cooperation between the Guangdong provincial government and the Hong Kong SAR politically possible, in part symbolized by CEPA (Closer Economic Partnership Agreement) established in 2003. This set the stage for international financial services firms in Hong Kong to feel more comfortable about transferring their back office jobs to Guangdong Province. In a sense this replicated the increasing comfort which Hong Kong's manufacturers felt during the early 1980s about moving their factories to the province, and once most of their concerns were alleviated, they began a pell–mell rush across the border.[17] The Asian financial crisis of 1997 and subsequent severe recession in Hong Kong, as well as in many Asian countries, however, delayed the restructuring of financial services firms. This led to a sharp temporary retrenchment in many global financial services businesses in Hong Kong.

The shift of back office jobs to Guangdong Province, including the nearby Shenzhen metropolitan area, conforms to movement of these types of jobs from major financial centres in North America and Europe to their surrounding suburbs or farther out to satellite cities. The forays of financial and related services firms to Guangdong province following the Asian financial crisis are identifiable around 2001 when Ernst & Young started a facility in Guangzhou. Over the next two years HSBC, Standard Chartered, and the Bank of East Asia in Hong Kong shifted back office jobs or enlarged their back offices across the border in Guangdong, even as they shifted some back office jobs from the main office areas in Hong Kong to peripheral sites within the city.[18]

By 2005 the choice of Shenzhen as a base for back office jobs had become a routine calculation. In 2006 HSBC reported that it had 3,500 back office jobs in China, though it did not specify the precise locations; nonetheless, it had been an early entrant to Guangdong Province. By that same year the Shenzhen government had institutionalized a programme to explicitly lure back office jobs from Hong Kong. The mayor of Shenzhen shrewdly argued that this programme was consistent with strengthening Hong Kong as an IFC because low-value, low-wage jobs would shift to his city, thus increasing the efficiency of the Hong Kong's financial services firms.[19]

Shenzhen's mayor possesses a sophisticated grasp of the dynamics of the transformation of Hong Kong as an IFC. For some years to come the shift of back office jobs to Shenzhen and elsewhere in Guangdong Province, such as the Guangzhou metropolitan area, probably will keep a lid on overall employment growth of financial services and associated producer services jobs, which also have back office components (e.g., routine accounting jobs). The reason: the back office sector is far larger than the sophisticated financial and producer services sectors. A movement of 500 back office jobs, for example, would not be matched by entry of the same number of high-level positions. Thus Hong Kong will increase its specialization and sophistication as an IFC even as aggregate numbers of jobs show little change. At some point in the near future, the shift of the largest number of back office jobs will wane and then growing numbers of sophisticated financier and producer service workers will contribute to net growth in Hong Kong.

Transformative specialized sectors

Growth of the private equity and hedge fund sectors epitomizes transformation underway in Hong Kong's status as an IFC. Individuals and firms in these sectors focus their activities on Asia, and they require deep knowledge of business opportunities in the region and of individuals and firms who manage firms and the funds in which they invest. Private equity firms operate within a complex political and economic environment because their investments generally are in assets that are fixed in place, whether they be banks, factories, retail stores, and so on. Hedge fund managers sometimes operate with private equity firms, and they also require confidential knowledge of the strategies and skills of lead managers of investment funds in the region.

Hong Kong dominates as the centre of private equity funds that invest in Asia. As of 2004, Japan had about the same aggregate amount of private equity funds under management, but almost 90% of this was invested in domestic companies. In contrast, Hong Kong is the reverse image; about 90% of its US$27 billion was invested outside Hong Kong and almost all of this was targeted elsewhere in Asia. Compared to Singapore's private equity funds, Hong Kong's funds manage about 2.5 times as much and their investments elsewhere in Asia are more than three times as much. Hedge fund management in Hong Kong is on a rapid upward trajectory. Between 2004 and 2006 the number of active hedge fund managers doubled from 58 to 118, the number of hedge funds jumped from 112 to 296, and the amount of assets under management almost quadrupled from US$9.1 billion to US$33.5 billion.[20]

These private equity and hedge fund firms come to Hong Kong because it is the pivot of the social networks of capital in Asia. Interweaving of the numerous foreign and Chinese individuals and firms across many business sectors, directly in finance and indirectly in corporate management and producer services, and the business networks which link them elsewhere in Asia provide private equity and hedge fund managers with unparalleled access to knowledge and expertise about Asia. They share this in Hong Kong within close social networks of friends and business acquaintances, as well as in the many venues where they share insights, including formal and informal meetings, lunches, dinners, parties, and so on.[21]

From the past to the future

Hong Kong became the pivot of the social networks of capital in Asia by the 1860s because it was the meeting place of the most sophisticated financiers and traders from the foreign and Chinese business networks. That position has never been lost over the past 150 years. An international financial centre must be conceptualized beyond traditional banking measures to a broader definition encompassing decision making about the exchange of finance and commodity capital. With this definition, Hong Kong has been the leading IFC in Asia since the 1860s. Fluctuations in its ranking from 1900 to 1980 as captured by traditional banking measures do not adequately reflect its long-term position as the Asian pivot of decision making for the exchange of capital.

The increasing scale of Hong Kong's financial and producer services sectors during the decades after 1960 coincided with Asian economic growth and development. Seeming stagnation which set in by the mid-1990s did not reflect deterioration of Hong Kong as an IFC. Some of the decline and/or stagnation consisted of temporary adjustments to recessionary conditions set off by the Asian financial crisis. At the deeper level, however, the financial sector, broadly defined, had entered a period of structural readjustment as firms shifted back office activities to Guangdong Province. Expanding sectors, such as private equity and hedge funds, are emblematic of increasing specialization and sophistication of finance, thus enhancing Hong Kong's status as an IFC.

The fundamental challenge to the future of Hong Kong as Asia's premier IFC emerged as political risk during the period leading up to the 'Joint Declaration' of 1984 between the United Kingdom and People's Republic of China, which would set the date of 1 July 1997 for the return of Hong Kong to China's sovereignty. That challenge never materialized because China boldly declared in article 7 and Annex 1 in the Joint Declaration that 'The Hong Kong Special Administrative Region will retain the status of an international financial center.' At the third session of the Seventh National People's Congress on 4 April 1990 the Basic Law governing Hong Kong was passed. In language almost identical to the Joint Declaration six years earlier, Article 109 said: 'The government of the Hong Kong Special Administrative Region shall provide an appropriate economic and legal environment for the maintenance of the status of Hong Kong as an international financial centre.'[22]

Beijing's leaders have never deviated from their support of Hong Kong as an IFC, and over the years various officials have repeatedly reaffirmed that position. Recent examples of this include Jia Qinglin, Chairman of the National Committee of the Chinese People's Political Consultative Conference, on a visit to Hong Kong in June 2006, and Shang Fulin, Chairman of the China Securities Regulatory Commission, in Beijing in November 2006. These officials typically stress the importance of cooperation between Hong Kong and the Mainland, and they often frame this in a supply and demand framework. The city supplies financial services to the Mainland, and its businesses and government organizations generate demand for Hong Kong services.[23]

The strengthening of the financial linkages between the Mainland and Hong Kong, therefore, stands high on the agenda of Beijing leaders. At the same time, financial leaders in Hong Kong reciprocate the motivation to expand financial integration. The Hong Kong Monetary Authority (HKMA) stated that as an aim in the 2005 Annual Report, and Joseph Yam, its Chief Executive, proposed a five-prong strategy to enhance that integration. Fred Ma, Secretary for Financial Services and the Treasury, repeated that theme of Hong Kong as an intermediary for

China in speeches which he gave in Hong Kong and around the world.[24]

Formal financial organizations in Hong Kong, including the HKMA, the Financial Secretary, the Securities and Futures Commission, and the Hong Kong Exchange, have the proper role of enhancing organizational, legal, and regulatory structures to strengthen Hong Kong as an IFC. Many of these issues have been itemized as a basis for evaluating the status of an IFC, such as a list developed by the Corporation of London and evaluated by the Securities and Futures Commission of Hong Kong.[25] Yet, attention also must be paid to providing a welcoming environment for sophisticated financiers, top corporate decision makers (regional headquarters and offices), and producer service providers from around the world to base themselves in the city. They constitute the fundamental building blocks of the social networks of capital in Hong Kong, and ultimately their agglomeration in the city and their interaction define it as a pivotal center of decision making for the exchange of capital. Because the growth of China generates enormous demand for sophisticated financial services which Hong Kong firms can provide, continued positioning of the city as China's window to global capital in both directions, when added to Hong Kong's Asia-Pacific financial services, will cement the city's rank as one of the three great global IFCs, behind London and New York.

Notes

1 Rebecca Buckman, 'Economic Ills Could Linger in Hong Kong', *Wall Street Journal* (June 23, 2003), A2; Mary K. Bumgarner and Penelope B. Prime (2000) 'Capital Mobility and Investor Confidence: The Case of Hong Kong's Reversion to China's Sovereignty', *Pacific Economic Review*, 5, 2, 263–78; Ben Edwards, 'Capitals of Capital', *Economist* (May 9, 1998); Bruce Gilley, 'Darkness Dawns', *Far Eastern Economic Review* (April 11, 1996), pp. 14–15; Y. C. Jao (1997) *Hong Kong as an International Financial Centre: Evolution, Prospects and Policies* (Hong Kong: City University of Hong Kong Press); Louis Kraar, 'The Death of Hong Kong', *Fortune*, 131, 12 (June 26, 1995), 118–38; H.C. Reed (1981) *The Preeminence of International Financial Centers* (New York: Praeger); Catherine R. Schenk (2001) *Hong Kong as an International Financial Centre: Emergence and Development 1945–65* (London: Routledge); E.R. Thompson (2004) 'The Political Economy of National Competitiveness: 'One Country, Two Systems' and Hong Kong's Diminished International Business Reputation', *Review of International Political Economy*, 11, 1, 62–97.
2 Corporation of London (2005) *The Competitive Position of London as a Global Financial Centre* (London: Z/Yen); Jao, *Hong Kong*; Charles P. Kindleberger (1974), *The Formation of Financial Centers: A Study in Comparative Economic History*, Princeton Studies in International Finance No. 36 (Princeton, N.J.:

Princeton University Press); Jessie P.H. Poon (2003), 'Hierarchical Tendencies of Capital Markets Among International Financial Centers', *Growth and Change*, 34, 2, 135–56; Reed, *The Preeminence*; Research Department, Supervision of Markets Division (2006), 'Hong Kong as a Leading Financial Centre in Asia', Research Paper No. 33 (Hong Kong: Securities and Futures Commission); Adrian E. Tschoegl (2000), 'International Banking Centers, Geography, and Foreign Banks', *Financial Markets, Institutions & Instruments*, 9, 2, 1–32.

3 David R. Meyer (2000), *Hong Kong as a Global Metropolis* (Cambridge: Cambridge University Press); Reed, *Preeminence*, appendix A.11, pp. 131–8.

4 Y. C. Jao (1974), *Banking and Currency in Hong Kong: A Study of Postwar Financial Development* (London, Macmillan); Reed, *Preeminence*, appendix A.11, pp. 131–8; Schenk *Hong Kong*.

5 John K. Fairbank (1992) *China: A New History* (Cambridge, Mass.: Harvard University Press); Jonathan D. Spence (1990) *The Search for Modern China* (New York: W.W. Norton).

6 Zhaojin Ji (2003) *A History of Modern Shanghai Banking* (Armonk, N.Y.: M.E. Sharpe); Meyer, *Hong Kong*, p. 132; Rhoads Murphey (1953) *Shanghai: Key to Modern China* (Cambridge, Mass.: Harvard University Press).

7 James Laurenceson and Kam Ki Tang (2005) 'Shanghai's Development as an International Financial Centre', *Review of Pacific Basin Financial Markets and Policies*, 8, 1, 147–66; Jon Ogden (2000) 'Shanghai Ready to Roll: Shanghai Seems to be Returning to its Former Glory as a World Finance Centre', *South China Morning Post* (August 15, 2000), *Business Post*, p. 12; William H. Overholt (2004), 'Hong Kong or Shanghai?' *China Business Review*, May–June, 44–7; 'Rivals More Than Ever: Which City, Hong Kong or Shanghai, Will Prosper Most in the New Century?' *Economist* (March 30, 2002); Louise D. Rosario, 'China: Shanghai makes up for lost time- China's largest city pulls out all the stops to regain the title of 'Global Financial Centre', *Banker* (March 1, 2003); Shahid Yusuf and Weiping Wu (2002), 'Pathways to a World City: Shanghai Rising in an Era of Globalisation', *Urban Studies*, 39, 7, 1213–40; Simon X. B. Zhao (2003), 'Spatial Restructuring of Financial Centers in Mainland China and Hong Kong: A Geography of Finance Perspective,' *Urban Affairs Review*, 38, 4, 535–71.

8 Jao, *Hong Kong*; Meyer, *Hong Kong*, pp. 228–30; Poon, 'Hierarchical Tendencies'.

9 'Chinese Cities Scramble to Host Regional HQ', *Industry Updates, China Daily Information Company* (February 12, 2007); Jean Chua, 'Real Challenge for Hong Kong is not Singapore; its Sister Cities such as Shanghai are Growing Blips on its Radar Screen', *Business Times Singapore* (January 26, 2005); K.C. Ho (2000), 'Competing to be Regional Centres: A Multi-Agency, Multi-Locational Perspective', *Urban Studies*, 37, 12, 2337–56; Jao, *Hong Kong*; Meyer, *Hong Kong*; Reed, *Preeminence*, appendix A.11, pp. 131–8; Kelvin Wong, 'High-End Bank Functions Outsourced to Singapore: Survey Finds Talent Pool and Business Culture Among Major Attractions', *Straits Times (Singapore)* (September 16 2005); Friedrich Wu (1997), 'Hong Kong and Singapore: A Tale of Two Asian Business Hubs,' *Journal of Asian Business*, 13, 2, 1–17; Hsiao-Wen Young, Ken Hung, and David C. Cheng (1999), 'Toward Asian Pacific Financial Centers: A Comparative Study of Financial Developments in Taiwan, Hong Kong and Singapore', *Review of Pacific Basin Financial Markets and Policies*, 2, 1, 29–55.

10 This discussion draws on Meyer, *Hong Kong*, ch. 2.

11 For the evidence on which the discussion of this section is based, see Meyer, *Hong Kong*, chs. 3–6.

12 'Advancement of Port Facilities in the Pearl River Delta Region: Opportunities and Challenges for Hong Kong' (2005), *Third Quarter Economic Report*, Economic Analysis and Business Facilitation Unit, Financial Secretary's Office (Hong Kong: Government of the Hong Kong SAR), Box 3.1; *Asian Development Outlook 2007* (Hong Kong: Asian Development Bank), 82–99; 'Offshore Trade and the Mainland's External Trade' (2006), *Third Quarter Economic Report*, Economic Analysis and Business Facilitation Unit, Financial Secretary's Office (Hong Kong: Government of the Hong Kong SAR), Box 2.1.

13 *Annual Report, 2005* (Hong Kong: Hong Kong Monetary Authority), table E, p. 198.

14 Data underlying figure 8.8 for Hong Kong; for Singapore see: http://www.edb.gov.sg/edb/sg/en_uk/index/industry_sectors/headquarters_and_professional.html

15 Census and Statistics Department, *Report of 2006 Annual Survey of Companies in Hong Kong Representing Parent Companies Located Outside Hong Kong* (Hong Kong: Government of Hong Kong SAR).

16 Evidence in this paragraph is based on websites of the commercial and investment banks and on news reports on their activities. Confidential interviews with top financiers in commercial and investment banking, private equity, hedge funds, private banking, and money management conducted by the writer in Hong Kong during 2006 and 2007 confirm this generalization about the city's significance as an Asia-Pacific headquarters of finance. That research is supported by National Science Foundation grant No. 0451945. Among major banks, Lehman Brothers stands as a prominent exception to the choice of Hong Kong as Asia–Pacific headquarters; it senior people operate from Tokyo, although it has a large office in Hong Kong.

17 Meyer, *Hong Kong*, pp. 172–8.

18 'Bank of East Asia to Transfer More Back Office Processes to Guangzhou', *AFX-Asia* (January 10, 2003); 'Banking Giants Draw Up Plans for Mainland', *Global News Wire, Asia Africa Intelligence Wire, The Standard* (September 17, 2002); Louis Beckerling, 'Leverage Opening', *South China Morning Post* (November 9, 2002), Business Post, p. 3; Bruce Einhorn and Manjeet Kripalani, 'Move Over India', *Business Week* (August 11, 2003), p. 42; 'HSBC to Hire 2700 in China, India, Hong Kong', *Emerging Markets Datafile, Hong Kong Imail* (April 5, 2002); Kelvin Wong, 'Swelling Bank Workforces Spark Hunt for Extra Office Space', *South China Morning Post* (January 6, 2005), Business Post, p. 1.

19 '113 of Top 500 Global Firms Find Home in Shenzhen', *Asia Pulse* (August 26, 2005); Jiang Bing He, 'Shenzhen Office Market, Quarter 2, 2005', *DTZ Quarterly Property Market Overview in North Asia* (July 20, 2005); Lee Yuk-kei and Carrie Chan, 'Shenzhen Out to Lure SAR Banks' Business', *Global News Wire, Asia Africa Intelligence Wire, The Standard* (April 13, 2006); Lee Yuk-kei and Yvonne Lee, 'Bank to Boost China Staff', *Global News Wire, Asia Africa Intelligence Wire, The Standard* (March 8, 2006).

20 'Private Equity Investment', *Half-Yearly Economic Report 2005*, Economic Analysis and Business Facilitation Unit, Financial Secretary's Office (Hong Kong: Government of the Hong Kong SAR); Securities and Futures Commission,

'Report of the Survey on Hedge Funds Managed by SFC Licensed Managers' (Hong Kong: Government of the Hong Kong SAR, October, 2006).

21   These generalizations are based on confidential interviews with leading financiers in Hong Kong conducted by the writer in 2006 and 2007, with funding from a United States National Science Foundation grant (No.: 0451945).

22   *The Basic Law of the Hong Kong Special Administrative Region of the People's Republic of China* (Hong Kong, 1992); 'Joint Declaration of the Government of the United Kingdom of Great Britain and Northern Ireland and the Government of the People's Republic of China on the Question of Hong Kong', Signed in Beijing, December 19, 1984.

23   'Chinese Consultative Body Chief: Beijing Supports Hong Kong as a Financial Centre', *Global News Wire, Asia Africa Intelligence Wire, BBC Monitoring International Reports* (July 5, 2006); 'CSRC Supports Mainland Firms Listing in Hong Kong', *Global News Wire, Asia Africa Intelligence Wire, Business Daily Update* (November 30, 2006).

24   Hong Kong Monetary Authority, *Annual Report, 2005* (Hong Kong: Government of the Hong Kong SAR), pp. 86–7; Fred Ma, 'Hong Kong: Financial Centre in the New Silk Road,' Financial Times China-Middle East Summit, Dubai, January 30, 2007; Joseph Yam, 'One Country, Two Financial Systems', British Chamber of Commerce, October 20, 2006.

25   Corporation of London, *The Competitive Position of London as a Global Financial Centre*; Securities and Futures Commission (2006) 'Hong Kong as a Leading Financial Centre in Asia', Research Department, Supervision of Markets Division, Research Paper No. 33 (Hong Kong: Government of the Hong Kong SAR).

Bibliography

Official Publications

Asian Development Outlook 2007 (Hong Kong: Asian Development Bank).

Census and Statistics Department, *Hong Kong Annual Digest of Statistics* (Hong Kong: Government of Hong Kong SAR).

Census and Statistics Department (2005) *2004 Gross Domestic Product* (Hong Kong: Government of the HKSAR).

Census and Statistics Department, *Report of 2006 Annual Survey of Companies in Hong Kong Representing Parent Companies Located Outside Hong Kong* (Hong Kong: Government of Hong Kong SAR).

China: The Maritime Customs Statistical Series, no. 3–5, *The Foreign Trade of China: 1926*.

Economic Analysis and Business Facilitation Unit, Financial Secretary's Office (2005) *Half-Yearly Economic Report* (Hong Kong: Government of the Hong Kong SAR).

Hong Kong General Chamber of Commerce *Annual Reports*.

Hong Kong Government (1932) *Historical and Statistical Abstract of the Colony of Hong Kong 1841–1930*.

Hong Kong Government, *Hong Kong Administrative Reports*.

Hong Kong Government (1930) *Report of the Currency Committee*.

Hong Kong Government, *Reports of the Economic Commission*.

Hong Kong Hansard.

Hong Kong Monetary Authority, *Quarterly Bulletin*.

Hong Kong Museum of History (2007) *The Development of Banks in Shanghai & Hong Kong* (Hong Kong: Hong Kong Museum of History).

Housing Department (2003) *Consultation Paper: Landlord and Tenant (Consolidation) Ordinance (LTO) (Cap.7) Security of Tenure* (Hong Kong, Housing, Planning and Lands Bureau).

Monopolies and Mergers Commission (1982) *The Hongkong and Shanghai Banking Corporation, Standard Chartered Bank Limited, The Royal Bank of Scotland Group Limited. A Report on the Proposed Mergers* (Cmnd 8472, HMSO).

Securities and Futures Commission (2006) *Hong Kong as a Leading Financial Centre in Asia*, Research Department, Supervision of Markets Division, Research Paper, No. 33 (Hong Kong: Government of the Hong Kong SAR).

Securities and Futures Commission (2006) *Report of the Survey on Hedge Funds Managed by SFC Licensed Managers* (Hong Kong: Government of the Hong Kong SAR), October.

Secondary Literature

Atkin, J. (1970) 'Official Regulation of British Overseas Investment', *Economic History Review*, 23, 2.

Atkinson, R.L.P. and Williams, A.K. (1970) *Hong Kong Tramways* (London: Light Rail Transport League).

Bank of China (Hong Kong) (2007) 'The RMB Appreciation and Its Impacts on Hong Kong', February. (http://www.tdctrade.com/econforum/boc/boc070201.htm).

Barnett, M. (1984) *Tramlines: The Story of the Hong Kong Tramway System* (Hong Kong: South China Morning Post).

Beckerling, L. (2002) 'Leverage Opening', *South China Morning Post*, November 9, Business Post.

Bell, P.W. (1956) *The Sterling Area in the Postwar World: International Mechanism and Cohesion, 1946–1952* (Oxford: Clarendon Press).

Birch, A. (1974) 'Control of Prices and Commodities in Hong Kong', *Hong Kong Law Journal*, 4, 2, pp. 133–50.

Birch, A. (1991) *Hong Kong: The Colony that Never Was* (Hong Kong: Guidebook).

Bloomfield, A.I. (1957) 'Some Problems of Central Banking in Underdeveloped Countries', *Journal of Finance*, 12, 2.

Buckman, R. (2003) 'Economic Ills Could Linger in Hong Kong', *Wall Street Journal*, June 23.

Bumgarner, M.K. and Prime, P.B. (2000) 'Capital Mobility and Investor Confidence: The Case of Hong Kong's Reversion to China's Sovereignty', *Pacific Economic Review*, 5, 2, pp. 263–78.

Chambers, G. (1991) *Hang Seng: The Emerging Bank* (Hong Kong: Hang Seng Bank).

Chan, A.K.T. (1995) 'A Warlord Regime and a Colony: A Comparative Study of the Economic Policies of the Canton and Hong Kong Governments, 1929–1936' (M. Phil. thesis, history, University of Hong Kong).

Chan, M.K. (1975) 'Labor and Empire: The Chinese Labor Movement in the Canton Delta, 1895–1927' (PhD dissertation, history, Stanford University).

Chan, M.K. (1995) 'All in the Family: The Hong Kong-Guangdong Link in Historical Perspective', in R. Kwok and A. So (eds) *The Hong Kong-Guangdong Link: Partnership in Flux* (Armonk N.Y.: M.E. Sharpe).

Chan, M.K. and Lo, S.S.H. (2006) *Historical Dictionary of the Hong Kong SAR and the Macao SAR* (Lanham: Scarecrow Press).

Chau, L.C. (1983) 'Imports of Consumer Goods from China and the Economic Growth of Hong Kong', in A. Youngson (ed.) *China and Hong Kong: The Economic Nexus* (Oxford: Oxford University Press), pp. 184–225.

Chen, T. (1927) 'Analysis of Strikes in China from 1918–1926', *Chinese Economic Journal*, 10–11.

Chesneaux, J. (1968) *The Chinese Labor Movement, 1919–1927* (Stanford: Stanford University Press).

Chiu, S.W.K. *et al.* (1997) *City States in the Global Economy: Industrial Restructuring in Hong Kong and Singapore* (Boulder: Westview Press).

Chua, J. (2005) 'Real Challenge for Hong Kong is not Singapore: its Sister Cities such as Shanghai are Growing Blips on its Radar Screen', *Business Times Singapore*, January 26.

Chung, R.L. (1969) 'A Study of the 1925–26 Canton-Hong Kong Strike-Boycott' (MA thesis, history, University of Hong Kong).

Clark, T. (2004) *Good Second Class* (Stanhope: The Memoir Club).

Clauson, G.L.M. (1937) 'Some Uses of Statistics in Colonial Administration', *Journal of the Royal African Society*, 36, 45, pp. 10–12.

Clauson, G.L.M. (1944) 'The British Colonial Currency System', *Economic Journal*, 54, 213.

Corporation of London (2005) *The Competitive Position of London as a Global Financial Centre* (London: Z/Yen).

Dalby, S. (1972) 'Riding the sterling crisis', *FEER*, Vol. 77, No. 28, 8 July, p. 21.

Davis, C.B. (1982) 'Financing Imperialism: British and American Bankers as Vectors of Imperial Expansion in China, 1908–1920', *Business History Review*, 56, 2.

Deng, K., and Lu, X. (eds) (1997) *YueGang quanxi shi, 1840–1984* (Hong Kong: Qilin Books).

Deng Zhongxia (1953) *Zhongguo zhigong yundong jianshi (1919–1926)* (Beijing: Renmin chubanshe).

Denny, D.L. (1975) 'International finance in the PRC', US Congress, Joint Economic Committee, *China: A Reassessment of the Economy*, 653–77, p. 663.

Eatwell, J., Milgate, M. and Newman, P. (eds) (1987) *The New Palgrave: A Dictionary of Economics* (London: Palgrave).

Edwards, B. (1998) 'Capitals of Capital', *Economist*, May 9.

Einhorn, B. and Kripalani, M. (2003) 'Move Over India', *Business Week*, August 11.

Fairbank, J.K. (1992) *China: A New History* (Cambridge, Mass.: Harvard University Press).

Feuerstein, S. and Grimm, O. (2006) 'On the credibility of currency boards', *Review of International Economics*, 14(5), pp. 818–35.

Findlay, R. and Wellisz, S. (1993) 'Hong Kong', in Findlay, R. and Wellisz, S. (eds) *The Political Economy of Poverty, Equity, and Growth: Five Small Open Economies* (New York: Oxford University Press).

Freris, A.F. (1991) *The Financial Markets of Hong Kong* (London: Routledge).

Friedman, M. (1993) 'Do We Need Central Banks?', *Monetary Management in Hong Kong* (Hong Kong: HKMA).

Ghose, T.K. (1987) *The Banking System of Hong Kong* (Singapore: Butterworths).

Gilley, B. (1996) 'Darkness Dawns', *Far Eastern Economic Review*, April 11.

Goodhart, C. and Dai, L. (2003) *Intervention to Save Hong Kong: The Authorities' Counter-Speculation in Financial Markets* (Oxford: Oxford University Press).

Goodstadt, L. (1971) 'Currency Realignments: Government Blow to Hongkong Exports', *FEER*, Vol. 74, No. 52, 25 December.

Goodstadt, L. (1972) 'The HK$ Compromise', *FEER*, Vol. 77, No. 29, 15 July.

Goodstadt, L. (1973) 'Greasy Palms', *FEER*, Vol. 81, No. 37, 17 September, p. 55.

Goodstadt, L. (1973) 'Soft spot for the HK dollar', *FEER*, Vol. 81, No. 26, 2 July.

Goodstadt, L. (2005) *Uneasy Partners: The Conflict Between Public Interest and Private Profit in Hong Kong* (Hong Kong: Hong Kong University Press).

Goodstadt, L. (2006) 'Dangerous Business Models: Bankers, Bureaucrats & Hong Kong's Economic Transformation, 1948–86', *HKIMR Working Paper No. 8/2006*.

Goodstadt, L. (2006) 'Government without Statistics: Policy-making in Hong Kong 1925–85, with special reference to Economic and Financial Management', *HKIMR Working Paper*, No. 6/2006.

Goodstadt, L. (2006) 'Painful transitions: the impact of economic growth and government policies on Hong Kong's Chinese banks, 1945–70', HKIMR Working Paper, 16.

Goodstadt, L. (2007) *Profits, Politics and Panics: Hong Kong's Banks and the Making of a Miracle Economy, 1935–1985* (Hong Kong: Hong Kong University Press).

Gray, J. (1994) 'Monetary Management in Hong Kong: The Role of the Hongkong and Shanghai Banking Corporation Limited', in *Proceedings of the Seminar on Monetary Management organized by the Hongkong Monetary Authority on 18–19 October 1993* (Hong Kong: HKMA).

Greaves, I. (1955) 'Dollar Pooling in the Sterling Area: Comment', *American Economic Review*, 45, 4.

Greaves, I. (1957) 'Colonial Trade and Payments', *Economica*, 24, 93.

Greenwood, J. (1982) 'Hong Kong: How to Rescue HK$: Three Practical Proposals', *Asian Monetary Monitor*, Vol. 6, No. 5 (September–October).

Greenwood, J. (1984) 'The Monetary Framework Underlying the Hong Kong Dollar Stabilization Scheme', *China Quarterly*, 99.

Greenwood, J. (2008) *Hong Kong's Link to the US Dollar: Origins and Evolution* (Hong Kong: Hong Kong University Press).

Guangdong sheng donganguan, comp., *Chen Jitang yanjiu shiliao 1928–1936* (Guangzhao: Guangdong sheng donganguan, 1985), p. 161.

Howe, C. (1983) 'Growth, Public Policy and Hong Kong's Economic Relationship with China', *China Quarterly*, 95.

Hanke, S. (1999) 'Reflections on Exchange Rate Regimes', *Cato Journal*.

Hanke, S. (2002) 'Currency Boards', *Annals*, 579.

Hanke, S. (2002) 'On dollarization and currency boards: error and deception', *Policy Reform*, 5(4), pp. 203–22.

Havinden, M., and Meredith, D. (1993) *Colonialism and Development: Britain and Its Tropical Colonies, 1850–1960* (London: Routledge).

Hazelwood, A. (1953–54) 'Colonial External Finance Since the War', *Review of Economic Studies*, 21, 1.

Hirschman, A. (1957) 'Economic Policy in Underdeveloped Countries', *Economic Development and Cultural Change*, 5, 4.

Ho, C. (2002) 'A survey of the institutional and operational aspects of modern-day currency boards', BIS working paper, 110.

Ho, K.C. (2000) 'Competing to be Regional Centres: A Multi-Agency, Multi-Locational Perspective,' *Urban Studies*, 37, 12, pp. 2337–56.

Hong Kong Securities and Futures Commission (2006) 'Hong Kong as a Leading Financial Centre in Asia', Research Paper 33.

Jao, Y.C. (1974) *Banking and Currency in Hong Kong: A Study of Postwar Financial Development* (London: Macmillan).

Jao, Y.C. (1988) 'Monetary system and banking structure', in Ho, H.C.Y. and Chau, L.C. (eds) *The Economic System of Hong Kong* (Hong Kong: Asian Research Service).

Jao, Y.C. (1997) *Hong Kong as an International Financial Centre: Evolution, Prospects and Policies* (Hong Kong: City University of Hong Kong Press).

Ji, Z. (2003) *A History of Modern Shanghai Banking* (Armonk, N.Y.: M.E. Sharpe).

Jiang, B.H. (2005) 'Shenzhen Office Market, Quarter 2', *DTZ Quarterly Property Market Overview in North Asia*, July 20.

Kindleberger, C.P. (1974) *The Formation of Financial Centers: A Study in Comparative Economic History*, Princeton Studies in International Finance No. 36 (Princeton, N.J.: Princeton University Press).

King, F.H.H. (1957) *Money in British East Asia* (London: HMSO).

King, F.H.H. (1966) 'Sterling Balances and the Colonial Monetary Systems', *Economic Journal*, 65, 260, pp. 719–20.

King, F.H.H. (1968) *A Concise Economic History of Modern China* (New York: Praeger).

King, F.H.H. (1988) *The Hong Kong Bank between the Wars and the Bank Interned, 1919–1950: Return from Grandeur* (New York: Cambridge University Press).

King, F.H.H. (1991) *The Hong Kong Bank in the Period of Development and Nationalism, 1941–1984. From Regional Bank to Multinational Group* (Cambridge: Cambridge University Press).

Kirby, E.S. (1951) 'Hong Kong and the British Position in China', *Annals*, 277.

Kraar, L. (1995) 'The Death of Hong Kong', *Fortune*, 131, 12, June 26, pp. 118–38.

Lam, R.P. (1983) *Currency of Hong Kong* (Hong Kong: Urban Council).

Latter, T. (1994) 'The Currency Board Approach to Monetary Policy – from Africa to Argentina and Estonia, via Hong Kong', in *Proceedings of the Seminar on Monetary Management organized by the Hong Kong Monetary Authority on 18–19 October 1993* (Hong Kong: HKMA).

Latter, T. (2004) 'Hong Kong's Exchange Rate Regimes in the Twentieth Century: The Story of Three Regime Changes', *HKIMR Working Paper No. 17/2004*, 13, 15–16.

Latter, T. (2007) *Hong Kong's Money: The History, Logic and Operation of the Currency Peg* (Hong Kong: Hong Kong University Press).

Latter, T. (2007) 'Rules versus Discretion in Managing the Hong Kong dollar, 1983–2006', *HKIMR Working Paper No. 2/2007*.

Laurenceson, J. and Kam, K.T. (2005) 'Shanghai's Development as an International Financial Centre', *Review of Pacific Basin Financial Markets and Policies*, 8, 1, pp. 147–66.

Ma, F. (2007) 'Hong Kong: Financial Centre in the New Silk Road', *Financial Times*, China-Middle East Summit, Dubai, January 30.

Ma, Y., Kueh, Y.Y. and Ng, R.C.W. (2007) 'A comparative study of exchange rate regimes and macro-economic stability in Singapore and Hong Kong', *Singapore Economic Review*, April, Vol. 52, Issue 1, pp. 93–116.

Mclean, D. (1976) 'Finance and "Informal Empire" before the First World War', *Economic History Review*, 29, 2.

Meltzer, A. (2003) *A History of the Federal Reserve System* (Chicago: University of Chicago).

Meyer, D.R. (2000) *Hong Kong as a Global Metropolis* (Cambridge: Cambridge University Press).

Miners, N. (1987) *Hong Kong under Imperial Rule, 1912–1941* (Hong Kong: Oxford University Press).

Motz, E.J. (1972) 'Great Britain, Hong Kong and Canton: the Canton-Hong Kong strike and boycott of 1925–26', PhD, Michigan State University.

Murphey, R. (1953) *Shanghai: Key to Modern China* (Cambridge, Mass.: Harvard University Press).

Myint, H. (1954) 'An Interpretation of Economic Backwardness', *Oxford Economic Papers*, 6, 2.

Ogden, J. (2000) 'Shanghai Ready to Roll: Shanghai Seems to be Returning to its Former Glory as a World Finance Centre', *South China Morning Post*, August 15.

Olakanpo, J.O.W. (1961) 'Monetary Management in Dependent Economies', *Economica*, 28, 112.

Orchard, D. (1930) 'China's use of the boycott as a political weapon', *Annals of the American Academy of Political and Social Sciences*.

Overholt, W.H. (2004) 'Hong Kong or Shanghai?', *China Business Review*, May–June, pp. 44–7.

Pennell, W.V. (1961) *History of the Hong Kong General Chamber of Commerce, 1861–1961* (Hong Kong: Cathay Press).

Poon, J.P.H. (2003) 'Hierarchical Tendencies of Capital Markets Among International Financial Centers', *Growth and Change*, 34, 2, 135–56.

Posen, A.S. (2006) 'Why Central Banks Should Not Burst Bubbles', *International Finance*, 9, 1.

Prest, R. (1963) *Public Finance in Underdeveloped Countries* (New York: Praeger).

Rajan, R.S. and Siregar, R. (2002) 'Choice of Exchange Rate Regime: Currency Board (Hong Kong) or Monitoring Band (Singapore)?', *Australian Economic Papers*, December, Vol. 41(4), pp. 538–56.

Reed, H.C. (1980) 'The Ascent of Tokyo as an International Financial Center', *Journal of International Business Studies*, 11, 3.

Reed, H.C. (1981) *The Preeminence of International Financial Centers* (New York: Praeger).

Reinhart, C. and Rogoff, K. (2002) 'A Modern History of Exchange Rate Regimes: a reinterpretation', NBER Working Paper, 8693.

Remer, C.F. (1933) *A Study of Chinese Boycott* (Baltimore: Johns Hopkins University Press).

Ricardo, D. (1956) 'Development of Banking in Hongkong during 1955', *Far Eastern Economic Review*, 2 February.

Rigby, R. (1980) *The May 30th Movement* (Canberra: Australian National University Press).

Robinson, A.N.R. (2001) *The Mechanics of Independence: Patterns of Political and Economic Transformation in Trinidad and Tobago* (Barbados: University Press of the West Indies).

Rosario, L.D. (2003) 'China: Shanghai makes up for lost time – China's largest city pulls out all the stops to regain the title of 'Global Financial Centre', *Banker*, March 1.

Russell, M.B. (1972) 'American Silver Policy and China, 1933–1936' (Ph.D. thesis, University of Illinois).

Sayer, G.R. (1968) *Hong Kong 1862–1919* (Hong Kong: Hong Kong University Press).

Schenk, C.R. (1993) 'The Origins of a Central Bank in Malaya and the Transition to Independence, 1954–60', *Journal of Imperial and Commonwealth History*, 21(2), 409–31.

Schenk, C.R. (1997) 'Monetary Institutions in Newly Independent Countries: the experience of Malaya, Ghana and Nigeria in the 1950s', *Financial History Review*, (4) 181–98.

Schenk, C.R. (2000) 'Another Asian Financial Crisis: monetary links between Hong Kong and China 1945–50', *Modern Asian Studies*, 34(3), pp. 739–64.

Schenk, C.R. (2000) 'Banking Groups in Hong Kong 1945–65', *Asia Pacific Business Review*, 7(2), pp. 131–54.

Schenk, C.R. (2000) 'Banks and the emergence of Hong Kong as an international financial centre', *Journal of International Financial Markets, Institutions and Money*, 12(4–5), pp. 321–40.

Schenk, C.R. (2001) *Hong Kong as an International Financial Centre: Emergence and Development 1945–65* (London: Routledge).

Schenk, C.R. (2003) 'Banking Crises and the Evolution of the Regulatory Framework in Hong Kong 1945–70', *Australian Economic History Review*, 43(2), pp. 140–54.

Schenk, C.R. (2004) 'The Empire Strikes Back: Hong Kong and the Decline of Sterling in the 1960s', *Economic History Review*, LVII (3), 551–80.

Schenk, C.R. (2009) 'Sterling, Hong Kong and China in the 1930s and 1950s', in N. White and S. Akita (eds) *International Order of Asia in the 1930s and 1950s* (Aldershot: Ashgate Publishing).

Searle, F. *et al.* (1950) 'Colonial Statistics', *Journal of the Royal Statistical Society, Series A (General)*, 13, 3.

Schuler, K. (1996) *Should Developing Countries Have Central Banks? Currency Quality and Monetary Systems in 155 Countries* (London: Institute of Economic Affairs).

Shao, Z. (1987) 'Shougou baiyin qianhou yishu', in *Guangzhou wenshi tziliao*, v. 37 (Guangzhou: Guangdong renmin chubanshe).

Sharp, I. (1970) 'Renminbi or Bust', *FEER*, Vol. 68, No. 19, 7.

Sinn, E. (1994) *Growing with Hong Kong: The Bank of East Asia, 1919–1994* (Hong Kong: The Bank of East Asia).

Smith, H. (1966) *John Stuart Mill's Other Island. A study of the economic development of Hong Kong* (London: Institute of Economic Affairs).

Spence, J.D. (1990) *The Search for Modern China* (New York: W.W. Norton).

Thompson, E.R. (2004) 'The Political Economy of National Competitiveness: 'One Country, Two Systems' and Hong Kong's Diminished International Business Reputation', *Review of International Political Economy*, 11, 1, 62–97.

Tom, C.F.J. (1989) *Monetary Problems of an Entrepot: The Hong Kong Experience* (New York: Peter Lang).

Tsai, J.F. (1993) *Hong Kong in Chinese History: Community and Social Unrest in the British Colony, 1842–1913* (New York: Columbia University Press).

Tsang, S. (2004) *A Modern History of Hong Kong* (London: I.B. Tauris).

Tschoegl, A.E. (2000) 'International Banking Centers, Geography and Foreign Banks', *Financial Markets, Institutions & Instruments*, 9, 2, 1–32.

Walters, A. (1992) 'Currency Board', *The New Palgrave Dictionary of Economics* (London: Palgrave Macmillan).

Wong, K. (2005) 'High-End Bank Functions Outsourced to Singapore: Survey Finds Talent Pool and Business Culture among Major Attractions', *Straits Times (Singapore)*, September 16.

Wong, K. (2005) 'Swelling Bank Workforces Spark Hunt for Extra Office Space', *South China Morning Post*, January 6, Business Post.

Woodhead, H.G. (ed.) *China Year Book* (Tianjin: annual editions, 1901–1928).

Wu, F. (1997) 'Hong Kong and Singapore: A Tale of Two Asian Business Hubs', *Journal of Asian Business*, 13, 2, 1–17.

Wu, Y. (2005) 'A modified currency board system; theory and evidence', *Journal of International Financial Markets, Institutions & Money*, October, Vol. 15, Issue 4, 353–67.

Yam, J. (2006) 'One Country, Two Financial Systems', British Chamber of Commerce, October 20.

Yam, J. (2006) 'The RMB and the HK$', *Viewpoint*, November. (http://www.info.gov.hk/hkma/eng/viewpt/index.htm).

Yao, Chishun (Kay F. Yiu) (1930) *Xianggang Jinyong* [Hong Kong Money Market] (Hong Kong).

Yip, P. (2005) 'On the maintenance costs and exit costs of the peg in Hong Kong', *Review of Pacific Basin Financial Markets & Policies*, September, Vol. 8(3), 377–403.

Young, H.W., Hung, K. and Cheng, D.C. (1999) 'Toward Asian Pacific Financial Centers: A Comparative Study of Financial Developments in Taiwan, Hong Kong and Singapore', *Review of Pacific Basin Financial Markets and Policies*, 2, 1, 29–55.

Yusuf, S. and Wu, W. (2002) 'Pathways to a World City: Shanghai Rising in an Era of Globalisation', *Urban Studies*, 39, 7, pp. 1213–40.

Zhao, S.X.B. (2003) 'Spatial Restructuring of Financial Centers in Mainland China and Hong Kong: A Geography of Finance Perspective', *Urban Affairs Review*, 38, 4, 535–71.

Zheng, B. (1996) *Tuplan Xianggang huobi* (Hong Kong: Joint Publishing).

Zhou Liangquan (1997) 'Xianggang jinrong tixi', in Wang Gungwu (ed.) *Xianggang shi xinlun*, v.1 (Hong Kong: Joint Publishing).

Newspapers etc.

Asian Monetary Monitor
South China Morning Post
China Mail
Economist
Hong Kong Daily Press
Far Eastern Economic Review
Hong Kong Telegraph
The New Leader
The New Republic
North China Herald
The Standard
Xianggang gongshang ribao

Index